Serpents in the Garden
Liaisons with Culture & Sex

CounterPunch

To Jim & Elsie

Serpents in the Garden
Liaisons with Culture & Sex

Edited by
Alexander Cockburn
and Jeffrey St. Clair

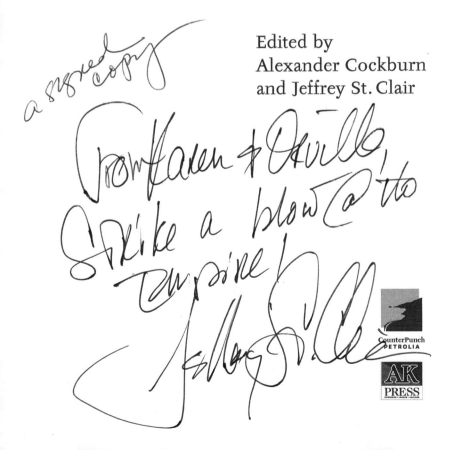

a signed copy

For Karen + Orville, Strike a blow @ the Empire!

CounterPunch
PETROLIA

AK
PRESS

First published by
CounterPunch and AK Press 2004
© CounterPunch 2004
All rights reserved

CounterPunch
PO Box 228 Petrolia, California, 95558

AK Press
674A 23ʳᵈ St, Oakland, California 94612-1163
www.akpress.org

PO Box 12766, Edinburgh, Scotland EH89YE
www.akuk.com

ISBN   1-902593-94-4

Library of Congress Cataloguing in-Publication data
Library of Congress Control Number: 2003113036

A catalog record for this book is available
from the Library of Congress

Typeset in Tyfa and Stainless.
Printed and bound in Canada.

Designed by Tiffany Wardle
Cover Illustration by Michael Dickinson

By Way of an Introduction: The Best Books of the Twentieth Century ix

Alexander Cockburn and Jeffrey St. Clair

By way of an Introduction:
The Best Books of
the Twentieth Century

WE EDIT COUNTERPUNCH, THE POPULAR RADICAL website and newsletter. We have fun doing it, and we spend a lot of time laughing, as we chat about the news, gossip and tasks of the day, on the phone between Petrolia, in Humboldt county, northern California, and Oregon City, Oregon, perched over the Clackamas, a few hundred miles north across the Siskiyous, in a whole different weather system. In the sixties and the eighties respectively, we both read English at college, Cockburn at Oxford and St. Clair at American. English is a discipline that says, or used to say before the critical theorists seized power and put pleasure to the sword, that it's okay to enjoy reading books and okay to put off more or less permanently what you're going to do when you grow up—yet another definition of being a journalist or a pamphleteer. We both like the blues and there's been a lot about the blues in *CounterPunch*. We both think that a big part of being radical in the best sense of the word is in enjoying, promoting, defending art and the spirit of freedom and pleasure and craft skills embodied in the arts. By the quality of life, art and freedom that the radicals commend, so will radicals prevail.

You want to know more about us and *CounterPunch*? A few years ago we asked ourselves and our friends, what would we include in the *CounterPunch* library of the hundred best non-fiction books in the riginal English, published in the twentieth century, more or less? The library we'd send to Other Planets, or to George W. Bush (though we know Laura the Librarian is doing her best...) Then we asked ourselves and our friends the same about books in translation. Actually we asked it about movies too, but you'll have to go to our website about that. There's way too much Hollywood-power as it is, and for more on that see the first essay in the book.

Culture, music, art, architecture and...sex. In the sixties the right thought the left had the best drugs, and the best sex. Now? Well, the left sort of won that battle. These days the right knows it's okay to have a good time and sneers at the left for staying at home to read up on theories of surplus value. But there are always subversion and revolutionary perspectives to be enjoyed in the The Garden of Eden. And in the battle to return to that delightful piece of real estate, there were heroes thus far unsung. Gershon Legman for example. Read Susan Davis' pioneering essay about him. For every pleasure we enjoy, there's a martyr in our past who paid the price.

Now for the list, so you can get acquainted with us.

First, the ones published in English.

Desert Solitaire: a season in the wilderness
Edward Abbey

Dynamite: the story of class violence in America
Louis Adamic

Inside the Company: CIA diary
Philip Agee

A Pattern Language: towns, buildings, construction
Christopher Alexander, Sara Ishikawa and Murray Silverstein

Confessions of a Muckraker: the inside story of life in Washington during the Truman, Eisenhower, Kennedy and Johnson years
Jack Anderson

Hollywood Babylon
Kenneth Anger

Eichmann in Jerusalem: a report on the banality of evil
Hannah Arendt

Mushrooms Demystified:
a guide to the fleshy fungi
David Arora

Spinster
Sylvia Ashton-Warner

The Devil Finds Work
James Baldwin

Los Angeles: the architecture
of four ecologies
Reyner Banham

The Crime and Punishment
of IG Farben
Joseph Borkin

A Treasury of Mississippi
River Folktales
B.A. Botkin

Ball Four
Jim Bouten

Labor's Untold Story
*Richard Boyer and Herbert
Morais*

The Encyclopedia of Organic
Gardening
*Marshall Bradley, Fern Bradley
and Barbara Ellis*

Labor and Monopoly Capital:
the degradation of work in the
twentieth century
Harry Braverman

Western Garden Book
Kathleen Brenzel

For the Earth's Sake
David Brower

Life Against Death: the
psychoanalytical meaning of
history
Norman O. Brown

The Road to Oxiana
Robert Byron

What Is History?
E.H. Carr

The Legacy of Malthus
Allan Chase

The Country Blues
Samuel B. Charters

The Fateful Triangle:
the United States, Israel
and the Palestinians
Noam Chomsky

Image of the People: Gustave
Courbet and the 1848
revolution
T.J. Clark

The Threat: inside the
Soviet military machine
Andrew Cockburn

I Claud
Claud Cockburn

Nature's Metropolis:
Chicago and the great West
William Cronon

French Provincial Cooking
Elizabeth David

My Journey to Lhasa
Alexandra David-Neel

Custer Died for Your Sins:
an Indian Manifesto
Vine DeLoria, Jr.

Geronimo: the man,
his time, his place
Angie Debo

War Without Mercy: race and
power in the Pacific War
John Dower

The Greeks and The Irrational
E.R. Dodds

The Souls of Black Folk
W.E.B. DuBois

Studies in the
Psychology of Sex
Havelock Ellis

Seven Types of Ambiguity
William Empson

Encyclopedia Britannica
11th Edition

The Dialectic of Sex: the case
for a feminist revolution
Shulamith Firestone

How to Cook a Wolf
M.F.K. Fisher

Modern English Usage
Henry Watson Fowler

Cezanne: a study of his
development
Roger Fry

An Anatomy of Criticism:
four essays
Northrop Frye

The Autobiography of
Malcolm X
Alex Haley and Malcolm X

The Long Haul: an
autobiography
Myles Horton

The Face of War
Martha Gellhorn

Detroit: I Do Mind Dying:
a study in urban revolution
*Dan Georgakas and Marvin
Surkin*

Growing Up Absurd
Paul Goodman

The Mismeasure of Man
Stephen Jay Gould

Exploring the Dangerous
Trades
Alice Hamilton

Native Planters in Old Hawaii:
their life, lore and
environment
*E.C.S Handy and Elizabeth
Handy*

Warriors: life and death
among the Somalis
Gerald Hanley

Themis: a study in the social
origins of Greek religion
Jane E. Harrison

The Gospel Sound: good
news and bad times
Anthony Heilbut

Kissinger: the price of power
Seymour Hersh

Bull Cook: Authentic Recipes
and Practices
*George Leonard Herter
and Berte Herter*

The World Turned Upside
Down: radical ideas during
the English Revolution
Christopher Hill

Fanshen: a documentary of
revolution in a Chinese village
William Hinton

Deschooling Society
Ivan Illich

The Fur Trade in Canada: an
introduction to Canadian
economic history
Harold A. Innis

The Death and Life of Great
American Cities
Jane Jacobs

The Black Jacobins: Toussaint
L'Ouverture and the San
Domingo Revolution
C.L.R. James

Home and Garden
Gertrude Jekyll

The Life and Work of
Sigmund Freud
Ernest Jones

Blues People: negro music
in white America
Leroi Jones

The Politics of War
Walter Karp

For Keeps: 30 years
at the movies
Pauline Kael

The General Theory of
Employment, Interest
and Money
John Maynard Keynes

The Kinsey Reports on
Human Sexual Behavior
Alfred Kinsey, et al.

The Thirty Years' Wars:
dispatches and diversions of a
radical journalist, 1965–1994
Andrew Kopkind

Harry Truman and the War
Scare of 1948: a successful
campaign to deceive the
nation
Frank Kofsky

Lame Deer Seeker of Visions
John Fire Lame Deer

The Divided Self
RD Laing

The Culture of Narcissism:
American life in an age of
diminishing expectations
Christopher Lasch

Etruscan Places
DH Lawrence

A Potter's Book
Bernard Leach

We The Jury: The Impact
of Jurors on Our Basic
Freedoms: Great Jury Trials
of History
Godfrey Lehman

North Star Country
Meridel Le Sueur

The London Hanged: crime
and civil society in the
Eighteenth Century
Peter Linebaugh

The Singer of Tales
Albert Bates Lord

A River Runs Through It
Norman Maclean

Eastern Approaches
Fitzroy McLean

Understanding Comics:
the invisible art
Scott McCloud

The Politics of Heroin:
CIA complicity in the
global drug trade
Alfred McCoy

Factories in the Fields:
the story of migratory
farm labor in California
Carey McWilliams

Advertisements for Myself
Norman Mailer

Heart of Rock and Soul:
the 1001 Greatest Singles
Ever Made
Dave Marsh

Remembrance
Hugh Massingham

The Snow Leopard
Peter Matthiessen

Prejudices: a selection
H.L. Mencken

The Air-Conditioned
Nightmare
Henry Miller

Listen Yanqui
C. Wright Mills

Japanese Homes and
Their Surroundings
Edwin Morse

Dada Documents
and Manifestoes
Robert Motherwell

Technics and Civilization
Lewis Mumford

Blues Fell This Morning:
meaning in the blues
Paul Oliver

The Oxford English
Dictionary

Deep Blues
Robert Palmer

A Field Guide to the Birds
Roger Tory Peterson

My Silent War
Kim Philby

The Great Transformation
Karl Polanyi

ABC of Reading
Ezra Pound

Architectural Graphic
Standards
*Charles Ramsey and Harold
Sleeper*

Autobiography
Bertrand Russell

Orientalism
Edward W. Said

The Class Struggle in the
Ancient Greek World
G.E.M. de Ste. Croix

A Month and A Day:
A Detention Diary
Ken Saro-Wiwa

Death Without Weeping:
the violence of everyday life
in Brazil
Nancy Scheper-Hughes

Shame of the Cities
Lincoln Steffens

The Myth of Mental Illness:
foundations of a theory of
personal conduct
Thomas Szasz

Religion and the Decline of
Magic: Studies in Popular
Beliefs in Sixteenth and
Seventeenth Century England
Keith Thomas

Sister of the Road:
an autobiography of
Box Car Bertha
Bertha Thompson

The Making of the English
Working Class
E.P. Thompson

Fear and Loathing
in Las Vegas
Hunter S. Thompson

A Biographical Dictionary
of Film
David Thomson

Across the Forbidden Sands
Robert Tench

The Phoenix Program
Douglas Valentine

Soma: divine mushroom
of immortality
Gordon Wasson

To the Finland Station
Edmund Wilson

Black Sun: the brief transit
and violent eclipse of Harry
Crosby
Geoffrey Wolfe

Rivers of Empire: water,
aridity and the growth of
the American West
Donald Worster

The Art of Memory
Frances Yates

In Translation

The South Pole: an account
of the Norwegian Antarctic
expedition, 1910-1912
Roald Amundsen

The Theater and Its Double
Antonin Artaud

Minima Moralia: Reflections
from a Damaged Life
Theodor Adorno

The Hour of Our Death
Philippe Aries

Mimesis: The Representation
of Reality in Western
Literature
Erich Auerbach

The Poetics of Space
Gaston Bachelard

Mythologies
Roland Barthes

Eroticism: death and
sensuality
Georges Bataille

The Egyptian, Syrian, and
Iraqi Revolutions: Some
Observations on Their
Underlying Causes and Social
Character
Hanna Batatu

Orson Welles: a critical view
Andre Bazin

Illuminations
Walter Benjamin

Black Elk Speaks
Black Elk

Feudal Society
Marc Bloch

Chinook Texts
*Franz Boas (Compiler and
Translator)*

Other Inquisitions
Jorge Luis Borges

The Mediterranean and the
Mediterranean World in the
Age of Philip II
Fernand Braudel

The Development of an
Aesthetic
Bertolt Brecht

Manifestoes of Surrealism
Andre Breton

The Evolution of Rock Art in
the Caves of France
Abbe Henri Breuil

My Last Sigh
Luis Buñuel

Homo Necans: the
Anthropology of Ancient
Greek Sacrificial Ritual and
Myth
Walter Burkert

Man, Play and Games
Roger Caillois

Reflections of Eden:
My Years with the
Orangutans of Borneo
Birute Galdikas

Memories of Fire
Eduardo Galeano

Gandhi: an Autobiography:
the Story of My
ExperimentsWith Truth
Mohandas Gandhi

How We Won the War
Vo Nguyen Giap

Travels in the Congo
Andre Gide

Mechanization Takes
Command
Sigfried Giedion

The Bog People: Iron Age
Man Preserved
P.V. Glob

Capitalism, Socialism,
Ecology
Andre Gorz

How New York Stole the Idea
of Modern Art
Serge Guilbaut

Art and Illusion
Ernst Hans Gombrich

Prison Notebooks
Antonio Gramsci

Episodes of the Cuban
Revolutionary War, 1956-58
Ernesto "Che" Guevara

A Theology of Liberation:
History, Politics and Salvation
Gustavo Gutierrez

Seven Years in Tibet
Heinrich Harrer

The Social History of Art
Arnold Hauser

Kon-Tiki
Thor Heyerdahl

This Sex Which is Not One
Luce Irigaray

Being and Time
Martin Heidegger

The Dialectic of
Englightenment
*Max Horkheimer and Theodor
Adorno*

Autumn of the Middle Ages
Johan Huizinga

The Gardens of Japan
Teiji Itoh

The Gnostic Religion
Hans Jonas

I Ching
(introduction by Carl Jung)

Memories, Dreams,
Reflections
Carl Jung

Kama-Sutra: Complete and
Unexpurgated Translation
Alain Danielou (translator)

Kamapua'a: The Hawai'ian
Pig-God
Lilikala Kame'eleihiwa

Shakespeare Our
Contemporary
Jan Kott

Psychopathia Sexualis
Richard von Krafft-Ebing

The Conquest of Bread
Petr Kropotkin

Montaillou: the Promised
Land of Error
Emmanuel Le Roi Ladurie

The State and Revolution
V.S. Lenin

The Coming of the French
Revolution
Georges Lefebvre

Critique of Everyday Life
Henri Lefebvre

The Broken Spears: the Aztec
Account of the Conquest of
Mexico
Miguel Leon-Portilla

Tristes Tropiques
Claude Levi-Strauss

Christ Stopped at Eboli:
the Story of a Year
Carlo Levi

The Periodic Table
Primo Levi

Russia: an Architecture for
World Revolution
El Lissitsky

Ornament and Crime
Adolf Loos

Man Meets Dog
Konrad Lorenz

History and Class
Consciousness
Georg Lukacs

Lumumba Speaks: the
Speeches and Writings of
Patrice Lumumba
Patrice Lumumba

Luxemburg Speaks
Rosa Luxemburg

The Diaries of
Alma Mahler-Werfel
Alma Mahler-Werfel

The Works of the People of
Old: Na Hana a Ka Po'E
Kahiko
Samuel Manaiakalani Kamakau

On Guerrilla Warfare
Mao Tse-Tung

Shadows of Tender Fury: the
Letters and Communiques of
Subcomandante Marcos and
the Zapatista Army of
National Liberation
*Frank Bardacke, Leslie Lopez and
the Watsonville, California,
Human Rights Committee (edited
and translated)*

The Economic and
Philosophic Manuscripts
of 1844
Karl Marx

The Gift: The Form and
Reason for Exchange in
Archaic Societies
Marcel Mauss

I, Rigoberta Menchu: An
Indian Woman in Guatemala
Rigoberta Menchu

Sense and Non-Sense
Maurice Merleau Ponty

A History of Russian
Literature: From Its
Beginnings to 1900
Dmitry Svyatopolk Mirsky

The Book of Five Rings
Miyamoto Musashi

Ecology, Community and
Lifestyle: Outline of an
Ecosophy
Arne Naess

Behemoth: the Structure and
Practice of National Socialism
1933–44
Franz Neumann

Hiroshima Notes
Kenzaburo Oe

Perspective As Symbolic Form
Erwin Panofsky

The Mind and Society
Vilfredo Pareto

My Life and the Beautiful
Game
Pele

Morphology of the Folktale
Vladimir Aioakovlevich Propp

Character Analysis
Wilhelm Reich

Renoir, My Father
Jean Renoir

For a New Novel: Essays on
Fiction
Alain Robbe-Grillet

Memoirs from the Women's
Prison
Nawal el Saadawi

Letters from Prison
Marquis de Sade

War Diaries: Notebooks from
a Phony War, 1939–40
Jean-Paul Sartre

Course in General Linguistics
Ferdinand de Saussure

Sabbatai Sevi: the mystical
messiah
Gershom Gerhard Scholem

Hibakusha: Accounts by
Survivors of Hiroshima and
Nagasaki
Gaynor Sekimori (Translator)

Memoirs of a Revolutionary
Victor Serge

Pillow Book of Sei Shonagon
Sei Shonagon

The Philosophy of Money
Georg Simmel

Critique of Cynical Reason
Peter Sloterdijk

Reflections on Violence
Georges Sorel

An Actor Prepares
Konstantin Stanislavski

The Russian Revolution, 1917
N. N. Sukhanov

Zen Buddhism
D.T. Suzuki

Popol Vuh: The Mayan Book
of the Dawn of Life
Dennis Tedlock (Translator)

Tibetan Book of the Dead
Robert Thurman (translator)

Curious Naturalists
Niko Tinbergen

The Social Teachings of the
Christian Churches
Ernst Troeltsch

The Films in My Life
Francois Truffaut

The Complete Letters
Vincent Van Gogh

Worlds in Collision
Immanuel Velikovsky

The Roman Empire
Paul Veyne

The Forty Days of Musa Dagh
Franz Werfel

The Protestant Ethic and the
Spirit of Capitalism
Max Weber

Oriental Despotism:
A Comparative Study
of Total Power
Karl August Wittfogel

Philosophical Investigations
Ludwig Wittgenstein

On the Passage of a Few
People Through a Rather Brief
Moment in Time: Situationist
International 1957–1972
Peter Woller

A World of Yesterday
Stefan Zweig

Culture

ALEXANDER COCKBURN

Milk-Bars, Hollywood and the March of Empires

SCARCELY MORE THAN A DECADE AFTER WINSTON Churchill had assured the British people that the German foe at last lay prostrate at their feet, the invasion against which Britain had been unable to defend itself was portrayed in lurid terms: "The milk-bars indicate at once, in the nastiness of their modernistic; knick-knacks, their glaring showiness, an aesthetic breakdown so complete that, in comparison with them, the layout of the living rooms in some of the poor homes from which the customers come seems to speak of a tradition as balanced and civilized as an 18th-century town house. Girls go to some, but most of the customers are boys aged between 15 and 20, with drape-suits, picture ties, and an American slouch. Compared even with the pub around the corner, this is all a peculiarly thin and pallid form of dissipation, a sort of spiritual dry-rot amid the odour of boiled milk. Many of the customers—their clothes, their hair-styles, their facial expressions all indicate—are living to a large extent in a myth-world compounded of a few simple elements which they take to be those of American life."

By the time Richard Hoggart thus savaged the innocent milk-bar (aka, in America, the soda-fountain) in *The Uses of Literacy*, published in 1957, the transatlantic contagion had ranged far beyond the milkshakes and "mechanical record player" that stirred him to such fury.

At the politer end of the national culture, *Encounter*, a politico-cultural monthly, was being covertly financed by the Central Intelligence Agency. And crucially, at the level of mass entertainment, Hollywood, after a fierce struggle, had carried all before it.

Until the French refusal to capitulate entirely to the US entertainment industry threatened to torpedo the GATT Treaty in 1993, most people had been unaware of the enormous importance attached not only by the US film industry but by Washington to unimpeded access of Hollywood product to foreign markets.

It was brought home to me forcibly in 1987, when Hollywood's top lobbyist of the period, President Ronald Reagan, suddenly departed from a numbing formal oration on the glories of US-Canadian free trade to lecture the Canadian prime minister, Brian Mulroney, in terse and uncharacteristically specific terms about legislation just passed by the Quebecois provincial legislature. The Quebecois bill threatened to prize loose movie distribution in the province from the grip of the American film industry.

That morning in Ottawa, as the press looked on uncomprehendingly, Reagan inquired sharply of Mulroney whether he really agreed with such plans to inconvenience the US president's former employers. Mulroney swiftly promised that no Canadian restrictive legislation would impede Hollywood's freedom of action. Reagan beamed with satisfaction.

Today, the number of countries sequestered from American cultural icons and imagery represented by the word Hollywood has dwindled almost to zero, and the hold-outs are looking increasingly frail. It is now only a matter of time before the former Soviet Union arrives at the vassal status of Great Britain or Brazil. (*The Hollywood Reporter* headlined the 1991 attempted coup by the Gang of Eight "Soviet Coup Blow to Piracy Fight", and called it a "potential major setback for the Motion Picture Association of America".) Even India, home of the largest domestic cinema industry on earth, is beginning to lower obstruction to foreign penetration.

In these days of the New World Order, Washington sets the political and Hollywood the cultural terms of world trade. Entertainment is, after aerospace, the US's second largest export, and exports are a matter of great import to the movie studios. In 1990, they took in $1.8 billion in rental fees inside the US and $1.6 billion in rentals from foreign distributors. American films take up more than 90 percent of all screen time in countries as disparate as Canada, Nigeria and Brazil. Jack Valenti, head of the film industry's international lobbying arm, the Motion Picture Export Association (MPEA), throws around the figure of a $3.5 billion trade surplus for his industry. In 1992 US audio-visual exports to Europe amounted to $3.7 billion in value, while equivalent EC exports to the US amounted to only $288 million. But though the march of political and economic empire has been the stuff of headlines ever since the days of Teddy Roosevelt's Rough Riders, the commercial victories of Hollywood on foreign soil have been the topic of far more discreet record. This most notable saga has been treated as something beautifully natural, like an Austrian child's sudden realization that McDonald's hamburgers and fries simply taste nicer than Knockwurst, Brot and Kartoffelsalat. So set now is Hollywood in the idiom of planetary universalism that it requires a conscious effort of memory to evoke the times, not long gone, when "Americanization" was something that in many countries was denounced and resisted by enemies such as nationalists, ecclesiastics, and local film-makers and entrepreneurs zealous to maintain concessions and patronage. Such were the barricades that Hollywood's salesmen and lobbyists aimed, from the 1920s onwards, to smash down.

Sometimes the American film industry's mundane economic interests were clothed in exalted language, as when the head of Paramount told the *New York Times* in 1946, "We, the industry, recognize the need for informing people in foreign lands about the things that have made America a great country, and we think we know how to put across the message of our democracy." (Of course those in Hollywood who tried to send out a different message in those crucial postwar years were swiftly red-baited out of the business by such FBI informers as Ron Reagan.) While mythology tells us that "the message" of American democracy was conveyed through the irresistibly combined charms of American stars, stories and production values, it has actually been force-fed to the world through the careful engineering of taste, ruthless commercial clout, arm-twisting by the US Departments of Commerce and State, threats of reverse trade embargoes and other such heavy artillery. By 1968, Valenti was boasting that 'the motion picture industry is the only US enterprise that negotiates on its own with foreign governments.'

THE MOMENT OF POLITICAL TRUTH THAT STRUCK ANTHONY Eden when President Eisenhower told him to call off the Suez adventure in 1956 had struck the British film industry, centred at Pinewood studios, nine years earlier. By the summer of 1947, American film corporations were taking more than $60 million out of Britain. This, coupled with Britain's war debt, helped trigger a severe balance-of-payments problem.

On August 6, 1947, the postwar Labour government, wishing to fortify cultural nationalism and repel invasion by Hollywood, imposed a 75 percent tax on the box-office earnings of Hollywood films. The tax was to be paid in advance, on the basis of estimated revenues. On August 9, Hollywood, in the form of the MPEA, retaliated with an indefinite suspension of all films to Britain. The co-founder of Pinewood studios, J. Arthur Rank, announced that to fill the breach he would undertake the production of 47 films at a vast capital outlay, the largest commitment to film ever made in Britain.

But the Labour government was buckling under fierce pressure from the US. On May 3, 1948, the 75 percent levy was abandoned and replaced by a ceiling on profits that could be repatriated to Hollywood. The Hollywood films came flooding back, just in time to sink the hastily produced and cheap material being put out by Rank. By the 1950s, all British resistance had collapsed. Across the Channel, the same battles were being fought and won by Hollywood. The US economic package designed to bail out a France bankrupted by war was withheld by US Secretary of State James Byrnes until Prime Minister Leon Blum agreed to annul the import quota that limited Hollywood to 120 American films a year. Blum told the French movie magnates that he was fully prepared to sacrifice the entire French film industry to get an agreement.

Surrender followed. The French war debt was erased and France given a 30-year, $318 million loan along with $650 million in credits from the Export-Import Bank. But the collapse on quotas dealt the French film industry a near-fatal blow. Half the studios closed and unemployment in the industry soon reached 75 percent. The number of workers employed in the French film industry dropped from 2,132 in 1946 to 898 in 1947. Another round of layoffs in 1948 chopped 60 percent of the remaining workforce.

This defeat duly produced an ironic sort of Vichy regime, in the form of young French cineastes immersing themselves in the American movies now flooding the country, evolving the auteurs and movie pantheon that had enthusiasts of my generation in the early Sixties scuttling from one end of London to the other, *Cahiers du Cinema* in hand, trying to track down B-pictures by Sam Fuller, Frank Tashlin and other Hollywood favorites of the French crowd.

If my own home in Ireland in the mid-1950s was anything to go by, US cultural imperialism was not meeting with much in the way of stiff resistance. My father toiled away, doing short stories for the *Saturday Evening Post. Time* magazine arrived each week. At school, under the leadership of Miles Kington, our jazz band (in which I played bass) rehearsed New Orleans blues.

The third record I ever bought was a blues '78 by Leroy Carr. We weren't alone. At the art schools around London, lads like Keith Richard were working their way through the classics of delta and Chicago blues, from Robert Johnson to Muddy Waters, Howling Wolf and B B King.

What Hoggart, stoutly defensive of British working-class culture and traditions, didn't quite get was that American culture was liberating, whether in the form of blues, jazz, rock or prose. Here was escape from airless provincialism, BBC good taste and the mandates of the class system, which Raymond Chandler caught so well in his discussion of style: "The tone quality of English speech is usually overlooked. This is infinitely variable. The American voice is flat, toneless and tiresome. The English tone quality makes a thinner vocabulary and a more formalized use of language capable of infinite meanings. Its tones of course are read into written speech by association. This makes good English a class language and that is its fatal defect. The English writer is a gentleman first and a writer second."

It was the difference between Dashiell Hammett and Agatha Christie, the Beats against the home crowd.

It's not hard to pick out the great defeats that signalled the true nature of the 'special relationship' and British inferiority in technology and R&B. Politically, Suez summed up the whole situation sharply enough. The Comet— Britain's effort to build a long-range passenger jet—kept crashing because the designers hadn't properly figured out the vibration stresses on the windows. In the early 1960s, Defense Minister Dennis Healey cancelled the TSR2, beaten into the ground by General Dynamics' F-111, itself a disaster, also a pay-off by JFK to the Chicago Mob. The staggering success of the MG and the Triumph sports cars, which helped make England, between 1947 and the early 1960s, the leading exporter of automobiles, inexorably wilted under the duress of managerial incompetence and archaic manufacturing processes. And yet the MG, brought back to the United States by American servicemen after the war, could have been described by some American nativist Hoggart as just the same intimation of invasive cultural imperialism as the milk-bar was to Hoggart himself. Detroit had no response, beyond the baroque glories of the tailfin era, which never answered the design or mechanical challenge of the MG and Triumph directly, but loudly changed the subject.

By the mid-Sixties, our American Hoggart was having to deal with the invasion of the Beatles in 1964 and subsequent years of dominance of British bands, whether The Who, the Rolling Stones, the Kinks, Led Zeppelin, Pink Floyd. There were Laura Ashley prints and Crabtree & Evelyn jams mellowing the rude shanties and preserves of the frontiersfolk. There was the British pub. And this was only the beginning.

I should at this point unveil the argument, already emerging in silhouette. We can show with copious illustration how America came to dominate British economic and, to a consider-able extent, political and cultural life. It wasn't long after Bill Clinton's victory in 1992 that political stylists from the Labour Party were studying his techniques with all the rapture of Elvis lookalikes lip-synching 'Love Me Tender'. This domination has extended gradually down the years, penetrating publishing, television, music and, on the bottom line, film.

But from the British side have come equally potent invasions. Benignly, the British music invasion saved American blues. When Keith Richard first saw Muddy Waters, the latter was painting the walls of the Chess recording studios because he had no musical work at the time. The Stones, mostly, put the great American blues singers back into the big time.

Malignly, from Albion's fatal shore came the glorification of the British class idea, at a particularly fraught moment in American political and cultural life, when—in the wake of the Watergate scandal—government and corporate institutions were in disrepute, and businessmen actually lower than journalists in public esteem. American Public Broadcasting, theoretically a venue for talent and ideas barred from the commercial TV networks, became a showcase for Masterpiece Theater, oil-company sponsored and devoted to endless episodes of "Upstairs, Downstairs" and well-mannered British actors togged up in Victorian or Edwardian fancy dress.

By the late Seventies, young American fogeys were aping Evelyn Waugh at his most loutish, with their noses dipped into Oakeshott or, more likely, getting their world history straight from Paul Johnson. Just as stylists from the Labour Party raced to mime the Clinton thing, the Reagan crowd before them had their model in Thatcherism, herald to the Age of Ron, same way Curtis LeMay, in the Pacific theater, held "Bomber" Harris in high esteem as his guide in the arts of killing very large numbers of civilians with high explosive and incendiaries. Masterpiece Theater brought gentrification to the TV screen, and the British hacks brought their vulgar arts to the *National Enquirer* and later, under Rupert Murdoch's supervision, the *New York Post*. Study the literature of the paranoid American right and you'll usually find, at the apex of the conspiracy to sap American freedoms, a 'British-Zionist' plot.

In a timbre certainly less drear than the shadow of Margaret Thatcher, the impact of Ian Fleming and of his creation, James Bond, nicely illustrates the British imperial contribution. Fleming wrote the memo that inspired the charter of General Donovan's Central Office of Intelligence, which later evolved into OSS, and still later into the CIA. In 1960 Fleming was taken to dinner at the home of Senator Jack Kennedy, and held the room riveted with an amusing scheme for the US to drop leaflets over Cuba, with the compliments of the Soviet Union, announcing that, due to American atom bomb tests, the atmosphere over the island had become radioactive; that radioactivity is held longest in beards; and that radioactivity makes men impotent. As a consequence, Cubans would shave off their beards and without beards Castro was doomed. The day after, Allen Dulles, head of the CIA, told a friend of Fleming that he was sorry he had not been present to hear Fleming's plan in person. Within two years the Kennedy brothers, along with Dulles, were hiring gangsters to help either in the murder of Castro or in his humiliation, the latter being attempted by proposed application of a dust that would make his beard fall out. In 1961 Hugh Sidey of *Time* magazine announced that the President had 10 favorite books, of which one Fleming was ninth, just ahead of Stendhal's *The Red and The Black*. (Sidey later admitted that he and Kennedy had made up most of the list, though probably not the Fleming) along with the widely broadcast fantasy that JFK read at a rate of 1,200 words a minute.

Bond became the embodiment of Western discourse on the Cold War. The ur-Reaganites watched *Thunderball* and conceived the idea that terrorists, probably Libyan, would steal atomic bombs and attack American cities. They watched the lasers in *Goldfinger* and *Diamonds Are Forever*, plus the "particle beam" in a Bond sequel novel called *For Special Services*, and came up with the space-based defense system later known to the world as SDI. Thus has evolved not so much a cultural imperialism but a mutually reinforcing culture of capital, with all the oft-advertised propensities of capital to degrade, vulgarize, constrict, or, as the argot has it now, 'tabloidize'. British TV executives justify the plunge into whatever unidimensional crudities they have in mind by pointing to the necessity of pleasing the American co-producers—and, putatively, American audiences—essential to financial survival. But while the transnational capitalist crowd has been happily co-operative in its manipulation and degrading of the cultures, outlaw cultures have made their brave, sometimes prosperous, and mostly brief stands. American blues nurtured the dreams and the fortunes of Lennon and Jagger. Fifteen years after, the dreams of youth utterly desolate or commercialized, British punk gave expression and a fighting spirit (if not much in the way of fortune) to dour and alienated American children previously transfixed by disco. Kurt Cobain, young, rich and dead, inherited and remodelled that tradition. There are lots of wrecks littering both sides of this two-way street. Fifty years on from VE Day, the big cultural entrepreneurs experience little hindrance in their zeal for the commodification and vulgarizing of more or less everything, but there's always still that space, at the margins, for originality, whose integrity may survive only for the briefest of moments. These are the moments nonethe less that prevent the cultures both sides of the Atlantic from becoming irrecuperably sterile.

MARSHA CUSIC

Jolene: On the Line in Detroit

ONCE WORKED IN A FACTORY WITH A GIRL NAMED JOLENE,.
We were 17 and lied to get hired; we couldn't legally work in
the plant for another year.She was white, from a suburb—
Taylor, "Taylor tucky" to some, a name that mocked the
Southern roots of its working-class and poor whites. She lived
near the plant and I lived in Detroit; without the factory we'd
never have met.

I was black, I still am as a matter of fact. We both were young
and shapely then, which now I'm not; I wouldn't know about
Jolene. She had just been hired and, like they say in prison, you
depended on those who know the lay of the land, even if it's a
day more than you.

The factory was a mechanical hell of extreme temperatures,
convoluted conveyors and steel, and people at all levels with
power, the wielding of which never did bode well.

Women wore hairnets for "quality control" but mostly to
prevent decapitation; the long-haired guys were bullied into
wearing them too. I wore braids down to my waist, long before
it was fashion, and the specter of hair and heads caught in gears
was so conceivable we wore the ugly nets in willing resignation,
one more theft of our outside, normal lives.

Jolene and I circled each other, cat-like—two girls used to
inhabiting the center of any attention—then relaxed in the
knowledge that our appeal could be divvied up without threat;
there were plenty male eyes for the both of us. We became
friends, revolving around each other like planets, the type of
friendship that burns too hot to last.

Ours was a work-hours friendship, walking our fast, hip-
rolling walk down the cement runways of the packing lines, lithe

and nubile. We flaunted our tiny waists and drum-tight thighs at the high senior ladies with tired feet and eyes who had left their younger bodies back in some other lifetime.

We ate in the cafeteria, laughed and drove men crazy and pretended we didn't know. We held court with the tradesmen and machinists, and flirted our way through the long, hard days. But I was dead serious, in ceaseless examination and contention with my surreal, hard surroundings; I was Alice fallen through the wrong side of the looking glass and wanted to know just where and why I had landed.

I was forced into the blue-collar world by pregnancy at 16 and a hard-headed refusal to return to school (my sixties-style protest against formal education and yes, the humiliation of too-young motherhood—this in the days when there was still shame in such things).

My desire to get a factory job met with the dismay of my businessman father and my mother, who had never worked a day in her life except in his employ, not returning to work after motherhood till she was widowed in middle-age. I lived where my peers were prepared for professional success and poised for a piece of the American pie. Mine had been a first black family in a neighborhood of doctors, bankers, salesmen; solidly middle class, in the days when that term didn't apply to blue-collar folk, before proletarians had stock options and portfolios.

The bottom line is, working in a factory was not exactly what was expected of me.

There were a handful of blacks in the plant, among them Miss Loretta, a bashful, hard-working woman who called the place we worked a "plant-ation" but worked all the overtime she could get; Indiana, small and yellow, who could pack boxes faster than anyone but fell behind so they wore her out like the machines; Fast Freddy, dressed like a technicolor pimp before he changed into his uniform each day, and years later had a five-page spread in GQ; Edna, bright and funny, worked with black eyes from a husband trying to kill her; Tie-tongue Bob, big and "slow", who never missed work and could lose his money to any woman so inclined; fine Lynnette, who looked like Pam Grier.

The blacks were an island in a sea of white; they kept their eye on me, lest I be too smart and fast for my own good or theirs, causing trouble with my brick shithouse body or rebelling against the way they had learned to live.

I was unaccustomed to the whites of the working class and I eyed with amazement these new folks at the plant—women like Willa Dean with a Tennessee twang and black-dyed hair, who knew the most important thing one could have was a good man and good work shoes.

Men like Reb from towns Down South that aimed dogs and hoses on dark girls like me; bikers who worked in full regalia with long chains on long wallets holding long money and extra-long Zig Zags for long days of work and long nights.

There were engineers and machinists like Earl and Tom, exacting and smug in the security of their skills; they more or less looked out for all of us—the machines and the people—and we grudgingly looked up to them, even if some of them spent hunting season with supervisors.

I managed a wary co-existence with my new co-workers at first, then settled into the realization that they were all "just people". Eventually, I became their leader. But that's another story.

Jolene was blond, the type of blond that's white in child-hood, what they call tow-headed; the blond that leaves a fuzz of white on the arms and brows white as snow. She had high cheek-bones from a Nordic ancestor, or maybe some tribe of Indian that gave her face hills and valleys in all the right places to made it perfect.

She had a mole near her mouth and perfect teeth and she laughed all the time at everything when she wasn't mad about something. She was as beautiful as the mod girls in my teen magazines and proof that good looks were not exclusive to the rich and high class.

Jolene was a young mother too; for me young and unwed meant not reaching my destiny—for Jolene, not escaping hers. For if work in the plant was for me a fall from grace, for her it was the height of fortune, the key to a future other than being trapped in a trailer home.

We wore skin-tight, high-waisted Levis, denim corsets that noosed our waists into tight circles small enough for a man's hands to wrap around and touch fingers front to back. Even childbirth could not destroy our strong, young curves, and motherhood gave us even more of what got us in trouble in the first place.

Our jeans had the threadbare wear in all the right places that implied rubbing against all the wrong things. We were locked together in beauty and failure and rebellion. We never buttoned our lab coat uniforms, the white hems flew behind us as we sashayed down cinder block halls. We raced past women with wisdom and seniority to get to the source of real attention, guys we looked right in the eyes as as we sneaked cigarettes on the loading docks. We let them think they were smarter than us and they might have a chance, never letting on they were wrong on both counts.

Bra's burned on TV and we didn't wear them, proud that nobody could make us, and mostly, because they stood quite nicely on their own.A supervisor, Phil, had his eye on us and when we'd burst into his office to report a mishap on the line or stomped about some new imposition, he'd sit up, unable to tear his eyes away from us at breast level. He called us "High Beams" as if he was being original, and we'd roll our eyes and swivel back to our machines, letting him know that whatever he was thinking was out of the question.

When the line broke down or shut down early, we jumped in cars and hit the gravel road behind the plant, and flew to the bar where we'd we stay till last call. If we got there too early, by closing time we'd be deep in beers and Southern Comfort and 7-Up, and if somebody else was buying, Jack Daniels with a Pepsi chaser. That was back in the days when I still ruined my liquor.

By closing time we'd be sloshed and stumbling, dancing with eye-lined, hard-drinkin' women and wanna' be cowboys chained to assembly jobs and wives who read Harlequin Romances. We sang, drunk and off-key:

> *You picked a fine time to leave me Lucille,*
> *With four hungry children and a crop in the field.*
> *I've had some bad times been through some sad times*
> *But this time the hurt it won't heal.*
> *You picked a fine time to leave me Lucille.*

The jukebox was full of those Kenny Rodgers songs and ballads of Elvis and Patsy Cline.

The barmaids took no shit; they could fight you like a man and sawdust and sickness lined the bathroom floors. I know I was watched by some God I didn't much believe in at the time those nights after last call; a drive home cold drunk on a coal black highway, hand over one eye to keep the center line from blurring into two. That I didn't die or kill I attribute to forces miraculous.

It was June, suddenly summer, and I'd been at the plant six months. The weather turned glorious and I left it outside each day while I went in for the afternoon shift at 3. Day after day I was missing the summer, getting off work at midnight, or 2 or 3 AM overtime. I should have been graduating and here I was punching a clock.

In an epiphany, it occurred to me that now there was no such thing as "summer vacation". You might get off a week or two with seniority, but not a whole summer like year after year since kindergarten. This revelation hit me like a bad surprise.

Jolene and I were working in separate departments, and the summer heat combined with the usual inferno inside turned the plant into a sauna. Grease oozed from the gears of the conveyor belts and even up out of the bricks in the floor; both working and walking were a dangerous proposition. We toiled in a steam-bath of production quotas, eight, ten, twelve hours a day.

Some vomited in the heat, a few passed out, the supervisors passed out salt tablets. If you stood on the catwalk you could see waves of heat quavering over our heads. In the flat and flickering fluorescent lights the machinery and sweating, moving limbs were a vision of a different kind of hell.

Angry conflicts spit into the air at the smallest provocation or supervisory order. There was talk of a walk-out but no one dared to face the wrath of the company and union both.

Still, in the parking lot on breaks and lunch, parties sprang from trunks of cars and stationwagons; eight-track tapes played Willie Nelson, Bowie, Marvin Gaye, the beer and weed hidden from security guards.

In this cauldron of heat, rage and music, love affairs bubbled up among single and married alike, in furtive grapplings behind storage rooms and rows of stacked wooden pallets, or full-blown trysts during the midnight shift in motel rooms that lined the roads on the way home.

Next day, no matter what you did the night before, it was still hot and you still went back to work.

One day, during a break-down on the line, I slipped away. Not far of course, for the line would start back up and I'd better be there, or else. I hid behind boxes and machines to furiously read a page or two of Flaubert, Hegel, Hershey.

Not just me, in the plant were real scholars, some discussing issues of the day like career diplomats from their designated spots in the lunchroom, others locked in silent, desperate reading, brief and hungry moments of escape.

I looked for the best route to dodge the foreman and slipped through the back of the line, careful on the oil-slick floors; past the press where a lady lost two fingers—one on one year and one the next—past the maintenance crib and tool shed, over a skid of supplies and past the bins of packing boxes, around the hi-lo repair shack and through inventory staging room. Finally, breathless, drenched in sweat, I reached my destination, the railcar dock.

Away from the suffocating heat in the plant, it was a fine June day, hot and bright new summer. I could smell the hay used to pack equipment and the blue wildflowers and wheat that grew by the tracks. The plant was built on old farm land, and there was still a rural beauty to anything that had escaped the industrial grasp.

The dock was a massive barn, high and open-ended so that train cars could be maneuvered in and out on the tracks embedded in the floors. A car would be uncoupled and unloaded for days, sometimes weeks, emptied of raw materials, then hitched back up and rolled down the tracks.

The wheels were higher than the top of my head; the train was a mammoth thing, a sleeping mastodon of black steel. Sometimes a car would be bright red or yellow depending on the cargo, or sometimes a huge tanker filled with oil.

Young guys, they too restless and trapped in the plant on a hot day, would climb up the sides and smoke a joint on top of the car, twenty feet high, unseen by hunting supervisors or worrisome chicks. I listened closely, I was lucky today, alone. I walked the length of the car and snatched off my hairnet to feel the breeze blow cool through my braids.

A beam of sunshine from a vent in the roof made a square on the floor ahead of me, the motes of dust and grain floated in a tube of light from the sky to the floor. I walked over and stood in the patch of sun, as if that square of light held the last of my old life.

Suddenly, reality and self-pity swirled around me in the light like a snow globe—my ruined life, my friends at proms and graduations, summer parties before going off to college. I was a teenager with a child who refused to let parents or welfare help too much, now paying the price for my young lust and pride, defiant and rebellious, tying my fate to those who labored.

I looked into the light but the sun held no answers, I shielded my eyes and let the sweet June heat take the place of the sauna that awaited me on the line; I saw myself movie-like from outside of myself, bathed in light, a dark, lonely seraph in a column of light and defeat. Well, I would stick it out a while longer, then decide what to do.

Thirteen summers later I was still there.

Well, I started out telling you about Jolene. Actually there's not that much more to say; we stayed friends for a while before she was fired. Her pretty smile didn't make up for her smart mouth after too many beers.

She started going with a man, the kind you couldn't be with and stay beautiful, you had to turn brittle and hard and ready to take an ass whippin'. I wonder if her face got that punched up look of too many schnapps and bar fights and back seats, if her pretty teeth were gone; if she added many children to that first one, if she met crack cocaine. I don't know what happened to her, after that first year or two of seniority I never saw her again.

It's been three decades since we met, but when I see a woman of means, I sometimes think of Jolene; if her life were different, Jolene would have been with the ladies who lunch, with her high cheekbones and white-blond hair. She was ever-after proof that wealth and beauty were not twins—and in my mind still young and raw and beautiful as the hills.

Looking back of course my life was not near over, my factory days were clearly no defeat; just another row of pieces in the puzzle of my life, just a stop for 13 years that will always stay with me.

Maybe I told you about her, and, really, I wanted to tell you about me—how once I was young with a waist so small that a man's hands could fit all around, with thighs like congas and hip-length braids that blew in the wind; how once upon a time I had another life.

I once worked in a factory with a girl named Jolene.

JEFFREY ST. CLAIR

The Butterfly Has Landed

UNDER THE CLEAREST OF NORTH COAST SKIES, FOUR DAYS before the winter solstice and the brightest moon for the next hundred years, Julia Hill, aka Butterfly, descended from her aerie in a redwood near Stafford, California, touching ground for the first time in two years, to a worshipful welcome from her cohorts, who call themselves the Circle of Life. Her way was prepared. Within 24 hours she was in New York, speeding to a rendezvous with *Good Morning America*, with Letterman lined up and other assignations with the press scheduled and brokered in a business-like manner.

In the deal that brought Madame Butterfly back to terra firma, Hill agreesdto pay Pacific Lumber $50,000, culled from donations, t-shirt sales and book royalties. In exchange, Pacific Lumber pledged that it won't log the Stafford Giant (which Butterfly calls "Luna"), the 1,300-year-old redwood that was her arboreal hermitage for two years. PL's parent, Maxxam, the timber company taken over by the piratical Charles Hurwitz, keeps the title to the land, and only Butterfly has a "perpetual right to visit the tree". The transaction is scarcely social in nature. Admittedly they had a lot more money but when the Rockefellers bought a redwood grove, at least it became a public amenity.

Pacific Lumber also promised that it won't clearcut within 200 feet of the redwood, although it reserves the right to conduct salvage logging inside the so-called buffer zone—all it was really able to do to begin with.

Every time money changes hands in the forests of Northern California, Senator Dianne Feinstein hovers, harpy-like, over the transaction. First, she sealed the bail-out scheme, that gave the corporate raider Hurwitz $480 million for the core Headwaters grove, along with a green light to log the hell out of the surrounding landscape. Feinstein called it a win-win solution. But the only winners were the senator and her husband's buddy, Hurwitz. Not only did Hurwitz get a hugely inflated price for Headwaters but the deal also makes it nearly impossible to protect lands outside the core Headwaters area. Ontogeny recapitulates phylogeny, as the psychoanalysts say. This time we see the process in miniature, with Butterfly paying her own ransom.

"I am very pleased this agreement has been reached," Feinstein said. "I've talked with all the parties involved. I believe Pacific Lumber did the right thing. I am now hopeful that the Headwaters agreement will be carried out. I believe that it is in the best interest of old-growth forest and sustained-yield of timber." In other words, let the logging commence.

The civil disobedience actions on Pacific Lumber lands near Stafford didn't start with Julia Hill, but with Earth Firstlers and local residents who feared that logging on those unstable slopes put their community at risk of killer landslides. On New Year's Day 1997, part of the logged-over hillside above Stafford gave way. Mud and rocks and stumps hurtled down on part of the town, damaging or destroying more than 30 homes. The landslide originated on Pacific Lumber lands. The company said the blow-out was an "act of God", offered the residents $1,000 each for their loss and busily began planning the logging of the remaining forest on the slope, including the stand containing the Stafford Giant. On October 7, 1997, Earth Firstlers began a tree-sit in the 300-foot tall redwood. They were cheered by local residents of this logging community, a scene that was repeated earlier this year by residents of the timber town of Randle, Washington, where the wives and daughters of loggers baked dinner for tree-sitters on steep hillsides that Plum Creek Timber Company wanted to clearcut.

Julia Hill came along in October of 1997, on a self-described journey of spiritual discovery. Hill is the daughter of an Arkansas preacher. On August 18, 1996, she was in a terrible auto crash that laid her up for nearly a year. Released from her doctor's care, Hill says she "headed West following my spirit to an unknown destination." Her journey brought her to northern California, a couple of hundred miles up 101 from San Francisco where she saw "the great majestic temple of the Redwood forest" for the first time. "My spirit knew it had found what it was searching for," Butterfly writes. "I dropped to my knees and began to cry, because I was so overwhelmed by the wisdom, energy and spirituality housed in these holiest of temples." After a night of prayer on the Lost Coast, Hill had a revelation. God spoke to her and told her that she should do what she could to save "the awe-inspiring" forests. Hill says she returned briefly to Arkansas, "settled my lawsuit, sold everything that I owned, said goodbye to the closest friends I ever had, and came back out west determined to do whatever I could to be of help."

On December 10 she ascended the Stafford Giant, a young woman, a dedicated seeker with little background in the environmental movement. She expected to stay up there a couple of weeks at most. The weeks turned into months, the months to years. Along the way something happened. Julia Hill became Butterfly and she christened the Stafford Giant "Luna", embodying it with a spiritual presence. "Luna and I have become one," Butterfly writes 79 days into her tree-sit. "Luna and I, with the amazing efforts of a wonderful support team, stand together in defiance of the destructive practices of corporate greed and paid-off politicians. Luna is our beacon of hope and truth. In all her majestic glory, she has become our platform to the world." Two years later, Butterfly came down a full-blown mystic, the Gurdjieff of the redwoods. The fiery anti-corporate rhetoric had been replaced by banal New Age homilies and awful poesy.

It is impossible to demean the courage of Butterfly's vigil. Tree-sitting is a hazardous avocation. In the winter with high winds and driving rains it's an especially dangerous business. Pacific Lumber also resorted to numerous intimidation tactics, such as cutting down ropes tied to surrounding trees, logging nearby lands with helicopters, setting security forces around Luna in attempt to starve Butterfly out by keeping her from being resupplied.

Tree-sits, especially ones that last for more than a year, are hardly ecologically benign forms of social protest. Had Butterfly's roost been constructed on federal lands, it would have required a full-blown environmental impact statement. In the swirl of hagiography, an important fact was overlooked: this is endangered species habitat. With all the action going on 180 feet up Luna, it's difficult to imagine spotted owls or marbled murrelets nesting there. Still, that's okay, if the tree were to stand as a representative of the ecosystem, where the ecological integrity of that particular stand could be sacrificed in the name of protecting the entire redwood ecosystem. But that's not what happened. Indeed, the equation was reversed. Luna was transubstantiated into a temple worthy of saving in itself because of its spiritual merger with Butterfly. The rest of the ecosystem be damned. This is exactly the kind of process that environmentalists have been trying to avoid for years. It's not about spotted owls, we said. They are only a symbol for the health of the ecosystem. But by protecting the owl, millions of acres of ancient forest could be cordoned from the chainsaw. The protection of Luna yields only Luna. It's possible to recognize the bravery of an act of resistance and at the same time remark on its folly. Butterfly's 774-day sojourn was a foolhardy exile among the arboreal titans, misbegotten and obsessive, amounting to a kind of ecological fetishism.

I've never met Butterfly. But I've listened to her cell-phone sermons, read her monologues from on high and her poems. Here's a sample from a poem called "Truly Blessed":

Varying shades of green raise their arms to embrace this magical beauty
I climb to the top of my perch reaching in to the heavens
raising my hands in absolute adoration to the spiritual wonderment of Creation.

Gary Snyder this is not. But Butterfly is articulate and telegenic. The photos of her, wrapped in the redwood fogs, depict a woman of haunting beauty with faraway eyes, like Falconetti's Joan d'Arc in Carl Dreyer's film. The beatification of Butterfly probably began the day steelworkers hoisted Bonnie Raitt and Joan Baez up to meet her in a scene worthy of the brush of a French neo-classical painter. This, a kind of eco-tele-evangelism, is perhaps one reason Butterfly became a national celebrity, while the less photogenic defenders of Cove/Mallard and Warner Creek waged similar campaigns to an indifferent (if not hostile) press.

Pacific Lumber wanted Butterfly to sign an agreement that she wouldn't seek to profit off her experience on their lands. She objected and the company relented. But Pacific Lumber got its point across. How many stylites (pillar-sitting mystics) signed book contracts? Now there is talk of a movie in the offing, with north coaster Wynona Ryder, the skin-and-bones actress from Petaluma, slated to play Butterfly.

But what is the message here? In the wake of her deal with Maxxam, Butterfly has said that Maxxam had taken "an unprecedented, courageous first step towards ending the timber wars. Their initiative in this agreement and covenant symbolizes hope that a new era of peace and cooperation has begun between the timber industry and environmentalists—between corporations and communities."

If the high priestess of Luna now says that Maxxam is all right, who could argue with her without being called a heretic? Well then, let us be heretical. This is the same company that has ravaged the redwoods, ripped off its workers' pension fund and looted a savings-and-loan. Now, once again, it is being paid not to destroy the environment. And what do we tell those steelworkers—the 3,000 men and women that Charles Hurwitz has locked out of Kaiser Aluminum plants in Washington, Iowa and Ohio—with whom environmentalists have lately made a fruitful alliance? It's going to be a meager Christmas for those workers and their families and I don't think Butterfly's blessing of Maxxam is going to sit very well with them. Indeed, it tends to confirm every worst prejudice they had about "tree huggers".

We shouldn't blame this turn of events on Butterfly, so much as the organizers who allowed her to stay up in the tree for that ridiculous period of time. After all, they could have got her down in speedy fashion, simply by telling her that they wouldn't be reprovisioning, and were sending up another sitter. But Butterfly was their *Ace in the Hole*, the title of a good movie years ago, when Kirk Douglas plays a reporter who realizes that the story will die as soon as the man stuck down a mine shaft is rescued. Up that tree Julia was a valuable commodity, and they didn't want to give it up.

The legacy of John Jr. and Laurance Rockefeller stack up pretty well next to Butterfly. Yes, given their incomprehensible wealth their efforts on behalf of the redwoods could be considered chintzy. They were undoubtedly ego-driven. Laurance wanted to know that his money had preserved the world's tallest tree (in Rockefeller Grove) so badly that he was willing to let an even taller one be secretly logged off in the Redwoods National Park further north to keep his record. But at least they bought up whole stands of trees, dozens of entire groves with some clearcut and high-graded lands mixed in. And they turned them over to public ownership, in national and state parks. Certainly, this act of checkbook environmentalism indirectly benefited the clearcutters, driving up the price of Lousiana-Pacific, Simpson and Georgia-Pacific holdings. But what the Rockefellers bought was at least ours, open for anyone to hike through and marvel at. Butterfly's deal with Hurwitz is another story entirely.

Even worse, the deal reaffirms the hostage-taking mentality of corporate raiders like Hurwitz, forcing enviros to buy endangered species habitat from corporations to keep it from being destroyed. This is a doomed strategy that will pad the pockets of corporations but do almost nothing to aid the environment. At $50,000 per tree, it will take something like $3 trillion to buy back the rest of the threatened big trees in the Pacific Northwest. In other words, the combined wealth of Bill Gates, Paul Allen and the Sultan of Brunei couldn't save what's left of the ancient forests.

Many enviros-in-training, a startling number of them Catholics, have felt themselves drawn to a particular breed of saint, the ascetics and eremites who went into the wilderness for forty years to stand alone against the forces of nature. One such was St. Anthony Aegyptus, about whom Flaubert wrote his beautiful novella, the *Temptations of St. Anthony*. For thirty years Anthony lived in solitude in an abandoned Roman battlement at Pispir in the heart of the Sahara, standing on a tall pillar from dawn to dusk, staring into the eastern reaches, awaiting revelations from above. He talked to lions, who helped him dig a grave for St. Paul of Thebes, and ravens, who brought him bread, his only sustenance. The desert winds ate away his flesh; his open wounds became a host for maggots, which, according to Athanasius' *Life of Anthony*, kept him from succumbing to gangrene. Anthony returned to Alexandria in time to crush the Arian heresy. In a small Gothic church in Tarcento, a village in northern Italy, the sacristy, a tomb-like room made of thick blocks of rock hewn from the Dolomites, contains the relics of

St. Anthony: an ancient bell, a sliver of a crucifix and a leathered strip of flesh said to be part of his tongue.

Decades from now what relics of Butterfly will pilgrims journey to Stafford to see? Her cellphone, Gore Tex jacket and book contract? Certainly, Luna won't be around. When the surrounding landscape is clearcut, this mighty redwood, exposed to brutal winter winds and rain, will come tumbling, a $50,000 piece of blow-down, whose meaning will be as inscrutable as that "colossal wreck", Shelley's "Ozymandias", an enigmatic, fallen statue in the desert sands.

ALEXANDER COCKBURN
Binti Jua's Family Values

I T SAYS MUCH FOR THE QUALITY OF AMERICAN POLITICAL culture in the high summer of 1996 that amid the gathering of the nation's two major political parties and limning of their overall vision of the future, the act of compassion deemed by millions to have advertised most succinctly our nobler, loving virtues was enacted by the child of an immigrant, and not even a human one at that: Binti Jua, the west African gorilla that lifted a toddler who fell into a cage at the Brookfield Zoo in Illinois, walked to the gate and laid him down for the keepers to retrieve.

In San Diego, the Republicans roared out their maledictions on thriftless mothers and their inconvenient children. In Chicago, the Democrats endorse a president whose welfare bill will pitchfork at least a million more children into poverty over the next three years. The numberless Americans who tuned out both gatherings preferred to get their political message from Binti Jua.

In the old days, political conventions used to be like zoos. Informed commentators would discuss the social anthropology of state delegations, which in turn often would defiantly display themselves in vulgar shows. "It's a zoo down there!" the radio reporters and TV commentators would cry. These days, the old zoo, with animals pacing about in cages adorned with notices giving information about their origins and Linnaean classifications, are mostly a thing of the past. These days, zoo staging has transmuted from older modes of confinement, whether cages or the moated enclosures that were pioneered in Germany and then this country by Carl Hagenbeck at the turn of the century. The trend now, fashioned by Jon Coe and Grant Jones, who designed the Woodland Park gorilla exhibit in Seattle in the mid-

1980s, is called "landscape immersion," with visitors enveloped in the appropriate habitat of the exhibit. The idea was to limit the peripheral vision of the onlookers, to shield them from distracting perspectives and immerse them in the total gorilla experience.

Conventionworld, the Republican gathering earlier this month in San Diego, showed how the impresarios had taken all this to heart. There was no moat between podium and audience. Landscape immersion was so complete that when, for example, Republican African-Americans were being "themed," the onlookers were allowed no peripheral vision of the mostly white human landscape surrounding the relatively few people of color in the hall.

San Diego was indeed a wonderful vantage point from which to study this dialectic between politics and zoos, humans and their fellow creatures. Near at hand, for Republicans eager to escape Conventionworld, were Sea World and the San Diego Zoo. Sea World, owned by the Anheuser-Busch Corp. and host to about 4 million visitors a year—same as the zoo—was a favored venue for convention events seeking to acquire reflected virtue from the kitsch atmosphere of aquatic purity, with dolphins and orca recruited to exhibit the fundamental harmony of creation under corporate auspices.

Sea World is non-union, with minimum wage levels for the attendants. The zoo is Teamster-organized, though there should be more interspecies union recruitment. We visited the same day Binti Jua brought warmth to every heart. In the polar bear exhibit (total immersion via a big new pool with enhanced underwater views) three of the bears had salmonella poisoning and were confined to what the guide brightly referred to as their "bedrooms". This meant compulsory overtime for 18-month old Chinook, who had been putting in 13-hour days for the duration of the convention.

Chinook appeared frayed and angry, but the guide insisted the cub was "doing a real good job" exhibiting bearishness to the audience. All the same, Chinook could do with a union rep, the same way poor Dunda the elephant needed one a few years back when it was discovered that she was being savagely beaten for disciplinary infractions. Don't trumpet, organize!

The onlookers looked at Chinook, and Chinook looked longingly at the antelope in the next exhibit. Unlike the scene taking place that very moment in the Brookfield Zoo, there was no uplifting moral we could take home, unless the sight of a caged creature is edifying. Zoogoers typically look at exhibits for about 90 seconds, and the two most frequently uttered questions are: "Where is the bathroom" and "Where is the snack bar?" Many visitors never break stride as they saunter past the exhibits, though they will pause for animals that beg, feed their young, make sounds or mimic human behavior.

And that's the line that many humans—embarrassed that a mere gorilla should be cleaning up in the compassion stakes—are taking about Binti Jua. She saved the baby because she was reared by humans and only thus acquired the instinct to cherish a human child.

So nothing truly ties us to Binti Jua. She's a themed exhibit on which only sentimentalists project their hopes for the human race. Future generations of gorillas nurtured by existing human standards in America will exhibit the acquired instinct: when that baby drops to earth, leave it lie. In Chicago, the Democrats had better visit only the old Field Museum, where the dioramas of stuffed animals never change, in frozen moments of time long gone.

BEN TRIPP

Take Two Hits and Call Me in the Morning

NOTE TO THE DEPARTMENT OF JUSTICE: ALL REFERENCES to the author's use of illegal drugs in this essay are purely satirical in nature. The author has never used drugs of any kind, although he once became high as the result of using PVC cement in a confined space.

'Medical marijuana' is one of those terms like 'friendly fire' or 'military intelligence' that just doesn't sound right—but who cares? Back in my day, when we smoked weed (my parents' generation smoked 'grass' or 'pot') we didn't have medical marijuana, and we would have laughed at the idea, our eyes as glassy and red as glazed hams. After all, dope or hemp was partially responsible for our low standing in academics, athletics and achievements; we were the first generation of teens more short-winded than our own grandparents. But we got laid like nobody's business.

We didn't need a note from the doctor. Little did we know, those were the good old days. The crumbly, brownish *cannabis sativa inferioris* we grew amongst the blueberry bushes on Mount Monadnock and similar eminences in southern New Hampshire was so inferior in quality you had to smoke the equivalent of fifty packs of unfiltered Marlboros to get properly stoned on the stuff. We didn't call it weed for nothing; you could eat it like salad and experience little more than a faint tingling in the molars. We'd have been better off smoking endive lettuce, but we only had iceberg. The local police would occasionally pull up the plants they stumbled upon whilst having sex with minors in the bushes, and if you got caught with a bud bag on you, they would lift your stash and maybe fine you $25. And then smoke the stuff themselves.

It was a reasonable system and everybody was a winner, staggering around in an acrid, reeking haze with cottonmouth and a soul-deep yearning for Cheetos. Was it worth it? Sure it was. Ganja took the sting out of acne, algebra and angst. It made us feel confident when we were not. It made our parents vaguely amusing, which they were otherwise not; and it made the interminable presidency of Ronald Reagan seem like a distant, unpleasant dream from which we would wake refreshed but dying for a quart of Mountain Dew. As long as we had a steady supply of wacky tobbaccy, those crappy jobs at Bradlees, McDonald's and Aubuchon's Hardware, were tolerable and we felt like we were earning money for a purpose, even if that purpose was to analyze the Ted Nugent "Double Live Gonzo" album for hidden metaphors. And with double albums you could use the fold in the record jacket to shake the seeds out of your latest dime-bag of Indian oregano.

They claim that marijuana is a "gateway" drug that leads to the use of more harmful and addictive substances; this is hokum. The eternal gateway drug is boredom. Is beer a gateway drug to drinking Aqua Velva? I quit the loco weed while George Bush Sr. was in office. I was in love with a woman who found me annoying when I was stoned, and I had other things to do with my time. Sometimes I miss it a little, usually right around election time, but I've never seriously considered lighting up again. It's been ages since I smoked anything more potent than a stale Cuban cigar.

Meanwhile, bud has been demonized, criminalized, and the drug war has been industrialized. There's more money to be made busting herb-smokers than there is in arresting drunk drivers, which is ironic, because drunk drivers kill thousands every year, while the only confirmed death from marijuana use was the result of a guy in Maui falling off a cliff while tending his crop of chronic green. The authorities have made a fortune fighting marijuana, classified since 1937 as an illegal substance in a bill signed by President Roosevelt, who seldom lit up himself. This was largely a formality, as nobody much cared and the government wasn't inclined to do much about this new law, but enforcement became popular by the 1950s as a way of busting Negro jazz musicians, white lefties, Mexicans and other undesirable types. In addition, defense lawyers had figured out they could get their clients out of trouble by claiming devil weed made the defendant go crazy. So as time passed, hemp got a bad name with the Establishment. Of course this meant that during the 1960's, everybody had to smoke it. You figure when the stoned youth of the sixties grew up, they'd decriminalize the doob, right? That's what my generation assumed would happen.

When Bill Clinton said he tried marijuana but never inhaled, he was, as often happened, stretching the truth. I guarantee you Bill didn't just inhale. Here was a man who could blaze a fattie and suck it down from fore to aft in a single Homeric drag until his eyeballs were as red as jawbreaker candies. Sinking back on the sofa, gripping the smoke in his lungs until the heart-crushing plumes were reduced to the faintest vapor upon exhalation to the applause of onlooking loose-breasted hippie chicks, he was stoned again. But Clinton in maturity became emblematic of the ex-radical's failure to reform the atavistic anti-marijuana stance of our government. To this day, a handful of dank nugs is considered as dangerous a narcotic as cocaine, heroin or morphine, and the sentences for possession or dealing are draconian and vigorously applied. Yet every single individual in power knows damn well the schmoke is mostly harmless, and most of them have enjoyed a toke or two themselves.

And why not? The days when you had to smoke an entire plant to get high are over; now a couple of tokes will take care of business for four hours of solid housecleaning or tax preparation. You don't need to smoke as much, so you're not getting all the tar and insecticide we inhaled in the good old days. Delivery systems have improved as well. We used to make pipes out of aluminum foil and a toilet paper tube, which would inevitably catch fire after a dozen hits; now there are filtered triple-chamber bongs and stainless steel micro mesh one-hitters which guarantee a degree of smoking comfort unknown in previous times. In addition, the supply system is streamlined, so your average high school student or corporate CEO can purchase the stuff without recourse to dark alleys and unsavory characters. Buying dope these days is more like a visit from the Avon Lady than anything else. Smoking it is a middle-class experience—and yet there is an entire population of stoners languishing in prison.

It makes no sense. Despite the brutal penalties against its use, marijuana is one of the mildest drugs—even the hairy, resinous super-breeds available today. And in recent times, the medical applications of this venerable herb known severally as grass, weed, pot, cannabis, dope, jay, skunk, kif or ganja have been documented by reputable professionals. Aside from the obvious effects such as inducing relaxation, improving social behavior, and making "Gilligan's Island" seem funny, Marijuana also helps people taking medications such as the AIDS cocktail or cancer drugs keep food in their stomachs. It has been found to ease the pain and symptoms of many diseases, such as epilepsy, MS, glaucoma and holiday gatherings. Yet the folks who self-medicate, or even take the stuff as allowed under local or state law, are suffering stormtrooper raids by the feds. These people are spending the last few precious months of their lives in prison or awaiting trial—as cruel and unusual as a punishment gets. Recent advertisements suggesting a causal link between the casual user and international terrorists just show how tenuous the case against cheeba really is.

I entirely support the idea that the herb, and its helpful cannabinoids, should be legal to take for medical conditions.

But is that what this is really about? I hope not. Let's call medical marijuana the gateway legislation, and pray that eventually we can drop the clinical side of the subject and acknowledge what this should really be about: everybody can get stoned. Can you really say that marijuana is dangerous? Have you ever had a problem with a stoned driver? Remember the old joke: a drunk speeds through the stop sign; somebody equally stoned waits for the sign to turn green. Are our hospitals filled with raving pot smokers, insane from reefer madness? Is it worth the money to have our government bust the kid who mows your lawn or serves you Slurpees? And what if a seed gets into your carpet and the feds raid your house for some other reason, as they are increasingly likely to do? You might hate the stuff, but it also might be growing wild behind your house, and that might be good enough to get you thrown in jail for life. Hell, your kid could have a nickel bag hidden in his room, and you'll go to jail, and so will your kid, and maybe the neighbor on the side of your house closest to your kid's room. None of this is your kid's fault: it's crazy laws, enforced for profit.

The situation is out of hand. We are a nation of quiet stoners, blazing up and smoking out in peace and harmony. Not everybody does it, but lots of people do; and a vast majority of Americans have done it at some point in the past. If marijuana were masturbation, the laws would have to change, or the entire nation would be behind bars. Marijuana smoking is not really all that different, and certainly little more harmful, than the time-honored practice of Onanism; the next time you revile pot smokers, try thinking of it that way. Just as wanking doesn't require a doctor's note, neither should pot-smoking. If we have to get medical exceptions first, and then dismantle the laws from there, that's dandy, but let's not fool ourselves. The best thing about marijuana is it's fun. And if you find masturbation disgusting and that analogy doesn't work for you at all, remember it's easier to get laid if everybody's a little high, and then we can all stop fondling our privates. Who knows, maybe that's the medical excuse we've been waiting for.

ALEXANDER COCKBURN
Hitler On Buchanan

THOUGH NOW 110 YEARS OLD AND IN POOR PHYSICAL shape, Adolf Hitler felt strong enough for a brief chat on the phone from his nursing home in Asuncion about the row over Pat Buchanan's new book.

COCKBURN: *Do you agree that America's entry into the First World War in 1917 prevented a compromise peace between Germany and its European antagonists, Britain and France, and ensured Germany's utter defeat, national humiliation, thus setting the stage for your own rise to power?*

HITLER: Nein. It was the sabotage from within Germany that rendered vain all the sacrifices and deprivations, the hunger and thirst of endless months, the death of 2 millions who died thereby --

To put it another way --

Would not the graves of all the hundreds of thousands open up, would they not open and send the silent heroes, covered with mud and blood, home as spirits of revenge, to the country that had so mockingly cheated them?

But, Herr Hitler--

Was it for this that boys of 17 sank into Flanders Fields? Was that the meaning of the sacrifice which the German mother brought to the fatherland, when with an aching heart she let her most beloved boys go away, never to see them again? Was it all for this that now a handful of miserable criminals was allowed to lay hands on the fatherland? Germany fell through the fantastic conception of a Niebelungen league with the Habsburg State cadaver.

But the Versailles Treaty --

Allow me to complete my thought. Germany was stabbed in the back, but of course the treaty was of boundless use to us, a means of whipping up national passions to the boiling point, until in the heads of 60 million men and women the same hate became a single fiery sea of flames out of whose glow a steely will arose, and the cry forced itself, WE WANT ARMS ONCE MORE!

Mr Buchanan argues that American intervention prevented a truce for Germany in the West with Britain and France that would have allowed Germany to turn east and crush the Bolsheviks.

Buchanan forgets that the ultimate goal of French diplomacy always stands in opposition to the final tendency of British state-craft. There was no necessary English interest in crushing Germany. The German people's irreconcilable and mortal enemy is and remains France. It does not matter who ruled or will rule in France, whether Bourbons or Jacobins, Bonapartists or bourgeois democrats, clerical republicans or red Bolsheviks, the final goal of her foreign-policy activity was always an effort to hold the Rhine frontier and to guarantee this stream by means of a disintegrated and dismembered Germany.

Some of Buchanan's critics --

... France both before, during and after the war remained the most terrible enemy. This people, which was constantly becoming more negro-ified, by its tie with the aims of Jewish world dominion constituted a grim danger for the existence of the European white race. For infection in the heart of Europe through Negro blood on the Rhine corresponded equally to the sadistic, perverse vengefulness of this chauvinistic, hereditary enemy of our people, and to the ice-cold plan of the Jews thus to begin bastardizing the European continent at its core and, through infection by inferior humanity, to deprive the white race of the foundations for a sovereign existence.

Herr Hitler, we have only a few minutes left --

Don't interrupt all the time, godammit. Now you've made me lose my train of thought. What was I saying?

You were talking about France, Herr Hitler.

Ach, Ja! What France, spurred by its own vengefulness, methodically led by the Jew, was doing in Europe was a sin against the existence of white humanity. Incidentally, we in the National Socialists learned much on these matters from your own great American thinkers, Madison Grant, Dr. Stoddard, Charles Davenport. As for attacking Russia, well of course in Russian bolshevism we saw Jewry's twentieth-century effort to take world dominion unto itself. To paraphrase Grant, whose *Passing of the Great Race* I still have here on my night table, the impotence of nations, their own death of old age, comes from the abandonment of their purity of blood. And the Jew guards this better than any other people of the earth. Thereby he continues to move further on his fatal course, until another force opposes him and, in a mighty struggle, once more pitches the stormer of the heavens back at Lucifer --

Herr Hitler, we're running out of time.

I'm almost through, and anyway the nurse here is telling me not to get over-excited. But just to finish the thought, for centuries Russia drew nourishment from a Germanic nucleus to its superior strata of thinkers. The Jews obliterated this. Jewry itself is not an organizing element,but a ferment of decomposition. Good to talk to you. Remind me if you call again to explain that the crucial watershed in the 1930s was my reoccupation of the Rhineland in 1936. If Britain and France had counterattacked our goose would have been cooked. Militarily, we were bluffing. It was a colossal gamble. But the British let me get away with it. As for your Roosevelt, well of course the Jews pushed him into the war. Okay, okay. *Auf wiedersehn* and don't forget to read Grant. Try reading his *Alien in Our Midst*. Buchanan probably knows it.

PETER LINEBAUGH

The Incomplete, True, Authentic and Wonderful History of May Day

A Beginning

THE SOVIET GOVERNMENT PARADES MISSILES AND marches soldiers on May Day. The American government has called May 1 "Loyalty Day" and associates it with militarism. The real meaning of this day has been obscured by the designing propaganda of both governments. The truth of May Day is totally different. To the history of May Day there is a Green side and there is a Red side.

Under the rainbow, our methodology must be colorful. Green is a relationship to the earth and what grows therefrom. Red is a relationship to other people and the blood spilt there among. Green designates life with only necessary labor; Red designates death with surplus labor. Green is natural appropriation; Red is social expropriation. Green is husbandry and nurturance; Red is proletarianization and prostitution. Green is useful activity; Red is useless toil. Green is creation of desire; Red is class struggle. May Day is both.

The Green

Once upon a time, long before Weinberger bombed North Africans, before the Bank of Boston laundered money or Reagan honored the Nazi war dead, the earth was blanketed by a broad mantle of forests. As late as Caesar's time a person might travel through the woods for two months without gaining an unobstructed view of the sky. The immense forests of Europe, Asia,

45

Africa and America provided the atmosphere with oxygen and the earth with nutrients. Within the woodland ecology our ancestors did not have to work the graveyard shift, or deal with flextime, or work from Nine to Five. Indeed, the native Americans whom Captain John Smith encountered in 1606 worked only four hours a week. The origin of May Day is to be found in the Woodland Epoch of History.

In Europe, as in Africa, people honored the woods in many ways. With the leafing of the trees in spring, people celebrated "the fructifying spirit of vegetation," to use the phrase of J.G. Frazer, the anthropologist. They did this in May, a month named after Maia, the mother of all the gods according to the ancient Greeks, giving birth even to Zeus.

The Greeks had their sacred groves, the Druids their oak worship, the Romans their games in honor of Floralia. In Scotland the herdsmen formed circles and danced around fires. The Celts lit bonfires in hilltops to honor their god, Beltane. In the Tyrol people let their dogs bark and made music with pots and pans. In Scandinavia fires were lit and the witches came out.

Everywhere people "went a-Maying" by going into the woods and bringing back leaf, bough, and blossom to decorate their persons, homes and loved ones with green garlands. Outside theater was performed with characters like "Jack-in-the-Green" and the "Queen of the May". Trees were planted. Maypoles were erected. Dances were danced. Music was played. Drinks were drunk, and love was made. Winter was over, spring had sprung.

The history of these customs is complex and affords the student of the past with many interesting insights into the history of religion, gender, reproduction and village ecology. Take Joan of Arc, who was burned in May 1431. Her inquisitors believed she was a witch. Not far from her birthplace, she told the judges, "there is a tree that they call 'The Ladies Tree'— others call it 'The Fairies Tree'. It is a beautiful tree, from which comes the Maypole. I have sometimes been to play with the young girls to make garlands for Our Lady of Domremy. Often I have heard the old folk say that the fairies haunt this tree...." In the general indictment against Joan, one of the particulars against her was dressing like a man. The paganism of Joan's heresy originated in the Old Stone Age, when religion was animistic and shamans were women and men.

Monotheism arose with the Mediterranean empires. Even the most powerful Roman Empire had to make deals with its conquered and enslaved peoples (syncretism). As it destroyed some customs, it had to accept or transform others. Thus, we have Christmas Trees. May Day became a day to honor the saints, Philip and James, who were unwilling slaves to Empire. James the Lesser neither drank nor shaved. He spent so much time praying that he developed huge callouses on his knees, likening them to camel legs. Philip was a lazy guy. When Jesus said "Follow me", Philip tried to get out of it by saying he had to tend to his father's funeral, and it was to this excuse that the Carpenter's son made his famous reply, "Let the dead bury the dead". James was stoned to death, and Philip was crucified head downwards. Their martyrdom introduces the Red side of the story, even the Green side is preserved because, according to the *Floral Directory,* the tulip is dedicated to Philip and bachelor buttons to James.

The farmers, workers and child-bearers (laborers) of the Middle Ages had hundreds of holy days that preserved the May Green, despite the attack on peasants and witches. Despite the complexities, whether May Day was observed by sacred or profane ritual, by pagan or Christian, by magic or not, by straights or gays, by gentle or calloused hands, it was always a celebration of all that is free and life-giving in the world. That is the Green side of the story. Whatever else it was, it was not a time to work.

Therefore, it was attacked by the authorities. The repression had begun with the burning of women and it continued in the sixteenth century when America was "discovered", the slave trade was begun, and nation-states and capitalism were formed. In 1550 an Act of Parliament demanded that Maypoles be destroyed, and it outlawed games. In 1644 the Puritans in England abolished May Day altogether. To these work-ethicists the festival was obnoxious for paganism and worldliness. Philip Stubs, for example, in *Anatomy of Abuses* (1585) wrote of the Maypole, "And then fall they to banquet and feast, to leape and daunce about it, as the Heathen people did at the dedication of their Idolles." When a Puritan mentioned "heathen" we know genocide was not far away. According to the excellent slide show at the Quincy Historical Society, 90 percent of the Massachusetts people, including chief Chicatabat, died from chicken pox or small pox a few years after the Puritans landed in 1619. The Puritans also objected to the unrepressed sexuality of the day. Stubs said, "Of fourtie, threescore, or an hundred maides going to the wood, there have scarcely the third part of them returned home again as they went."

The people resisted the repressions. Thenceforth, they called their May sports, the "Robin Hood Games". Capering about with sprigs of hawthorn in their hair and bells jangling from their knees, the ancient charaders of May were transformed into an outlaw community, Maid Marions and Little Johns. The May feast was presided over by the "Lord of Misrule", "the King of Unreason", or the "Abbot of Inobedience". Washington Irving was later to write that the feeling for May "has become chilled by habits of gain and traffic". As the gainers and traffickers sought to impose the regimen of monotonous work, the people responded to preserve their holyday. Thus began in earnest the Red side of the story of May Day. The struggle was brought to Massachusetts in 1626.

Thomas Morton of Merry Mount

In 1625 Captain Wollaston, Thomas Morton, and 30 others sailed from England and months later, taking their bearings from a red cedar tree, they disembarked in Quincy Bay. A year later Wollaston, impatient for lucre, left for good to Virginia. Thomas Morton settled in Passonaggessit, which he named Merry Mount. The land seemed a "Paradise" to him. He wrote, there are "fowls in abundance, fish in multitudes, and I discovered besides, millions of turtle doves on the green boughs, which sat pecking of the full, ripe, pleasant grapes that were supported by the lusty trees, whose fruitful load did cause the arms to bend".

On May Day, 1627, he and his Indian friends, stirred by the sound of drums, erected a Maypole 80 feet high, decorated it with garlands, wrapped it in ribbons, and nailed to its top the antlers of a buck. Later he wrote that he "sett up a Maypole upon the festival day of Philip and James, and therefore brewed a barrell of excellent beare". A ganymede sang a Bacchanalian song. Morton attached to the pole the first lyric verses penned in America, which concluded with the proclamation that the first of May at Merry Mount shall be kept holly day.

The Puritans at Plymouth were opposed to the May Day. They called the Maypole "an Idoll" and named Merry Mount "Mount Dagon" after the god of the first ocean-going imperialists, the Phoenicians. More likely, though the Puritans were the imperialists, not Morton, who worked with slaves, servants, and native Americans, person to person. Everyone was equal in his "social contract". Governor Bradford wrote, "They allso set up a Maypole, drinking and dancing aboute it many days together, inviting the Indean women for their consorts, dancing and frisking together (like so many fairies, or furies rather) and worse practise."

Merry Mount became a refuge for Indians, the discontented, same-sexers, runaway servants, and what the governor called "all the scume of the countrie". When the authorities reminded him that his actions violated the King's Proclamation, Morton replied that it was "no law". Miles Standish, whom Morton called "Mr. Shrimp," attacked. The Maypole was cut down. The settlement was burned. Morton's goods were confiscated, he was chained in the bilboes and ostracized to England aboard the ship *The Gift* at a cost, the Puritans complained, of 12 pounds 7 shillings. The rainbow coalition of Merry Mount was thus destroyed for the time being. That Merry Mount later (1636) became associated with Anne Hutchinson, the famous midwife, spiritualist, and feminist, surely was more than coincidental. Her brother-in-law ran the Chapel of Ease. She thought that god loved everybody, regardless of their sins. She doubted the Puritans' authority to make law. A statue of Robert Burns in Quincy near to Merry Mount, quotes the poet's lines,

> *A fig for those by law protected!*
> *Liberty's a glorious feast!*
> *Courts for cowards were erected,*
> *Churches built to please the priest.*

Thomas Morton was a thorn in the side of the Boston and Plymouth Puritans, because he had an alternate vision of Massachusetts. He was impressed by its fertility; they by its scarcity. He befriended the Indians; they shuddered at the thought. He was egalitarian; they proclaimed themselves the "Elect". He freed servants; they lived off them. He armed the Indians; they used arms against Indians. To Nathaniel Hawthorne, the destiny of American settlement was decided at Merry Mount. Casting the struggle as mirth vs. gloom, grizzly saints vs. gay sinners, green vs. iron, it was the Puritans who won, and the fate of America was determined in favor of psalm-singing Indian-scalpers whose notion of the Maypole was a whipping post.

Parts of the past live, parts die. The red cedar that drew Morton first to Merry Mount blew down in the gale of 1898. A section of it, about eight feet of its trunk became a power fetish in 1919, placed as it was next to the president's chair of the Quincy City Council. Interested parties may now view it in the Quincy Historical Museum. Living trees, however, have since grown, despite the closure of the shipyards.

On Both Sides of the Atlantic

In England the attacks on May Day were a necessary part of the wearisome, unending attempt to establish industrial work discipline. The attempt was led by the Puritans with their belief that toil was godly and less toil wicked. Absolute surplus value could be increased only by increasing the hours of labor and abolishing holydays. A parson wrote a piece of work propaganda called *Funebria Florae, Or the Downfall of the May Games*. He attacked "ignorants, atheists, papists, drunkards, swearers, swashbucklers, maid-marians, morrice-dancers, maskers, mummers, Maypole stealers, health-drinkers, together with a rapscallion rout of fiddlers, fools fighters, gamesters, lewd-women, light-women, contemmers of magistracy, affronters of ministry, disobedients to parents, misspenders of time, and abusers of the creature, &c."

At about this time, Isaac Newton, the gravitationist and machinist of time, said work was a law of planets and apples alike. Thus work ceased to be merely the ideology of the Puritans, it became a law of the universe. In 1717 Newton purchased London's 100-foot Maypole and used it to prop up his telescope.

Chimney sweeps and dairy maids led the resistance. The sweeps dressed up as women on May Day, or put on aristocratic periwigs. They sang songs and collected money. When the Earl of Bute in 1763 refused to pay, the opprobrium was so great that he was forced to resign. Milk maids used to go a-Maying by dressing in floral garlands, dancing and getting the dairymen to distribute their milk-yield freely. Soot and milk workers thus helped to retain the holyday right into the Industrial Revolution.

The ruling class used the day for its own purposes. Thus, when Parliament was forced to abolish slavery in the British dominions, it did so on May Day 1807. In 1820 the Cato Street conspirators plotted to destroy the British cabinet while it was having dinner. Irish, Jamaican and Cockney were hanged for the attempt on May Day 1820. A conspirator wrote his wife saying "justice and liberty have taken their flight... to other distant shores". He meant America, where Boston Brahmin, Robber Baron and Southern Plantocrat divided and ruled an arching rainbow of people.

Two bands of that rainbow came from English and Irish islands. One was Green. Robert Owen, union leader, socialist, and founder of utopian communities in America, announced the beginning of the millennium after May Day 1833. The other was Red. On May Day 1830, a founder of the Knights of Labor, the United Mine Workers of America and the Wobblies was born in Ireland, Mary Harris Jones, aka "Mother Jones". She was a Maia of the American working class.

May Day continued to be commemorated in America, one way or another, despite the victory of the Puritans at Merry Mount. On May Day 1779 the revolutionaries of Boston confiscated the estates of "enemies of Liberty". On May Day 1808 "twenty different dancing groups of the wretched Africans" in New Orleans danced to the tunes of their own drums until sunset when the slave patrols showed themselves with their cutlasses. "The principal dancers or leaders are dressed in a variety of wild and savage fashions, always ornamented with a number of tails of the small wild beasts", observed a strolling white man.

The Red: Haymarket Centennial

The history of the modern May Day originates in the center of the North American plains, at Haymarket, in Chicago—"the city on the make"—in May 1886. The Red side of that story is more well known than the Green, because it was bloody. But there was also a Green side to the tale, though the green was not so much that of pretty grass garlands as it was of greenbacks, for in Chicago, it was said, the dollar is king.

Of course the prairies are green in May. Virgin soil, dark, brown, crumbling, shot with fine black sand, it was the produce of thousands of years of humus and organic decomposition. For many centuries this earth was husbanded by the native Americans of the plains. As Black Elk said, theirs is "the story of all life that is holy and is good to tell, and of us two-leggeds sharing in it with the four-leggeds and the wings of the air and all green things; for these are children of one mother and their father is one Spirit". From such a green perspective, the white men appeared as pharaohs, and indeed, as Abe Lincoln put it, these prairies were the "Egypt of the West".

The land was mechanized. Relative surplus value could be obtained only by reducing the price of food. The proteins and vitamins of this fertile earth spread through the whole world. Chicago was the jugular vein. Cyrus McCormick wielded the surgeon's knife. His mechanical reapers harvested the grasses and grains. McCormick produced 1,500 reapers in 1849; by 1884 he was producing 80,000. Not that McCormick actually made reapers members of the Molders Union Local 23 did that, and on May Day 1867 they went on strike, starting the Eight Hour Movement.

A staggering transformation was wrought. It was: "Farewell" to the hammer and sickle. "Goodbye" to the cradle scythe. "So long" to Emerson's man with the hoe. These now became the artifacts of nostalgia and romance. It became "Hello" to the hobo. "Move on" to the harvest stiffs. "Line up" to the proletarians. Such were the new commands of civilization.

Thousands of immigrants, many from Germany, poured into Chicago after the Civil War. Class war was advanced, technically and logistically. In 1855 the Chicago police used Gatling guns against the workers who protested the closing of the beer gardens. In the Bread Riot of 1872 the police clubbed hungry people in a tunnel under the river. In the 1877 railway strike, federal troops fought workers at "The Battle of the Viaduct". These troops were recently seasoned from fighting the Sioux who had killed Custer. Henceforth, the defeated Sioux could only "go to a mountain top and cry for a vision". The Pinkerton Detective Agency put visions into practice by teaching the city police how to spy and to form fighting columns for deployment in city streets. A hundred years ago during the street car strike, the police issued a shoot-to-kill order.

McCormick cut wages 15 percent. His profit rate was 71 percent. In May 1886 four molders whom McCormick locked out was shot dead by the police. Thus, did this "grim reaper" maintain his profits.

Nationally, May 1 1886, was important because a couple of years earlier the Federation of Organized Trade and Labor Unions of the United States and Canada, "RESOLVED... that eight hours shall constitute a legal day's labor, from and after May 1, 1886."

On May 4, 1886 several thousand people gathered near Haymarket Square to hear what August Spies, a newspaperman, had to say about the shootings at the McCormick works. Albert Parsons, a typographer and labor leader spoke next. Later, at his trial, he said, "What is Socialism or Anarchism? Briefly stated it is the right of the toilers to the free and equal use of the tools of production and the right of the producers to their product." He was followed by "Good-Natured Sam" Fielden, who as a child had worked in the textile factories of Lancashire, England. He was a Methodist preacher and labor organizer. He got done speaking at 10:30 PM. At that time 176 policemen charged the crowd that had dwindled to about 200. An unknown hand threw a stick of dynamite, the first time that Alfred Nobel's invention was used in class battle.

All hell broke lose, many were killed, and the rest is history.

"Make the raids first and look up the law afterwards", was the Sheriff's dictum. It was followed religiously across the country. Newspapers screamed for blood, homes were ransacked, and suspects were subjected to the "third degree". Eight men were railroaded in Chicago at a farcical trial. Four men hanged on "Black Friday," 11 November 1887.

"There will come a time when our silence will be more powerful than the voices you strangle today", said Spies before he choked.

May Day Since 1886

Lucy Parsons, widowed by Chicago's "just-us", was born in Texas. She was partly Afro-American, partly native American and partly Hispanic. She set out to tell the world the true story "of one whose only crime was that he lived in advance of his time". She went to England and encouraged English workers to make May Day an international holiday for shortening the hours of work. Her friend, William Morris, wrote a poem called "May Day."

Workers

They are few, we are many: and yet, O our Mother,
Many years were wordless and nought was our deed,
But now the word flitteth from brother to brother:
We have furrowed the acres and scattered the seed.

Earth

> *Win on then unyielding, through fair and foul weather,*
> *And pass not a day that your deed shall avail.*
> *And in hope every spring-tide come gather together*
> *That unto the Earth ye may tell all your tale.*

Her work was not in vain. May Day, or "The Day of the Chicago Martyrs" as it is still called in Mexico "belongs to the working class and is dedicated to the revolution", as Eugene Debs put it in his May Day editorial of 1907. The A. F. of L. declared it a holiday. Sam Gompers sent an emissary to Europe to have it proclaimed an international labor day. Both the Knights of Labor and the Second International officially adopted the day. Bismarck, on the other hand, outlawed May Day. President Grover Cleveland announced that the first Monday in September would be Labor Day in America, as he tried to divide the international working class. Huge numbers were out of work, and they began marching. Under the generalship of Jacob Coxey they descended on Washington DC on May Day 1894, the first big march on Washington. Two years later across the world Lenin wrote an important May Day pamphlet for the Russian factory workers, in 1896. The Russian Revolution of 1905 began on May Day.

With the success of the 1917 Bolshevik Revolution the Red side of May Day became scarlet, crimson, for 10 million people were slaughtered in World War I. The end of the war brought work stoppings, general strikes and insurrections all over the world, from Mexico to Kenya, from China to France. In Boston on May Day 1919 the young telephone workers threatened to strike, and 20,000 workers in Lawrence went on strike again for the eight-hour day. There were fierce clashes between working people and police in Cleveland as well as in other cities on May

Day of that year. A lot of socialists, anarchists, bolsheviks, wobblies and other "I-Won't- Workers" ended up in jail as a result.

This didn't get them down. At "Wire City", as they called the federal pen at Fort Leavenworth, there was a grand parade and no work on May Day 1919. Pictures of Lenin and Lincoln were tied to the end of broom sticks and held aloft. There were speeches and songs. *The Liberator* supplies us with an account of the day, but it does not tell us who won the Wobbly-Socialist horseshoe-throwing contest. Nor does it tell us what happened to the soldier caught waving a red ribbon from the guards' barracks. Meanwhile, one mile underground in the copper mines of Bisbee, where there are no national boundaries, Spanish-speaking Americans were singing "The International" on May Day.

In the 1920s and 1930s the day was celebrated by union organizers, the unemployed, and determined workers. In New York City the big May Day celebration was held in Union Square. In the 1930s Lucy Parsons marched in Chicago at May Day with her young friend, Studs Terkel. May Day 1946 the Arabs began a general strike in Palestine, and the Jews of the Displaced Persons Camps in Landsberg, Germany, went on hunger strike. On May Day 1947 auto workers in Paris downed tools, an insurrection in Paraguay broke out, the Mafia killed six May Day marchers in Sicily, and the Boston Parks Commissioner said that this was the first year in living memory when neither Communist nor Socialist had applied for a permit to rally on the Common.

1968 was a good year for May Day. Allen Ginsberg was made the "Lord of Misrule" in Prague before the Russians got there. In London hundreds of students lobbied Parliament against a bill to stop Third World immigration into England. In Mississippi police could not prevent 350 black students from supporting their jailed friends. At Columbia University thousands of students petitioned against armed police on campus. In Detroit with the help of the Dodge Revolutionary Union Movement, the first wildcat strike in fifteen years took place at the Hamtramck

Assembly plant (Dodge Main), against speed-up. In Cambridge, Mass., black leaders advocated police reforms while in New York the Mayor signed a bill providing the police with the most sweeping "emergency" powers known in American history. The climax to May '68 was reached in France where there was a gigantic General Strike under strange slogans such as

> Parlez a vos voisins! L'Imagination prend le pouvoir! Dessous les paves c'est la plage!

On May Day in 1971 President Nixon couldn't sleep. He order 10,000 paratroopers and marines to Washington DC because he was afraid that some people calling themselves the May Day Tribe might succeed in their goal of blocking access to the Department of Justice. In the Philippines four students were shot to death protesting the dictatorship. In Boston Mayor White argued against the right of municipal workers, including the police, to withdraw their services, or stop working. In May 1980 we see Green themes in Mozambique where the workers lamented the absence of beer, or in Germany where 300 women witches rampaged through Hamburg. Red themes may be seen in the 30,000 Brazilian auto workers who struck, or in the 5.8 million Japanese who struck against inflation.

On May Day 1980 the Green and Red themes were combined when a former Buick auto-maker from Detroit, one "Mr. Toad", sat at a picnic table and penned the following lines,

> *The eight hour day is not enough; We are thinking of more and better stuff.*
> *So here is our prayer and here is our plan,*
> *We want what we want and we'll take what we can.*
> *Down with wars both small and large,*
> *Except for the ones where we're in charge:*
> *Those are the wars of class against class,*
> *Where we get a chance to kick some ass..*

For air to breathe and water to drink,
And no more poison from the kitchen sink.
For land that's green and life that's saved
And less and less of the earth that's paved.
No more women who are less than free,
Or men who cannot learn to see
Their power steals their humanity
And makes us all less than we can be.
For teachers who learn and students who teach
And schools that are kept beyond the reach
Of provosts and deans and chancellors and such
And Xerox and Kodak and Shell, Royal Dutch.
An end to shops that are dark and dingy,
An end to Bosses whether good or stingy,
An end to work that produces junk, An end to junk that produces
work,
And an end to all in charge—the jerks.
For all who dance and sing, loud cheers,
To the prophets of doom we send some jeers,
To our friends and lovers we give free beers,
And to all who are here, a day without fears.
So, on this first of May we all should say
That we will either make it or break it.
Or, to put this thought another way,
Let's take it easy, but let's take it.

Law Day/ U.S.A.

May Day was always a troubling day in America; some wished to forget it. In 1939 Pennsylvania declared it "Americanism Day". In 1947 Congress declared it "Loyalty Day". Yet, these attempts to hide the meaning of the day have never succeeded. As the Wobblies say, "We Never Forget".

Likewise in 1958, at the urging of Charles Rhyne, Congress proclaimed May 1 "Law Day/U.S.A." As a result the politicians had another opportunity for bombast about the Cold War and touting their own virtues. Senator Javits, for instance, took a deep historical breath in May 1960 by saying American ideas were the highest "ever espoused since the dawn of civilization". Governor Rockefeller of New York got right to his point by saying that the traditional May Day "bordered on treason". As an activity for the day Senator Wiley recommended that people read Statute Books. In preaching on "Obedience to Authority" on May Day 1960, the Chaplain of the Senate said he believed it was the first time in the twentieth century that the subject had been addressed. He reminded people of the words carved on the courthouse in Worcester, Massachusetts: "Obedience to Law is Liberty". He said God is "all law" and suggested we sing the hymn, "Make Me a Captive, Lord, and Then I Shall be Free". He complained that TV shows made fun of cops and husbands. He said God had become too maternal.

Beneath the hypocrisy of such talk (at the time the Senate was rejecting the jurisdiction of the World Court), there were indications of the revolt in the kitchens. In addition to the trumpeted Cold War overtones, frightened patriarchal undertones were essential to the Law Day music. Indeed, it attempted to drown out both the Red and the Green. Those who have to face the law-and-order music on a daily basis, the lawyers and the orderers, also have to make their own deals.

Among the lawyers there are conservatives and liberals; they are generally ideologues. On Law Day 1964 the president of the Connecticut Bar wrote against civil rights demonstrators, "corrupt" labor unions, "juvenile delinquency", and Liz Taylor! William O. Douglas, on the other hand, on Law Day 1962, warned against mimicking British imperialism and favored independence movements and the Peace Corps by saying "We need Michigan-in Nigeria, California-in-the-Congo, Columbia-in-

Iran", which has come true, at least judging by what's written on sweat shirts around the world. Neither the conservative nor the liberal, however, said it should be a holiday for the lawyers, nor did they advocate the eight-hour day for the workers of the legal apparatus. In Boston only the New England School of Law, the Law and Justice Program at UMass. and the College of Public and Community Service celebrate the Green and the Red.

Among the orderers (the police) Law Day isn't much of a holiday either. Yet police, men and women, all over the United States owe a lot to May Day and the Boston police. It is true that more than 1,000 Boston men of blue lost their jobs owing to Calvin Coolidge's suppression of the Boston police strike of 1919. They had been busy earlier in the summer during May Day. At the same time there were lasting gains: a small pay increase ($300 a year), shorter hours (73-90 a week had been the norm) and most important, free uniforms!

An Ending

Where is the Red and Green today? Is it in Mao's Red Book? or in Col. Khadafy's Green Book? Some perhaps. Leigh Hunt, the English essayist of the nineteenth century, wrote that May Day is "the union of the two best things in the world, the love of nature, and the love of each other". Certainly, such green union is possible because we all can imagine it, and we know that what is real now was once only imagined. Just as certainly, that union can be realized only by red struggle, because there is no gain without pain, as the aerobiticians say, or no dreams without responsibility, no birth without labor, no green without red.

The children used to celebrate May Day. I think schools stopped encouraging them sometime around when "Law Day" was created, but I'm not sure. A correspondent from East Arlington, Massachusetts writes that in the late 1940s, "On any given Saturday in May, anywhere from 10-30 children would dress up in crepe paper costumes (hats, shirts, &c.); we would pick baskets of flowers and parade up and down several streets (until the flowers ran out!). The whole time we would be chanting, 'May Party, May Party, rah, rah, rah!'. A leader would be chosen, but I don't remember how. (Probably by throwing fingers out). Then, we would parade up to Spy Pond at the edge of the Center off Lake Street and have a picnic lunch." This correspondent now teaches kindergarten. "In recent years", she continues, "I have always decorated a May Pole for my kindergarten class (they do the decorations actually), and we would dance around it. It would always attract attention from the older children."

Music

DANIEL WOLFF

From Gospel to the Birth of Soul: Sam Cooke and The Soul Stirrers

IVE MEN IN CRISP WHITE SUITS STAND SHOULDER TO shoulder, ready to go to work. In front of them is a single microphone. Their white suits and white shirts and white-tipped shoes shine so brightly that you can barely see their faces, but even so and even at a distance, the four men in the back are clearly older. They stand in a semi circle, like a crescent moon, with the fifth—the youngster—in the middle.

The work they're about to do is very precise: they are going to try to bring the divine spirit down into this room. And the measurement of their success is equally precise. Out beyond the microphone sits a congregation of eager people dressed nearly as sharply as the men on stage. Amongst them—amongst the extended families, the grandparents, the fidgety children, the adolescents eyeing each other from pew to pew—there are women of a certain age who go by the generic name of Sister Flute. If the men in the white suits do their job right, Sister Flute will start to moan. She may stand where she is and wave one hand in the air, or rock her head back till her broad- brimmed Sunday hat threatens to drop off. And if the men are truly suc-cessful, if they shout the house, Sister Flute's moans will turn to shrieks. Her legs will stiffen, and the heels of her best shoes will start to drum the floor, and, as the spirit gathers, she may col-lapse, or throw herself into the arms of the deacons, all the time shouting the praises of an almighty and present God.

How do the men in the white suits make this happen? Well, they are the Soul Stirrers, a gospel quartet, and after twenty years on the road they've devised certain proven methods. One is to sing in a glittering harmony as carefully constructed and intense as stained glass. The man on the far left, bass singer J.J. Farley, lays down a deep foundation that seems to be hooked into the very bedrock beneath the building. Next to him is Paul Foster, a rough-voiced, dark- skinned man in eyeglasses whose growl can be modulated into a gravelly counterpoint. R.B. Robinson sings baritone, twining his voice with that of the first tenor and manager of the group, S.R. Crain. Sometimes, all Sister Flute needs is to hear that first immaculate hum of harmony, and she'll start to moan.

The white suits are part of the job, too. This isn't show business—no, no, as the singers often say, "We're here for chu"—but it is a performance. The Soul Stirrers tend toward the formal: standing upright, not moving much, Crain keeping the beat by clapping softly. Others in their line of work—the Blind Boys, for instance, or the Sensational Nightingales—will charge the room, rushing off the stage and right down into the pews. The Soul Stirrers get just as passionate—but with style.

Of course the songs make a difference. They're the vehicle that the spirit rides in on. It helps to have a musical hook that grabs the listener, or a story so familiar to the congregation that as soon as they hear the premise—maybe that Mother's died, or a Bible tale they've been told since childhood—they nod their heads in recognition, ready to be transported.

Finally, all successful gospel groups have a gifted lead singer to spark the holy fire. From 1937 through 1950, the Stirrers had one of the very best: Rebert H. Harris. His proud high voice could beg or boast, mourn death or trumpet victory. But in 1950, Harris leaves. His replacement is that youngster in the middle: an unknown 19- year-old son of an itinerant preacher. Reverend Cook's boy, Sam (he would not add the last "e" to his name until years later) has a pretty face, an even prettier voice, and a couple years experience touring with the teenage Highway QC's. But stand him up next to the hard-won professionalism of the

Soul Stirrers, and it's not surprising if Sister Flute eyes the new kid and wonders whether he can do the job.

The Stirrers' record producer shares this skepticism. "Art Rupe didn't actually think too much of him" is how Crain recalled it. "Actually, Art Rupe didn't like nobody but Harris". That's because R.H. sold records. His February 1950 version of "By and By" shipped some 25,000 copies, a major hit in the gospel Fields. Now, a year later and with that single still selling, the Stirrers show up at Universal Recording Studio #2 in Hollywood with this new kid. It's as if Rupe had bought the Yankees only to discover that DiMaggio had decided to retire.

The Soul Stirrers' main source of income isn't from record sales (not at the pay rate of two cents a double-sided single) but from the group's almost constant touring. Still, a record is yet another factor in getting Sister Flute. If it precedes them—if she knows the song and the sound beforehand—she's that much more willing to give herself up into familiar arms.

Rupe looks the fresh-faced Cook over and then turns to J.W. Alexander, manager of the Pilgrim Travelers and Specialty's gospel scout.

"Can he sing?"

"Yeah, he can sing" is J.W.'s response.

"Well, I'll try him", Crain remembered Rupe saying, "but I don't care too much for taking chances".

Rupe covers his odds by conducting a marathon session. From 2:15 in the afternoon into the evening of March 1, 1951, Rupe tests the new singer. Usually, a session consists of four songs, eight at the most. This one stretches to eleven cuts, with an emphasis on sure things: strong traditional compositions by established gospel writers.

They begin with "Come Let Us Go Back to God" by Thomas Dorsey, the author of "Precious Lord" and one of the founding fathers of modern (which is to say bluesier) postwar gospel. Paul takes the first, measured lead as the Stirrers gather in solemn harmony behind him. Outside the studio, the Korean conflict is in its second year, and Foster warns us that "what happens across the sea // may come to you and me". The anxious, Cold War lyrics depend on the singer conveying a sense of doom. Cook, who's never cut a record before, has had some trouble figuring out how far to stand from the microphone. When he does come in, his young voice doesn't quite convince us that "death has marked a path we trod". There's no doubt Sam can hit the notes; the question is whether he can strike the emotion.

He's more successful on "Peace in the Valley", another Dorsey standard, best known at that time through its country-western interpretation by Red Foley. Sam's innocent voice suits this material better, as he declares that we will be "led by a little child". But Paul carries the tune with his raspy shouts, as Cook joins the rest of the Stirrers responding to and magnifying these calls. On Crain's "I'm Gonna Build on That Shore" the group relies on its almost ragtime sense of rhythm; the undubbed version of "I'm on the Firing Line" uses the soft insistence and lifting harmony that made the Stirrers famous; and on the triumphant ending of "Joy, Joy to My Soul", they produce the ringing sound of some huge cathedral. This is group music, a collaborative effort. Rupe wouldn't hear the rookie's individual strengths until the eighth cut, a narrative written by the great gospel composer, Lucie Campbell.

The plot of "Jesus Gave Me Water" concerns the woman from Samaria. She meets the Savior at the well, then goes back into town to convince the locals that she's witnessed a miracle. As Campbell has constructed it, this is a story-song about the power of story-telling. And the lead singer's challenge is the same as the Samarian woman's: to evoke the inexpressible. Crain sets the succinct lyrics to a bubbling, joyful arrangement, and, in a sense, all Cook has to do is ride the current. But he accomplishes that with a grace and confidence beyond his years, meanwhile adding his own telling narrative flourishes. Hear him describe the miraculous liquid as "living, loving, lasting" and, at the end, riff on the word "water" till the song cascades to its conclusion.

The session, already long, should end there. But the last three cuts appear to be a kind of challenge. All have been sung earlier by R.H. Harris; now it's as if the rookie is taking on the memory of the absent veteran. Technically, Cook's voice can't match Harris's. It's too light (which may be the same as saying too modern) to quite fit the sober, traditional arrangement of "He's My Rock"—a song that went all the way back to Trinity, Texas, where the Stirrers formed in the 1920s. On "How Far Am I From Canaan?"—the tune Sam had auditioned with just a month or so earlier—he sounds dutiful and technically in control but not particularly passionate. And Cook's version of "Christ Is All" doesn't stand up to the one the Stirrers cut with Harris just a year before. Still, the rookie's earned a place on the team as the five of them rise together to hit that shared note that affirms, "Christ is *all*".

For Rupe, the true test is in the marketplace. After waiting a few months, he releases "Peace in the Valley" with "Jesus Gave Me Water" on the flip side. It answers any remaining doubts, nearly tripling the sales of Harris's "By and By" and ushering the Soul Stirrers into a new era.

The group doesn't record again for almost a year. That's typical. Right after the 1951 recording session, the Stirrers do a program up in Oakland. In April, they host their regular Mother's Day event at DuSable High School in their home base of Chicago. The Easter program is usually in Detroit, at Reverend C.L. Franklin's church (where the Reverend's daughter, Aretha, gets a look at what she calls the "just beautiful" Sam Cook). In the spring, the group tours the South from Birmingham to Norfolk, then follows the warm weather up into the Northeast: D.C., Philadelphia, Newark. It's mostly night work, on some high school stage or at a big Baptist church, then driving till dawn to do it again the next day. In the summer, they might dip down into the Southwest, cutting through Memphis to get to Oklahoma and Texas. Then, it's the Carolinas in time for the tobacco harvest, Florida in the dead of winter and, by February, back to California and the recording studio. When they arrive, they come with another set of finely honed, road-tested songs.

"Actually", Art Rupe has declared, "I dug gospel music even more than rhythm and blues", and the producer often made his own crucial modifications to the songs. In 1952, he seems to hear a new, beat-heavy sound on the horizon. A month after this Stirrers' session, he'll go to New Orleans and cut "Lawdy Miss Clawdy", a runaway number one R&B hit by Lloyd Price that sells to both white and black fans. Here, Rupe approaches from the gospel end, adding drums to the Stirrers' usual mix.

At first, it's an awkward fit. Compare the single of "It Won't Be Very Long" to the alternative takes, and you can hear the predictable beat dumbing down the complex rhythms. But toward the end, an odd synthesis starts to happen. The lead voices jump with urgency, and the group seems to open up and let the drums in. Social critics have argued that the concept of the teenager was an invention of the 1950s. If so, here's evidence that it happened not just in the malt shop but across the street, in church.

What Rupe calls "the best number we did today" is another attempt at W.H. Brewster's standard, "How Far Am I From Canaan?" With the drums added, we lose the genius of the Stirrers' arrangement: Farley's bass thrum and the incredible use of pauses and silence. But Cook has clearly matured in a year, and Rupe puts his voice way forward, capitalizing on the young singer's knack for intimacy. This, the Specialty owner seems to be arguing, is the future. In that context, Cook's first recorded composition, "Just Another Day", sounds like a debate between the modern and the traditional, with Sam's reedy vision of the coming day playing tug-of-war with Paul's deeper, more patient view.

That tension is even more obvious a year later. Rupe let his gospel talent scout, J.W. Alexander, supervise the 1953 session, and he seems caught between. Despite the presence of drums, piano and organ, the first single highlights the more traditional sound that J.W. and the Stirrers helped forge. Crain's "He'll Welcome Me" and his arrangement of "End of My Journey" are country: you can almost smell the piney air over the Trinity, Texas, sawmills. These old-timey battle cries are proven weapons in the spiritual war, yet the single will barely sell. As the Stirrers have begun to notice on the road, the nature of their job is changing. Yes, Sister Flute is still the key. But pushing past her, migrating to the front, are the young city girls—eager to see if this Cook boy is really as pretty as he sounds.

One of the songs that signals the shift is by an up-and-coming gospel writer, Alex Bradford. The flamboyant Bradford has a pop sensibility which will eventually land him on Broadway in "Your Arms Too Short to Box With God". His song here, "He's My Friend Until the End", has more froth than the Stirrers' old tunes and a strolling, contemporary beat. It also relegates the Stirrers to back-up singers. Cook, way up front, uses the spotlight to showcase a technique he's been developing out on the road: a high yodel that breaks a note into pieces and then seems to string it back together. This will become Sam's trademark, and, more and more, the group will look for opportunities to have him soar like this, drifting through the air while the girls cry out in wonder.

As Cook's style develops, the Stirrers don't give up on tradition as much as add to it. Five months later, Rupe and the others are incorporating Bob King's electric guitar into the mix. Listen to the three takes of "Come and Go to That Land", and you can hear them trying to figure out where the popular instrument might fit. At first, King's high notes ride over the parts Cook,

Robinson and Crain normally take. Though it works better with Paul's low voice, the result is a mess. Then, Rupe brings up the drums and backs off the guitar so that Sam's repeated cries of "Joy! Joy! Joy!" break through the mix. On tunes such as "I Gave Up Everything to Follow Him" and "I'm Happy in the Service of the Lord", the guitar mostly provides backup; the drama is in the thrilling shared leads of Paul (roaring out his faith) and Sam (perfecting the glissando of his yodel.)

The finishing touch in Cook's vocal education comes through one of gospel's true master singers, Julius "June" Cheeks. In 1954, Cheeks temporarily left the Sensational Nightingales to ride the gospel highway with the Stirrers. Cheeks was a shouter, unstoppable, and an onstage mover who rushed the floor to get Sister Flute—and pushed Cook to do the same. June's eloquent urgency was social as well as spiritual: he was one of gospel's most outspoken critics of segregation. And his stint with the Stirrers coincides with the Supreme Court's *Brown vs. Board of Education* decision which helped launch the modern civil rights movement.

The one recording we have of Cheeks and Cook together, "All Right Now" is a raving, extended lesson in dynamics. The first full take goes on nearly four minutes, much of it June repeating "All right now" in a voice that threatens to blow out the recording equipment. Though he cuts a minute off that in Take #4, it's still a convincing argument that distortion and feedback aren't the sole invention of rock and roll. Listen closely to the climax, as June simultaneously rages and exults, and you can hear the Stirrers shiver in excitement, as if they're about to throw down their stylish harmonies and just testify.

Sam Cook is far from the center of this astonishing maelstrom, but the other cuts show him, as Crain has said, "in his power". That includes a pretty good roar of his own toward the end of "He'll Make A Way", a yearning, upward melody that Sam navigates like some daredevil tightrope walker. While "Jesus, I'll

Never Forget" has the Stirrers' traditional interwoven arrangement (listen to how they end each other's sentences), the emphasis is clearly on Cook's confident lead. And the smooth ballad "Any Day Now" seems designed to show off the 23-year old. You can imagine the church girls rushing forward on this number—and imagine how Cook must have begun thinking that, with the right song, the same thing might just happen outside of church.

"Any Day Now" is written by the woman pianist on the 1954 session, Faidest Wagoner. Finding strong material continues to be a challenge. Crain provides some memorable originals; many of the others—including Bradford's and Brewster's—come from Kenneth Morris, the famed Chicago song-writer and, with Sallie Martin, publisher. "Whenever we were in town", Crain reported, "we'd go by the studio ... 42nd and Indiana. Little old dumpy place. Wasn't enough room in there for the piano and the books he had stacked up". In 1955, they came out with a song by the keyboard player for the Caravans, James Cleveland. "One More River" caps the group's adaptation to instruments, with Willie Web's organ swelling like a death shroud behind the exquisite harmonies.

But the songwriter who really emerges at this session is Sam Cook. He provides both sides of the first single. "Be With Me Jesus" is a traditional sounding, "dying hour" song that showcases Paul's deep solo work. It's the A-side, "Nearer to Thee", that proves, as Crain wrote Rupe after the session, a house wrecker. It will turn out to be the Stirrers' most successful single since "Jesus Gave Me Water", and it sounds like Cook's been studying Lucie Campbell's narrative technique. "There's a story", he declares, "in every song we sing" and that story can "lift heavy burdens". The hook here is the traditional hymn "Nearer My God to Thee", which Cook builds into the chorus, making the old the focus of the new. That way, Sister Flute gets a shot of recognition and can instantly sing along, while the younger generation can marvel at Sam's sophisticated flight through the verses. As the session makes clear, Cook's talents shine in these higher, lighter regions. On Crain's "I'm So Glad", for example, hear how Paul takes the parts about sin while Sam is the messenger of gladness.

No one produced better sounding records than Art Rupe and his master engineer, Bunny Robyn: these two to three minute gems still jump out at us a half- century later. But for the Stirrers and the other gospel groups on Specialty, the records were always secondary to their live performances. In July of 1955, Rupe sent his new A&R man, Robert "Bumps" Blackwell, to record a big gospel program at the Shrine Auditorium in Los Angeles. The result is an extraordinary opportunity to hear just how the Stirrers did their job. Getting Sister Flute involves three songs extended over 20 minutes. Note that all three are written by no-longer-rookie Cook. His "I Have a Friend" is a warm-up, both for the group and the crowd. At the first note from Sam, a female shouts her approval, and he goes on to work the rough, June Cheeks end of his voice. (One indication of how effectively Sam suppressed this gospel roar on his pop records is that, 30 years later, when his "Live at the Harlem Square Club" is released, rock and roll fans and critics are surprised at how "soulful" he sounds.)

"Be With Me Jesus" charges right at the Shrine audience, Paul leading with Sam singing flat out ugly encouragement in the background. About three minutes on, you can hear the "midnight hour" that Wilson Pickett turned into a soul hit a decade later. But while Paul's persistence sweats the crowd, it doesn't carry them over. That work is done during the eight and a half minutes of "Nearer to Thee". There's nothing very subtle about Cook's approach here: he's going to push till the walls fall down, adding lyrics not on the studio version and hammering at the chorus. Finally, six minutes down this rough road, the sweet-faced singer testifies that bad company can make a good child stray—and Sister Flute starts to go, screaming all the way.

Between the two of them, Paul and Sam lift her higher and higher till she seems to rise right through the suddenly open roof of the Shrine: manhandled into paradise.

If this sounds like the passion of rock and roll, part of what the box set of the Soul Stirrers shows is that history is more complicated than that. By 1955, cross-pollination is everywhere. A month after the Shrine concert, Blackwell will go to New Orleans and record "Tutti Frutti" with that young student of the gospel shout, Little Richard. Meanwhile, Elvis Presley is acting out his own kind of possession over at Sun Records. Strangely, the Stirrers' session that takes place just a month after the Shrine yields no singles—until fifteen years later when an over-dubbed chorus turns the old Methodist hymn "The Last Mile of the Way", into "contemporary" gospel.

By the February 1956 session, categories are dissolving. Is the lilting "Wonderful" a pop ballad in disguise, or are R&B croon-ers like Specialty's own Jesse Belvin singing gospel? Just before this session, Cook and Crain sign separate contracts that for the first time give them larger cuts than the rest of the group. From now on, the billing might as well be Sam Cook and the Soul Stirrers. Sam not only takes the lead on "Farther Along", a song that calls for Paul's rasp, but it isn't until near the end of the session that Foster gets any solo at all, trading leads on "Must Jesus Bear the Cross Alone?"

Cook both writes and sings the session's most stunning song, "Touch the Hem of His Garment". What makes the spirit of this first-person, biblical narrative so modern (call that spirit rock and roll if you want) is not only the yodeling focus on what "I" did, or the return of Bradford's strolling beat, but the declara-tion of need that's at the heart of the song. Sam embroiders the phrase "if I could just touch" till it's all about want and possibil-ity: how to be "made whole" in an unforgiving world. The song is recorded barely two months after Rosa Parks demands to be treated as a human being on a segregated Alabama bus.

It's at the end of this year, 1956, that Sam cuts his first pop recordings. "A Friend I've Been Knowing For Quite A While", Cook writes Rupe in his careful handwriting, "Asked Me If I Would Consider Recording Some Popular Ballads...". Sam has "One of the Major Recording Companies" interested and material ready: a five-song audition tape. He just needs Rupe's permission. "We most certainly would be very happy to record you in the pop Fields ourselves", Rupe quickly replies—and sends Bumps Blackwell to meet Sam in New Orleans. There, under the name Dale Cook, they cut four tunes. "Lovable" is simply a remake of "Wonderful" with the subject switched from the divine "He" to a secular "she". The other three numbers—less songs than melodic riffs—barely engage the talents of the first-rate musicians, including drummer Earl Palmer. What does emerge is a talented singer searching for a new persona. Starting from his gospel role as the good child gone astray, Cook feels his way toward a kind of vulnerable sexiness. But he still seems confused about exactly what his new job entails. Apparently, it will have less to do with how "I", the singer, transport "you" than how you will send me.

These first tries at popular music don't sell. (Later, Rupe will overdub Sam's audition tape of "I'll Come Running Back to You" and get a major hit, but only after Cook—by then Cooke—is already a rock and roll star.) Sam hurries back from New Orleans to New York City's Apollo Theater, where the Stirrers are appearing on a Christmas program. But his gospel days are numbered. The group cancels their annual February recording date. When they do get in a Chicago studio, in April of 1957, it will be their final session together.

Dale Cook is nowhere to be found on the traditional "Lord Remember Me". This is old-fashioned gospel with Sam's cracked vocal conjuring up the raging "storm of life". Closer to the secular is the one original tune Cook brings in, "That's Heaven to Me", which defines paradise as "the things that I see as I walk along the streets". While the Lord does get mentioned, the lyrics and the fluting vocal focus on the beauty to be found right here on earth. Recorded only a couple of months before Cook splits from the Stirrers, the tune can be heard as both an apology and a statement of purpose: he may be leaving gospel, but he's also bringing it with him, expanding its definition.

The traditional "Were You There?" shows what Cook couldn't bring along. The group struggles to set a tempo that can express the excited awe of being at the crucifixion and still allow Sam enough time to tell the story. Like many of the greatest Soul Stirrers songs, this narrative is about bearing witness. Was he really there when they pierced the Savior in the side? Claps of encouragement shout Cook forward to testify that not only was he there, but it made him tremble. Sam uses all his skills on this one—his June Cheeks shout, his yodel, that clear diction—in a performance as convincing as it is passionate. It's tempting to say he never achieved this level of direct urgency in his pop music. But that's not fair because he had different goals and a different audience. Better to say that those who knew him from gospel instantly recognized the well he drew from for "Bring It On Home to Me" and "A Change Is Gonna Come".

Reflecting on the session's final cut, "Mean Old World", Crain recalled, "That was an old song. Sam had that when he came to us". The opening line—if not the entire melody—is a variation on T-Bone Walker's seminal electric blues, also called "Mean Old World", recorded in 1942. Yet, from the rolling bass intro through the syncopated handclaps right to Cook's last gorgeous and, somehow, chilling falsetto, this is a song of the spirit. God isn't mentioned once, but His absence is the driving force. "It's a mean old world to live in—all by yourself."

All by himself is how Sam entered rock and roll. He didn't leave gospel completely behind, still attending programs occasionally and recording the Soul Stirrers for his own SAR record label. But the 26-year -old would never again stand before an audience in that semibcircle of group singing, that crescent moon. As these remarkable sessions come to an end—six years and some fifty songs later—we hear Sam Cook saying good-bye to his gospel family in order to make his mark in a larger, meaner world. One job is over, the next just begun.

DAVID VEST

From Birmingham to Nashville: The Making of Tammy Wynette

FIRST ENCOUNTERED THE LEGEND KNOWN AS TAMMY Wynette on my car radio one afternoon in 1966. I had just come from my steady gig at Ireland's Pub in Nashville, across the street from Vanderbilt University. As I started my yellow Corvair, unsafe at any speed but fun to drive if you didn't know that, I heard the opening lines of "Apartment Number 9", her first released recording.

I recognized the voice at once. I'd have known it anywhere. It was my old friend, Wynette Byrd, born Virginia Wynette Pugh, with whom I had worked and played and recorded in Birmingham for the past few years. She had not long ago kissed me goodbye outside the Pussycat-a-Go-Go club down under the viaduct, where we had gone to hear some blues. I turned the radio up in my car as loud as it could go. Damn, she sounded good! And the material was right for her.

When the song ended, I was surprised to hear the singer identified not as Wynette Byrd but as a "new" artist named Tammy Wynette. I can still remember how strange that felt.

God knows, playing piano at Ireland's was already weird enough. Half the audience were musicians, many of them well-known artists unwinding after sessions on Music Row a few blocks away. As I discovered during my standing gig, an unknown musician performing for a famous audience is usually way too innocent for his own good.

Joan Baez was there one night. She walked out after complaining to the management that I was playing too loud when she was trying to have a conversation (thanks, Joan). On another day I looked up to see three of The Byrds staring across the piano at me as I played "Hickory Wind". I pretended not to recognize them.

Charlie McCoy sat at the bar and told me of a Bob Dylan session he'd been called in to play bass on. It was for the album *John Wesley Harding*.

"I can't figure it out. So far it's just drums, bass and Bob's acoustic guitar. I reckon they'll overdub the rest of the stuff later", he said, "unless it's just a demo".

A couple of the Foggy Mountain Boys told wonderful Lester Flatt stories and talked about playing for college audiences. "Man, them hippies loved Earl Scruggs", they said.

So I was used to strange. Learning that yet another favorite cowboy singer was gay ("Why do you think he likes all them sparkly suits and everything?") would no longer have shocked me.

But hearing this familiar voice on my radio attributed to a "Tammy" was something else. "I can't feature that", we'd have said in the musician's parlance of the day.

So I sat in my car and speculated to myself about what "they" had done to her. I imagined her sitting on a sofa with her hands folded above her knees while "they" paced around an office.

"What's your name again? Wynette? What kind of a name is that? Is that even a name, Bob? What do you think? Am I right? It's more like a last name. You need a first name". And then somebody who had probably seen a Debbie Reynolds movie would have suggested *Tammy*. "But you don't look like a Tammy. No problem, we can fix that. We'll have to do something with your hair".

In truth, there has never been a reason to suggest she was less than a willing accomplice. Self-creation is the great American dream. We long to shed the ordinary like a husk. Remember when you could "drink milk for a new you"?

Perhaps to her it was an attempt at self-transformation, not a corporate make-over. It had elements of both. Shedding the last name of an ex-husband cannot have been entirely unattractive. Maybe by renaming herself, or allowing herself to be renamed, she was declaring herself her own woman, willing to carry no man's name from this point onward.

Anyway, what choice did she have, unless she wanted to go back and work in a beauty shop the rest of her life?

For the Wynette I had known in Birmingham, country music was about telling the truth, not keeping facts straight. I had been in the car with her when she had furiously changed the radio dial to avoid hearing "crap" on country stations. Around her, conversation stopped cold when Charlie Louvin or Melba Montgomery were on the juke box. To watch her listen to great music was an intense experience.

I had played with her maybe a hundred times, and I had never seen her do anything to "sell" a song. She stood there, she went into it, and she sang it from deep inside. Sometimes a line from a song got past her inner defenses and she broke down, unable to continue. Usually, she fought it off and went on, singing in a harder tone. She did nothing out of the ordinary to call attention to herself, but if you didn't drop whatever you were doing when she sang, if time didn't stand still in your world as well as hers, you weren't human. She was that powerful.

But then, I knew her when all she ever sang were the greatest songs in the country and western repertoire, songs like "She's Got You", "Let's Go All the Way" and "Don't Touch Me". Her taste was infallible. With rare exceptions, and never by choice, she sang nothing she didn't believe in. She knew exactly where the center of the great tradition lay. She lived in it.

If it felt strange to hear her voice associated with a new name, that was nothing compared with the strange power of "Stand By Your Man", one of the greatest vocal performances (and still the best-selling single) in the history of country music.

Today we know it was the voice of a battered woman, a wife who stood by men who came home too drunk to stand up by themselves, a little girl whose father died and left her. It was the voice of courage and longing, not submissiveness, that we were hearing.

If the song's lyrics seemed to be lifted from an official document of the patriarchy, she managed somehow to get a message past the words, speaking to us like a political hostage blinking out the truth in code while reading a statement written by her captors. She connected on a fundamental level as only a few have done. Thousands, even millions of women identified with her, wanted to be her, felt she spoke to and for them.

It had nothing to do with playing a supporting role or being true to anyone other than oneself. For one thing, the song ignored men altogether and spoke directly to women. Significantly, women also identified with "You and Me", in which she sang about lying in bed with her husband, who has just made love to her, and fantasizing about being with another man.

I have read that she started singing, early on, as a way to support her children. That's not entirely true. I'm sure she did use the money she earned to support them, because she lived (and dressed) very simply in those days. But the reason she sang was because she was a singer. She always knew what she wanted. The only doubt in her mind was about how to get there.

She also knew exactly how good she was, that her voice entitled her to a place among the best in her fields, that her peers were people like Patsy Cline, Loretta Lynn and George Jones.

I know that she was offered and refused gigs for good money, turning them down because they had nothing to do with getting her where she wanted to go. Indeed, she left steady work behind in Birmingham to stage her assault on Nashville.

When she arrived there, she was a hard-core country singer trying to break into an industry that believed hard-core country was over. A town that was attracting Dylan, Baez and The Byrds because of its roots connection was moving to the suburbs as quickly as possible. Dylan might be stripping the music to its bare essentials and trying to sing like young Eddie Arnold, but old Eddie Arnold was trying to sound like Perry Como with fifty Italian strings. Flatt and Scruggs were covering Lovin' Spoonful songs. Willie Nelson was singing "Norwegian Wood".

But Nashville had also discovered women and their issues. Loretta Lynn was singing about "the pill". Women were also becoming more openly assertive about their sexuality, as in Lynn's amazing "Somebody, Somewhere (Don't Know What He's Missing Tonight)".

"Apartment Number 9" and "Your Good Girl's Gonna Go Bad" were early attempts to work this vein, before Wynette and producer Billy Sherrill found the motherlode with "Stand By Your Man".

She had an incredible run. Her vocals on "You and Me" and "Till I Can Make It On My Own", songs worthy of her talent, were as good as anything ever recorded by a country artist.

By the end of it all, the industry that had taken everything she had to offer for as long as she could give it wouldn't play her music on the radio anymore, and she was never really invited to the video revolution.

Along with all the number one hits had come drug addiction and the usual attendant insanity. (The music biz corporate bio-flicks about country music entertainers with drug problems usually have a sentence beginning something like this: "To cope with the increasing pressure of his career and the loneliness of life of the road, Cowboy B needed help, so he turned to... " In other words, you'd take dope, too, if you had all the problems of a superstar entertainer in a luxury custom bus.)

Tammy Wynette, we are told, was addicted to pain relief medication. That she suffered real pain seems not to be in doubt. There were thirty-five surgeries, some of them rumored to have been badly botched. I have written elsewhere that she once told me she had often fantasized about having her fears surgically removed.

There was also at least one attempt at detox at the Betty Ford Clinic (by one published account, she left there in an ambulance to go someplace where they'd give her pain medication). After selling millions and millions of records she was forced to file for personal bankruptcy.

Stories too incredible to be believed but too bizarre not to have some basis in fact kept coming out. She had been kidnapped, beaten and abandoned 80 miles from Nashville. No, wait, she had kidnapped herself for "publicity". In yet another version, she had been battered by one of her husbands and was so terrified of him that she faked the kidnapping to cover for him.

The last time I saw her on television, she appeared nervous and desperately uncomfortable, afraid to answer even the simplest question.

After her death there were public disagreements between her fifth husband and her children, who demanded an autopsy. Her corpse was exhumed. Dueling memoirs were published.

You can't argue with success, but you can damn sure argue with death.

Tammy Wynette had a full measure of both success and misery. Will her music outlast everything it was supposed to "symbolize"? I hope that it will, but it's way too soon to know. Country music has forsworn memory, and music store bins now typically carry just her greatest hits. Most of her recordings don't sound "rootsy" enough to be retro, yet. And it's been a while since I heard a young female country singer do any of Tammy Wynette's material.

But that doesn't mean they don't want to be her.

LENNI BRENNER

How Dylan Found His Voice: Big Joe Williams, the Lower East Side, Peyote and the Forging of Dylan's Art

DON'T SAY I WAS BOB DYLAN'S ROOM MATE. CALLING someone your room mate means that at least one of us paid rent. It was the winter of 1961. I was crashing at banjo-picker Paul Shoenwetter's pad on East 4th Street between Avenues C and D, in what is now called the East Village but which we knew as the Lower East Side, along with Vince Hickey, a jazz drummer, and Tom Condit, a socialist buddy, when St. Paul brought in yet another stray, Bob Dylan.

Vince married black, to the daughter of Victoria Spivey, an ol' timey blues singer. He was an encyclopedia on ragtime. Tom and I were up to our asses in the civil rights struggle. Bob, at 19 going on 20, four years younger than me, was our junior colleague. He couldn't be expected to say much that was new or interesting or amusing to us worldlings. However we recognized a marvelous musician, and welcomed him into our fraternity of the rebellious, brilliant and crazy.

The highpoint of one chat is chiseled into stone. Peyote was still legal. The problem was that it tasted like tiger piss going down. Then it upset your stomach. But that's the best news it ever had. That means the veggie was kickin' in. It gave me spectacular eyes-closed color visions and the tummy-ache vanished.

Tom processed some. He ground-up a batch of dried up fist-sized buds, and put the powder into gelatin caps. That solves the taste problem. He laid 50 caps on me and split. I took 30 and was waiting for them to come on, when Bob walked in. I gave him the 20. He downed them, told of a nearby party and left. After my technicolor show came on, I walked over.

I vote the winter of 1961 as New York's greatest. Four fulsome blizzards had left huge mounds everywhere, and then, on Friday night/Saturday morning, February 3-4, another storm dumped 17.4 inches on the city. The total accumulation was the greatest ever. For the first time, the mayor had to ban nonessential traffic so plows could clear a lane down the side streets, with many parked cars buried for months under humongous glaciers. For me, high, those streets, with icicles as big as they get, hanging off tenement fire-escapes, were the once-in-eternity Siberia-in-the-Apple, well past any piddling prophet's paltry Paradise.

The party was at the home of *Village Voice* cartoonist Jules Feiffer. Bob was adding whiskey to the peyote, as he, Mark Spoelstra and other folkies played in a back room.

After dawn on Sunday, the 5th, I left for Paul's. I was alone when Bob came in, 20 minutes later. We chatted about the night, and I got on him about a southern song they sang, "Just lookin' for a Home".

"Bob", I said, "you never saw a boll weevil. Mark never did. None of us have. If one flew in the window, or crawled in under the door, or whatever the hell they do, we wouldn't recognize it. Stop singing about boll weevils and sing about your own life and times".

He was slouched on a couch. In a hot second he was upright, his smiling young face suddenly electrically alive: "That's what Joe Williams told me!" His new maturing face mirrored his thinking as the implications of what we said sank in. Others have that experience. Someone tells us something but it doesn't click until someone else slams it in.

It is idle to speculate as to whether Bob could have eventually figured out by himself that he had to do his own thing. I say with certainty that Big Joe and I were, in life, the agencies that propelled him to his destiny. I remember nary another word.

But his expressions were unforgettable. Here was the most gifted young musician-poet of his time and place suddenly getting his act together as an adult and performer.

For at least the first minute, almost two, after his exclamation, his thoughts put themselves spontaneously onto his face. His initial reception of my statement was followed by a series of self-induced facial shocks as he silently cooked our old/new ideas in his pot. Then he regained his composure, leaned toward me with his elbows on his thighs and we talked for a few more minutes. Then, as we had been up for a heap of hours, we crashed. There was no doubt that both of us thought a profound thing had happened to him.

Of course I had no idea that he would make such an impact on the world. But that visual scene was hardly one that anyone could forget, even if it happened with a nobody. To be sure, it wasn't quite as if the scales immediately fell from his eyes and he received sight forthwith and arose and was baptized, as with Saul becoming Paul. But through his cogitations he did spring up and go. The few words remembered and circa 10 minutes forgotten are how the mind sometimes turns events into memory. A highlight stands in for a whole conversation. The physical details are so vivid because the night was so spectacular and my vision was keyed up by peyote.

As his career took off shortly after, in the full bloom of our friendship, I had further reason to think about that morning, and lock in the incident. I'm sure that he saw it the same way. For the next two years, I was his wise buddy, who pulled his coat on a crux matter for him as a poet and person. In any case, we got up in the winter dark. We had no food. Bob cleared out first, saying "I have to do some writing". Yea verily, a bright young fellow came into that pad, a full man went out.

I never asked him what Big Joe actually said. But we get the spirit of it in Robert Shelton's *No Direction Home*. Williams recalled that "Bob...wrote me thanking me for the advice I had given him about music. What he earned, what he done, he got it honest. They ask me: 'Is he real?' And I tell them that they should let him live his own life".

Being in on the pad's chats, he understood my "sing about your own life and times" to be more ideologically loaded than Williams' "live his own life". I was also able to musically critique him because I had heard many of the best folk singers of the day and had listened to thousands of folk songs on records. In that period, Dave Van Ronk introduced me to Alan Lomax, the great field collector. After listening to them, I read Lomax on the complex stylistic evolution of American folk music. It was obvious to me that what we call the folk music tradition was actually innumerable singers doing the old songs and making up new ones about their lives and times.

The ideological level varied from none to highly political. It is a myth that folk singers were all poor and illiterate or nearly so. And some were musically highly cultured via their churches. Accordingly, Bob welded our notions together because I added the obligation that his art should reflect our times—his, Mark's, mine—its experiences and demands, to Williams' down-home blues sagacity.

Yet note again how the kingly power, chance, plays with us. If I had to be ahead of time to drink with Woody, I had to be the second to hit Bob like the sun, moon and stars falling on him. We ran into each other over the next two years, at Gerde's Folk City and other hangouts, notably Dave and Terri Thal's crib. Terri was Bob's first manager. They were fellow Trotskyists. Bob was there, sometime after his return from his 1962 trip to Europe. Boll weevil Bob told me how he didn't like to work in clubs for pay because "the people I want to play for can't afford the admission".

He ground on, all about how his record company took advantage of his youth to screw him financially, and how he had to make bootleg British records as Blind Boy Grunt. Management atrocity tales were boring old news to a seasoned red, so I tried to get him off himself. "That's very deep Bob". He shot back: "How deep is deep? Forty inches? Six feet?" With him completely wrapped up in his career, my like-it-is sarcasm zipped over his self-centered head. But his verbal facility was evident even in that answer that ain't an answer.

I bumped into him on 6th Avenue and Waverly in the Village in the Spring of 1963. I offered to pay the bill for a coffee. I explained that I had sold a silver goblet boosted from a Reform Jewish Temple. He smiled and we went to what was then a plain American greasy spoon, now the Waverly Resturant, got us a table and enjoyed the fruits of what we knew was a crime.

My ex-Christian ex-gal had taken me to a Village Episcopal church. After the ceremony, I went up to the alter and did partake of my first communion, without benefit of clergy. I took a wafer from a vessel. Yea, verily, Jerusalem Slim's body is like unto a Napoleon pastry. So, in return for certainty on a subtle point of Christian ritual that had perplexed Jewish minds for centuries, I led her through the open doors of an empty sanctum we happened upon in those innocent, pre-crime wave days, down the aisle and onto the raised rabbi's platform. The ritual goblet held some of what looked like wine, except that it didn't smell of alcohol. Coke, in a sacred vessel before an altar, is, by American law, a religion, to be protected from desecration. Good. Even great. I'm describing a legal transgression that doesn't merit repetition. But, in the real American twentieth century, that Temple wasn't Judaism. And in the twenty-first century Reform ain't even religion. It's what a minority of Jewish kids grow up doing if they live in our secular Coke present but are hung up on their parents' ancestral religion. A book of proverbial truths, spiritual fantasies and barbaric war stories, also reduced, in the physical world, from the perpetual miracle of intoxicating wine, down to flat soda, in an empty shrine. Bob approved of the double miracle, the conversion of a profaned vessel into capitalist lucre, and then into coffee and snacks, because he also had a contemptuous familiarity with Reform's instant platitudes.

I don't remember every word that passed between us. I told him I was heading back to the Bay Area and its politics. After maybe an hour, he felt "a song coming on". "You know I love to hear you say that". I left my buddy pen in hand.

Shortly after, I took off for Berkeley. We've had no contact since. If history records me, it will be as a historian and political activist. Beyond that, my advice to Bob that winter morning will be seen as my proudest artistic contribution. His radical songs will live on. But do a good deed and throw it into the sea. His later theological trapeze act, swinging between Jesus and the late Lubavicher rebbe, Menachem Schneerson, can only be described as the all-time-most-pathetic American Jewish tragi-comical shtik.

Bruce Jackson

The Myth of Newport '65: It Wasn't Bob Dylan They Were Booing

OB DYLAN PERFORMED AT THE NEWPORT FOLK FESTIVAL on August 3, 2002, and apparently it went very well. All the articles I've read and reports I've heard on radio and seen on TV say there was none of the angry booing that so famously accompanied his 1965 performance, when he appeared on stage with members of Paul Butterfields's blues band at the Sunday night closing concert.

The July 25, 1965, audience, the story goes, was driven to rage because their acoustic guitar troubadour had betrayed them by going electric and plugging in. The booing was so loud that, after the first three electric songs, Dylan dismissed the band and finished the set with his acoustic guitar.

There's a host of other associated narratives about goings-on in the wings: Pete Seeger and other Newport board directors were so repulsed and enraged they struggled to kill the electric power; Pete was frenetically looking for an axe to chop the major power line; people were yelling, screaming, crying, beating breasts, rending garments. Greil Marcus tells some of those stories really well at the beginning of his 1998 Dylan book, *Invisible Republic*.

Great stories. But not one of them is true.

I was one of the directors of the Newport Folk Festival and I was in the wings during Dylan's Saturday night performance. Every time I heard those stories retold, I'd say, to whoever was talking", That's not how I remember it. Nobody made a move for the power. Nobody took a swing at the sound man. It wasn't Dylan the audience was booing".

After Dylan's August 3, 2002, concert occasioned all those retellings of the Legends of 1965, I decided to check both the legend and my memory: I took down the original tapes made from the stage microphones during that performance. (I have in my office at the University of Buffalo all of the Newport board's audiotapes, save some that Peter Yarrow borrowed and, to my knowledge, never returned, and some that were made for us by a Providence recording company that shortly thereafter went belly-up and disappeared, along with our half-inch four-track master tapes.)

The entire event, from the beginning of Peter Yarrow's introduction to the beginning of Peter's introduction of the next performer, takes 37 minutes. You can hear the audience very clearly throughout. Yarrow's talk is clear, the musician's performances are clear, the audience's responses are clear. No doubt the sound of the people in the front of that great open-air theater come through more loudly than people far in the back, but there's no reason to assume that they didn't cheer and boo the same things.

This is what is on the tape, what people on stage, in the wings, and throughout most of the audience heard:

YARROW: *One, two. Can I have some volume on this microphone? Hello. One, two. Ladies and gentlemen, at this time there's a little microphone setup to be done. Cousin Emmy's a gas, right?*

[laughter, applause]

There's someone that's coming on to the program now, as a matter of fact, the entire program tonight was designed to be a whole group of small performances. You know I will be performing later with the group that I'm a part of, you know. [Yarrow was a member of a pop-folk group named Peter, Paul & Mary.]

[light applause]

And we are all limited in the time that we can be on stage for a very specific reason. The concept of the program tonight is to make a program of many, many different points of view that are together and yet without the huge expanse of the performing of any group. We will be very limited in time and so will each person who comes up. The person who's coming up now

[a single note from each string of an electric guitar struck by someone apparently checking the tuning]

Please don't play right now, gentlemen, for this second. Thank you.

[three more guitar notes]

The person who's coming up now is a person who has in a sense

[two brief bursts of feedback hum]

changed the face of folk music to the large American public because he has brought to it a point of view of a poet. Ladies and gentlemen, the person that's going to come up now

[Yarrow pauses a long time, drawing it out; a few hoots at the pause from the audience]

has a limited amount of time

[very loud booing and yelling, shouts of "No, no, no"]

his name is Bob [pause] Dylan

[enthusiastic and sustained cheering and applause from the audience that had watched the electric band set up and that was now watching Dylan plug in his own electric guitar]

[a minute or so of noises of things being moved around, levels checked, voices talking about where to set things. No hoots, jeers, calls or yells from the audience. Minutes 0:00_7.32 on the tape]

DYLAN AND GROUP: *"Maggie's Farm"*

[applause, retuning, a voice says "Ready?" a little more tuning, Dylan says "Okay". 7:32–8:25]

DYLAN AND GROUP: *"Rolling Stone"* 8:25–14:19

[applause, returning, murmur of musician's voice, 14:19–15:03]

DYLAN AND GROUP: *"It Takes a Lot to Laugh, It Takes a Train to Cry"* 15:03–18:26

[applause, musician's voices saying "Let's go, man, let's go". Sounds of movement, which I take to be Dylan and the band moving off the stage, followed by audience yelling "No, no, no". 18:26–18:44]

YARROW: *Bobby was*

[booing]

Yes, he will do another tune, I'm sure. We'll call him back. Would you like Bobby to sing another song? I don't know where he is.

[huge applause, happy yelling "Yes, yes, yes".]

Listen, it's the fault of the, he was told that he could only do a certain period of time.

[audience yells]

Bobby, can you do another song, please? He's going to get his axe.

[audience chants: "We want Dylan, we want Dylan".]

He's coming.

[audience continues chanting: "We want Dylan. We want Dylan".]

He's going to get an acoustic guitar.

[audience continues chanting at the same level: "We want Dylan. We want Dylan".]

Bobby's coming out now. Yes, I understand, that's okay. We want Bobby, and we do. The time problem has meant that he could only do these few songs. He'll be out as soon as he gets his acoustic guitar.

[audience continues chanting: "We want Dylan. We want Dylan". Then bursts into enthusiastic applause. 18:44–20:26]

[bit of microphone hum, harmonica testing, Dylan says "Peter, get" then a few words I can't make out. Tunes guitar. Dylan says, "You got another one?" A bit more tuning, mumbled conversation, occasional sounds from the audience 20:52–22:42]

DYLAN: *"It's All Over Now, Baby Blue"* 22:42–27:37

[applause 27:37–28:32, someone in the audience yells "Tambourine, Bobby". Someone else yells, "Tambourine Man". Dylan says, "Okay, I'll do that". Tunes, fusses. Dylan says, "All right". 29:13]

DYLAN: *"Mister Tambourine Man"* 29:13–35:29

[applause. Dylan says, "Thank you very much". Audience calls, "More, more". 35:29–35:40]

YARROW: *Bob Dylan, ladies and gentlemen. Thank you, Bob. Thank you. The poet, Bob Dylan. Thank you, Bob. [audience continues applauding through this.] One, two. One, two. Thank you, Bob. Ladies and gentlemen, the next group that's coming up*

[audience: "No! Bob!" boos. Rhythmic clapping]

is the group from which all this music started. You know the tradition of blues in our country originally came from the African tradition and the African tradition

[boos and rhythmic clapping continue]

Ladies and gentlemen, Bob can't come back. The African tradition, when it was brought over originally, was brought over into the deep South, and the music became, to a large extent

[boos and yells continue]

Ladies and gentlemen, please be considerate of Bobby. He can't come back. Please don't make it more difficult than it is. (35:40–37:04)

That's what is on the tape made on stage at Newport, Rhode Island, on the night of July 25, 1965.

Three things stand out.

First, you can hear a lot of individual things yelled by the audience and the general responses of the audience.

Second, all the booing you can hear from the stage is in response to things Peter Yarrow said, not to things Bob Dylan did.

Third, it was Peter Yarrow who first started drawing attention to what guitar Dylan was using. He twice said that he was coming back with an acoustic guitar, and he stressed it each time. I remember wondering at the time why Peter was making such a big deal of what instrument Dylan was going to use.

I've heard people say that Dylan himself gave proof of how upset he was at the boos when he came back to do those encores with that acoustic guitar rather than two more electric songs with the Butterfield group. Nonsense: Dylan and the blues band did three songs together because that was all the songs they'd prepared to perform together. They hadn't prepared more because they'd been told beforehand by us Newport board members that three songs was all they'd be allowed to do.

I know that at some subsequent performances Dylan's electric guitar was indeed booed by people in the audience. But I've never known if those boos were from people who were really outraged and affronted at the electric power, or from people who read some of the first renderings of the Legend of Newport

'65 and thought that was the way they were supposed to behave to be cool. After all, by the end of that summer everybody knew Dylan had gone electric, so why go to a concert if you knew beforehand that you were going to be unhappy and your ears were going to hurt? Maybe to have a good time, screaming and yelling, the way kids do.

After listening to the original recording, I can't help wondering if that whole short period of public rage at Bob Dylan's electric guitar wasn't just one more passing fad manufactured out of some warped stories that came out of a performance that just about everyone who was really there, at the time, if not in the reconstructions of memory, thought was pretty damned fine.

Jeffrey St. Clair
Seduced by a Legend:
The Return of Jimmy T99 Nelson

U SUALLY, LLOYD ALLEN, THE DYNAMIC SINGER AND guitar slinger for the Cannonballs, is, among his many other talents, a walking fashion statement.

But on this Independence Day evening at the Waterfront Blues Festival in Portland, Allen wisely choose to tone down (for him anyway) his attire. Even the flamboyant Allen knew there was no way he could compete with the splendor of the Cannonballs' guest singer for the night, the Jimmy T99 Nelson, the greatest living blues shouter and one of the true progenitors of rock and roll.

Midway through the Cannonballs' rollicking set Nelson strolled onto the stage in a cerulean-colored suit that shimmered so brightly it looked as if it had just been painted by Raphael. Adorned with a captain's cap and fighter pilot shades, T99 looked like he was ready to rock all night. And damned if he didn't! Indeed, the 83-year-old blues shouter dominated the stage not only with the Cannonballs, but with a host of other top-notch acts including guitarist Duke Robillard, piano player Marcia Ball and harp master Paul DeLay, stealing the show at what has become one of the nation's biggest blues festivals.

Nelson grabbed the microphone, waved one of his big paws at the crowd, then turned and chided the band. "Slow it down, boys, I'm gettin' too old to sing it that fast. Heh, heh". The little chuckle told the whole story. There was nobody on that stage who was going to outpace Nelson on this night. "The older a blues singer gets, the better he sounds!" Nelson told me later. "It's all those life experiences, man".

With David Vest on piano, you could almost imagine you were hearing Big Joe Turner and Pete Johnson in their prime, back when the R&B sound was being invented and ripped apart at the same time. Vest can do almost anything with a keyboard. But he'd met his match with Nelson. Nothing he did with those keys on this night could detour much attention from the magic and power of Nelson's voice. Vest knew it too. You could see him smiling as Nelson ripped through "Shake, Rattle and Roll", man-handling the band and hypnotizing the audience. This was no surprise to Vest. The two were old friends from Houston, where Vest had played piano in Nelson's band in the 1990s, as T99 resurrected a career that had lain dormant for nearly 30 years.

Nelson is known as a blues shouter. But it's a misnomer. "Shouter" gives the impression of a singer who attracts attention by uncontrolled screaming. That's not T99. Nelson brings the whole package. He can be as smooth as Jackie Wilson, as nuanced as his friend Percy Mayfield and urgent as Wynonie Harris. Nelson earned his stripes singing a variety of styles, from straight blues and jump blues to big band and swing to R&B and soul crooner. "It all depended on the audience, man", Nelson told me. "Back then some of those white cats couldn't really understand the blues. You had to sing them something they could relate to".

On this Independence Day night, the largely white audience would have adored anything Nelson chose to sing for them. By the time Nelson finished "Flip, Flop and Fly" and "Roll 'Em Pete", the crowd was in a frenzy, begging Nelson for more. But he just smiled, waved and strolled off the stage. "You got to know when to walk off", Nelson said later. "You've got to leave them wanting more. That's one of the great secrets of life in the music business".

Jimmy Nelson has a lifetime of those secrets, and on Saturday afternoon he shared a few with me and my wife Kimberly, along with David Vest and Teresa McMahill. We spent a couple of hours together at Pete's Coffee House in downtown Portland.

The first thing you notice about Jimmy, when he removes his ubiquitous shades, are his extraordinary eyes: light hazel in color, clear as crystal, lively, intelligent and impish. He was in Portland as an emergency replacement for Ruth Brown, who'd been taken ill. He flew into Portland and expected to stay a day. Instead, after his blow out opening night performance with Duke Robillard, the promoters demanded that he stay around for the entire five days of the festival. He'd brought one set of day clothes and his blue suit. He'd left his razor in Houston. He stayed five days and tore the place up each afternoon and evening.

"Man, I only have that one suit", Nelson joked. "If I don't change it soon, people are going to think I'm poor".

That wasn't going to be a possibility. Jimmy Nelson could look sharp in coveralls.

These days Nelson is marketed as "the Texas blues singer". But he's really an all-American musician, who was able to absorb the gospel sound, west coast blues and New Orleans R&B and transform it into his own unique, vibrant style. He was born in Philly, in 1918. It was a musical family, but a divided one. His father, Big Boy Nelson, was a featured sax player in Doc Hodges' band for many years. But Jimmy's father wasn't around very much. "He met my mother at a dance where he was playing sax", Nelson recalled. "And they got together hot-and-heavy right away, you know, and he dropped his seed and that was about it. When I was young, he didn't even come around to buy us milk. But, man, he always fascinated me. Leading the life of a musician".

His mother, Florence, was a singer and a very good one by his account. But she was religious and stuck to gospel songs and church settings. "She didn't play no clubs", says Nelson. "She didn't go for that. And she didn't like my father and didn't want me to be a musician. She wanted something better for me, I guess, and she got me in one of those 'Holy Roly' churches in Chester, Pennsylvania. She told me if I ever got in show business she'd whup me".

But the blues had captured Nelson's heart and soul and, at the same time, he was growing more and more curious about his father's life. "One day I hopped a street car in south Philly to a sale at a music store", Nelson said. "I bought a clarinet for $4.50 and then on the way home I bought this kitten. My mother came home from work. She saw the clarinet and the kitten, grabbed them, went up to the second story window and threw them out on to the sidewalk. That like to broke my heart, man. And I decided to leave right then. Everybody was always kicking my dad down to me. But I wanted to find out what show biz was like".

Most people think that the blues traveled north, from the Mississippi Delta up through Memphis and St. Louis to Chicago. Much of it did, of course. But not all of it. Jimmy Nelson was one of those who went west. Many of the R&B greats, such as Big Joe Turner and Nat King Cole, headed to California. So too did many of the Texas blues musicians, such as T-Bone Walker and Pee Wee Crayton. That blend of Texas jump blues and swing and urban R&B melded to form a West Coast sound that was not only distinct from what was being produced by Muddy Waters and Howlin' Wolf in Chicago at roughly the same period but rivaled it in quality.

So at the age of 17, Jimmy hopped a train and headed for the Pacific coast. "I went with my friend Head, who knew everything about riding trains", Nelson said. "But he didn't tell me how dangerous it was, especially on a passenger train. We was hiding between cars and you know if one of those guards, one of the bulls, found a black man crouched down there they'd just shoot them and leave them lying by the rails".

Jimmy eventually made it all the way to Seattle. He was headed for Port Orchard, a small town on the Olympic Peninsula to see his uncle Jimmy Luck. He took the ferry from Bremerton across Puget Sound. "I didn't have his address", Nelson said. "But he was the only black man in that town, so he was easy to find".

Jimmy stayed with his uncle only a couple of weeks before he headed south. "I roomed with him and his girlfriend until she got frisky, started looking for some fresh meat, you know?" Nelson said. "So I decided I need to get out of there before any trouble started".

"How old were you then, Jimmy? You must've been very young", Kimberly asked.

Nelson's face expanded into a devilish grin. "Oh, I was old enough for that honey, believe me, I sure was".

He landed in Sacramento, where he soon got a job in the fields, toiling as a farmworker picking tomatoes, cotton, strawberries and hops. "Oh mercy it was hot down there in those fields", Nelson said. "But I didn't mind the work. I was glad to be on my own and have some money".

One night he ventured into an Oakland club and heard Big Joe Turner, fronting the Kansas City Rockers. "It turned my life around", Nelson said. "We were listening to this band and they were pretty good, but then the biggest man I'd ever seen in my life stepped out on stage. He opened his arms wide and started to sing the blues and man I said that's for me. That man stood flat-footed and delivered the blues, man! He didn't need a microphone, he didn't need nothing. I said to myself, this guy's got something I need to have. That was Big Joe Turner. He was my inspiration to be a singer".

Eventually, Jimmy and Turner would become fast friends. They would perform together, travel together and drink together. "Booze, that was Big Joe's sickness", Nelson said. "He would drink and drink. Anything and everything. But he had a magic trick. He'd eat a lot. Oh, he'd eat mountains of food. And it kept him from passing out from the booze, you know. We were working in Mississippi once. There was this great smell coming up the steps of the hotel. We went down to see what was cooking. It was a big pot of chitlins. Joe bought the whole pot. And we ate all those chitlins with mustard. Oh, they was good, and we used to laugh about that day for years. Chitlins and hot mustard, oh yeah".

Sometimes the food didn't do the trick and Turner would get so drunk that he couldn't perform. On a few occasions, Nelson would go on stage for Joe. Sometimes, usually in some rural outpost, Nelson would actually go on stage as Joe Turner. "In a lot of towns in California people think I'm Joe Turner", Nelson said. "Clubs would hire me because I sounded like Joe, and Joe would be too juiced to make the gig. I did all of Joe's numbers".

"Do you think the music business treated Joe right?" Vest asked.

"Hell no", Jimmy said, slapping the table. "Joe Turner never did get his royalties. Look at all those hits: 'Lucille', 'Piney Town Blues', 'Wee Baby Blues', 'Shake Rattle and Roll'. And he didn't see hardly nothing. You know Joe couldn't even write his name. That's why he always had his valet with him. But they robbed him because of that. All those guys was robbed".

In the mid-1940s, Nelson began entering singing competitions, going up against the likes of that Bay Area great, Jimmy Witherspoon. At that point his talent may have been raw, but it was also evident to anyone with a feel for the new urban blues sound. He recorded a few songs for the small Oliet label, but back then Nelson was more interested in performing than recording. He soon landed a gig at a Richmond club called the Tapper's Inn, where he both sang and served as emcee. "I remember the night T-Bone Walker first came there to play", Nelson said. "He'd let it be known that he thought I talked too much when I gave the introductions. So when it came time to introduce him later that night all I said was 'T-Bone Walker'. Oh was he ever mad. He thought he deserved more fanfare than that. But we worked it out. We never had no problems after that. And T-Bone could play some guitar, man. People thought he was half-crazy, wailing away with a guitar that's got electricity flowing through it, and then plucking those strings with his tongue. It looked like he'd kill himself".

Many of the West Coast scene's best blues artists passed through Tapper's Inn, including Pee Wee Crayton, Percy Mayfield, Eddie "Cleanhead" Vinson and Lowell Fulson. "Those were the tender days of the blues", Nelson said. "Those old-timers could lay on the blues. Make you cry, if they wanted. I remember Ivory Joe Hunter. That man had the biggest feet in the world. When he sat on the bandstand, he didn't need no drummer. He'd just slap his foot and everybody'd start dancing to that stomping. And some night poor Lowell Fulson would come down with his guitar. They wouldn't let him sit in, because he was never in key and couldn't sing hardly at all. Finally, this guy from LA got Lowell, gave him this chic-a-boom beat, and he put that in "Everyday I've Got the Blues" and went flying to the top. I'm oo proud of Lowell. These white cats who play the blues today think they doin' blues. But a lot of them just don't have the feel, you know? It's a shame they didn't get to see people like Big Joe or Pee Wee".

Jimmy's best friend in Oakland was Percy Mayfield, the brilliant songwriter and singer. "Oh, Percy was great, but you know a lot people couldn't stand to be around him because he talked so much", Nelson said. "I mean he just couldn't stay quiet. Percy and I were in the Masonic Lodge together. But I didn't get to see him much because he was in the higher orders, in the inner sanctum. But Percy could be cheap too. One time I had to borrow his bus to take my band down to San Diego. He wasn't using it. But he still charged me $100. Oh, I loved Percy Mayfield like a brother, though".

Later Jimmy moved across the bay to the Long Bar Showboat Club on Fillmore Avenue in San Francisco, a fully integrated club with Chinese bartenders. "That was one of the wildest places, man", said Nelson. "And they worked you hard. The music would start at 9 PM and continue straight through until 10 in the morning. They demanded three new songs a week from the singers, four new songs from the band and even new songs from the shakedancers".

It was here that Nelson became friends with Louis Armstrong and Billie Holiday. By all accounts, Holiday was treated roughly by the management. "Billie, oh she would cry and cry", Nelson recalled. "Finally the owner got mad at her and paid her off in one dollar bills...700 one dollar bills. And he made her sit there and count them. That was cold, man".

Louis Armstrong was one of the original vitamin freaks and had something of a mean streak, particularly with women. "I never seen anyone pop as many pills as Louis Armstrong", Nelson said, shaking his head. "A big plate filled with all these different kinds of vitamins and stuff. Whew. You know Louis could be kind of rough on the ladies. But Louis's wife Lucille didn't stand for that. She carried a knife and told Louis if he hit her she'd cut him".

There were legendary singing contests at the Long Bar. "We was into cutting heads back then", Nelson said. "You know what cutting heads is? It was like a heavyweight fight on stage. You wanted to take on the top singer and cut his head on stage, man. I mean crack his skull open, upstage him, take his spot. Me and PeeWee Crayton and Percy Mayfield used to go at it with cats like Wynonie Harris. Oh boy, nobody dressed like Wynonie Harris. And his songs, they had some crude, cussin' stuff in there. But he was a mean man. Really mean to people. You know I always thought you had to be nice. You can't go around stepping on peoples' heads when you climb to the top cause there won't be no one around when you hit bottom. When Wynonie hit bottom there wasn't nobody there".

One day in 1951, Jimmy got a call from the Bihari Brothers, owners of Modern Records, asking him to perform at the club in Oakland with the Peter Rabbit Trio. That night they recorded four songs. Six weeks later "T99 Blues" (named after an old highway running out of Ft. Worth) hit the airwaves and Nelson was the hottest property in R&B. The emphasis here is on property. It's the old story of the relentless exploitation of black musicians and songwriters. His record was a big hit, but Nelson was pinned down at the Long Bar for another year. "I wanted to go on tour and take advantage of my record", Nelson recalled. "So I told the owner of the Long Bar that I needed to leave. He said, 'Son, come here, I want to show you something. This is a contract. You can't leave now.' That was an early lesson in how the music business owns you".

Like other blues artists of his time, Nelson also didn't see much profit from the brisk sales of his record, which climbed to the top of the charts. "We just wanted to make records to advertise ourselves and our club dates. We didn't know these records were going all over the country. And, of course, it wasn't in the Bihari Brothers' interest to tell us. Eventually, I learned from that, man, about the copyright laws. But only after everything died down".

When Nelson was finally free to hit the road, he got signed up with Los Angeles promoter Ben Waller. One of the first thing Waller did was to take Nelson to a tailor. "I go out to the tailor's shop", Nelson said. "My eyes got big. I saw all this material. I want that blue one, that gold one, that white one. Back in those days, black cats dressed sharp and sing your ass off. So I got to DC with all of these suits and then I got my first paycheck. And it wasn't much. And I called Ben Waller said, where's the rest of my money? And he says, in those suits. And then there was his 15 percent off the top. Early lessons in the music biz, man. Lots of tickets being sold, lots of money being made, but not by the singer".

Things haven't changed much. These days recording artists are routinely socked with the bills for overpriced videos deemed necessary to sell their records.

For the next two years, Nelson toured the country at a grueling pace, playing the Apollo in Harlem and the Howard Theater in Washington. The constant touring meant that Nelson didn't have time to record any new songs and left him too tired to write new music.

Nelson's voice has been a touchstone for some of the great singers who've followed him, perhaps none more so than B.B. King. Indeed, the success of "T99 Blues" prompted the Bihari Brothers to summon the young B.B. King from Memphis to Los Angeles for a recording session. Those cuts have recently b'een reissued and if you listen to them, along with "T99 Blues, you'll hear how deftly King incorporated Nelson's stylings into his own vocal approach, creating one of the signature sounds of postwar blues. Many years later King told Nelson: "If it hadn't been for singers like you, I would not have gotten in the business".

When the Bihari Brothers latched on to B.B., they ended up letting Jimmy go. "The Bihari Brothers said they wanted to record this kid from Memphis", Nelson said. "and that was BB King. Those sessions turned out one, two, three, four, five hit records in a row. 'It was three-o'clock in the morning...' Oh, yeah, B.B. was on his way. And it wasn't long before I got my 'Dear John' letter from them. They didn't have that much money and decided to put it all in promoting B.B. But I'm not bitter about it. I see B.B. from time to time and we chuckle about those days. He says, he wouldn't have made it without singers like me, without the money the Biharis made off of "T99 Blues". But I look back and say, it all works out in the end. B.B. became one big star and we've all been able to enjoy that great music".

"Yeah, but the Bihari Brothers blew it, Jimmy", Vest said. "They could have signed you and B.B. and had you recording great songs for them for the next fifty years".

I asked him what he thought about the advent of rock and roll and whether he felt ripped off that the white bands were making so much money off of black music. "Oh, man, that was nothing", he said. "We'd been doing rock 'n roll forever before those guys came along, Wynonie Harris, Big Joe, even Fats Waller. They rocked long before Elvis. I did like that Little Richard, though. I met him in a club in Atlanta. This was before I knew he was that way, if you know what I mean. He took us upstairs and said, 'Have some of this.' I drank it, thinking it was water, you know, but that stuff was the sweetest white lightning I'd ever tasted. And I just kept drinking it. Here's a secret for you: put a little grape juice in there with that stuff and you could go all night". Nelson playfully flicks his index finger up and down. "Heh, heh. But, you know, Richard got to the point where he stopped writing and doing new material. He's spent years and years performing the same old stuff and it shows. I can't do that".

In 1955, Nelson settled in Houston, where he became, along with Lightnin' Hopkins, Eddie "Cleanhead" Vinson and T-Bone Walker, one of the giants of the Texas blues scene. While in Texas, he continued to record, including the remarkable "Free and Easy Mind" for Chess. He also fell in love with the woman who would become his wife, Nettie. But with the advent of rock and roll, blues wasn't attracting as much attention or money. Records and club dates didn't pay the bills, so Nelson got a full-time job at Hartney Construction Company, where he worked for the next 20 years as a bricklayer and mason. He's very proud of pouring the concrete for the Astrodome and not very impressed with the Astros' new digs, Enron/Minute Maid Field.

"There came a time when working construction paid more money than playing music, and when you're married you've got to think about those things", Nelson said.

Over the next couple of decades, Nelson's chops weren't idle. He played local clubs in the Houston area and he continued to perfect his songwriting skills. Jimmy Nelson isn't just one of the greatest blues singers of his time. He's also one of the great song-writers in the history of the genre, including such standouts as "Meet Me With Your Black Dress On", "House of Blues" and "Free and Easy Mind". His songs can be ironic, funny, chilling, heartbreaking, raunchy and just flat out rocking. "I don't look back. I don't have any interest in redoing "T99 Blues". I'm writing new kinds of music. My new songs are seven chorus long. Now songs that long can get boring. So you have to work in some channels and utilize the band. Put some solos in there. The older I got the more I knew how to write. When I was young, I just put a bunch of silly things together. And if nothing comes to you, you get a block, just take another drink and shout the blues, man. It'll be all right".

In 1998, Jimmy Nelson made an audacious return to the recording studio, producing "Rockin' and Shoutin' the Blues" released by Rounder. This nine-song CD featured five new songs by Nelson and extensively rearranged covers of Leroy Carr's seminal "How Long Blues", Doc Pomus's "Boogie Woogie Country Girl" and his old friend Eddie "Cleanhead" Vinson's, "Sweet Mr. Cleanhead". Jimmy was backed by a first-rate band of Texas musicians, led by the great guitarist Clarence Hollimon along with two horn players from Roomful of Blues, Rich Lataille and Doug James. The music sounds new and fresh, the band finds deep grooves and stays in them. Even so, Nelson dominates the record with a voice that is both polished and thunderous, sly and playful.

The record was nominated for five W.C. Handy Awards, the Grammies of the blues. Nelson was invited to Memphis for the awards show. "I can't brag on Memphis", Nelson said. "My trip to Memphis was miserable. I paid my airfare, cab fare and hotel at $190 a night. They didn't pay the entertainers. I wish they wouldn't nominate me anymore. I'll go broke. I wondered why the Bobby Blue Bland and Etta James were reluctant to go down. Now I know".

Nelson also says that Rounder didn't do much to promote the CD. "Yeah, they didn't treat me right. They sent out thousands of copies of the cover with my picture on it, but the CD inside was religious music. Can you imagine that?"

This summer Nelson will release a new CD titled "Take Your Pick", featuring Duke Robillard on guitar. "After all these years, I finally found out the secret of life", Nelson concluded. "Own your own record label. My session cost $10,000. If I find a penny on the ground, it goes to my sessions. I pay the fees and the musicians and I can do what I like".

On the closing night of the blues festival the skies above Portland opened and the rains came pouring down. The crowd of 10,000 or so huddled together, grooving to Marcia Ball and her scorching band. Midway through her set, she brought out Nelson, looking splendid in that same blue suit. Jimmy ripped through two smoking blues and then waved goodbye. But the crowd wouldn't let him go. They demanded more, and he gave it to them.

There were many there who'd probably never heard of Jimmy T99 Nelson before that stormy night. And that's a damn shame, a sign of how quickly the living history of the blues can evaporate even among connoisseurs. But it only took a few moments for that sound to be resurrected and taken to heart. Those rain-soaked blues fans left in amazement, with no doubt that they'd just been seduced by a legend.

Ron Jacobs

A Conversation with the Blues: The Music of Big Bill Broonzy

BACK IN THE EARLY 1970S I WORKED AT AN INTERNATIONAL House of Pancakes in a suburban Maryland town. The pay was lousy, the work was hot and rapid-fire, and my fellow workers were all pretty cool. There was one in particular who sticks out in my mind. He was the manager (not that that means anything in the food service business except that one works more hours for not much more pay than the folks he or she supervises)-a 40-year old black man from Kansas City who had done a little time in prison and a lot of time in the streets. His wit was remarkably cutting at times. Other times it was full of warmth and humanity. The thing I liked best were his stories and his singing. The man was a treasury of tunes, especially old blues and R&B.

We both worked a shift every Friday and Saturday night that kept us in the kitchen from 6 in the evening until 6 the following morning. Fortunately, I had a friend who was a pharmacist's assistant. She managed to save a couple of pills out of every shipment of speed and was more than happy to share them with my co-worker and me. It was after the pills kicked in on these evenings when the songs began to roll. They might include anything from the Coasters' "Charlie Brown" to "They all ask for me, The cows ask, the pigs ask, they all ask for me". I was working with a human jukebox. My favorite of his songs was a blues that the late Big Bill Broonzy wrote called "Black, Brown and White". When my boss got to singing this song, he had every cracker in the restaurant looking toward the kitchen. It always seemed to me that they were afraid that their just desserts were coming out the kitchen door any minute. It was all just a little speed-fueled fun, but the white folks didn't know that.

Big Bill Broonzy was born in Mississippi in late June of 1893. Soon afterward his family moved to Arkansas. He lived the life of a poor black in America's South. One of seventeen children, he began work in the fields early and was sharecropping by 1915. However, when the drought ruined the harvest a year later, he went off to work in the mines, and in 1917 he was called into the Army. When he came back home he was restless and bored. He got a job on the trains and headed to Chicago, where he picked up guitar playing. By the 1930s he was making records on small "race record" recording labels. As with so many other folk-blues musicians of his time, it was John Hammond who brought Broonzy to a larger audience. This occurred when he performed at a Carnegie Hall concert in 1939 titled "Spirituals to Swing". Even with the greater commercial success Big Bill experienced in the wake of his wider audience, he was never wealthy. Like so many other African-Americans of his time, most of the money never reached his pockets.

Although Broonzy and others in his genre were often called to play spirituals, he considered himself a blues musician through and through. When asked why, he would tell a story about a turtle he caught to eat. After his uncle chopped off the turtle's head, the turtle walked headless back to the stream where Bill had caught it. As Bill told the story, his uncle told him, "There's a turtle who's dead and don't know it". Big Bill would continue: "And that's the way a lot of people is today: they got the blues and they don't know it". According to his autobiography, Big Bill Blues, he first played a fiddle he made out of a cigar box when he was 10. It was after he worked as a Pullman porter that he learned guitar.

Much of Big Bill's repertoire is the standard stuff that blues are made of. You know–women doing him wrong or spending all his money or women spending all his money and then doing him wrong. Other songs in his pocket are full of sexual innuendo and bravado. Still others are a variation of the blues lament. My favorite from this group has a verse that goes like this: "The men in the mine baby/They all lookin' down at me/Gal I'm down so low baby/I'm low as I can be/Yeah now baby/Girl I'm down as I can be/Gal I'm down so low baby/Ooh Lord everybody's lookin' down on poor me". All of this, of course, sung to the melodic guitar play backed up with a percussive thumb stroke on those lower strings.

Broonzy's songs weren't all women, whiskey and everyday hard luck, though. Some of his best songs dealt with tragedy and injustice. These excerpts from his 1937 "Southern Flood Blues" evoke a fear and sense of loss that every person who's been the victim of natural disaster can feel to their bones:

I was hollerin' for mercy, and it weren't no boats around
Hey I was hollerin' for mercy, and it weren't no boats around
Hey that looks like people, I've gotta stay right here and drown
Hey my house started shakin', started floatin' on down the stream
Hey my house started shakin', went on floatin' on down the stream
It was dark as midnight, people began to holler and scream

Listen to this piece and you're on the roof of your house going down a river whose rage is relentless—a rage with little hope of being soothed. This same sense of rage seethes just underneath the surface of my two favorite Broonzy songs, barely keeping the volcanic ash of his anger from raining down on the listener: "I Wonder When I'll Get to Be Called a Man", and "Black, Brown And White". These are songs about the most despairing blues of all. Those are the blues that don't have to be. Blues that exist not because of a misunderstanding in love or a poor crop or even a terrible flood, but because of ignorance and fear and the hatred that combination spawns.

The first song asks the question at the end of every verse: "I wonder when I'll get to be a man?" Big Bill asks the listener (and the system that keeps his people down) what does it take? He's been in the man's military and fought for him overseas, he's worked on the levee and chopped down his trees. He's played all their games and he's gone to school. "When", he wonders, "when will I get to be called a man/Do I have to wait till I get 93?" The second song, "Black, Brown and White", was the song my co-worker used to sing. Like "I Wonder When I'll Get to Be Called a Man", the song is a litany of injustices done to African-Americans in the US solely because they aren't white. From the verse about a bar where he was refused service to the verse about his trouble finding a job, this song leaves no doubt about how the system sees him. The title's reference to brown is a not-so-subtle dig at the gradations of prejudice based on how dark one actually is. In other words, the darker one's skin is, the less chances this country provides. I think Big Bill sums it up in the final verse and chorus:

> *I hope when sweet victory*
> *With my plough and hoe*
> *Now I want you to tell me brother*
> *What you gonna do about the old Jim Crow?*
> *Now if you was white, should be all right*
> *If you was brown, could stick around*
> *But if you black, whoa brother, git back git back git back.*

JEFFREY ST. CLAIR

Waylon Jennings, 1937–2002: An Honest Outlaw

"**T**O LIVE OUTSIDE THE LAW YOU MUST BE HONEST", sings Bob Dylan in "Absolutely Sweet Marie", a tune that has always struck me as kind of a comic rejoinder to Leadbelly's great prison song "Midnight Special". But those lines could also be an epitaph for the life and career of Waylon Jennings.

Jennings was an outlaw in all the right respects, not least as an outlaw to a corrupt industry that was exploiting him and his cohorts. At great professional risk, Jennings defied the pious and rigid lords of Nashville, the country purists of the Opry, who sneared at pop sounding songs and banned full drum sets from their stage. He fought as fiercely as Chuck D or Pearl Jam against the bosses of the record biz, who defile the sound and content of recordings, and treat performers as cattle.

When you look back on Jennings' life and music you're struck by his honesty, his courage and, as Dave Marsh points out his "humor".

Jennings was born in LittleFields, Texas, in 1937 and moved to Lubbock in 1954, where he worked as a DJ and played in rockabilly bands. He was to develop an inimitable rough-edged and rumbling sound, a voice as arid and tough as a west Texas wind. But he got his start working for one of the smoothest voices in rock history, Buddy Holly. From 1958 to 1959, Jennings toured as Holly's bassplayer in Holly's band, the Crickets.

In his book *Country*, Nick Tosches writes that of all the great rockabilly artists Holly was the only one never to top the country charts. It's a ferocious indictment of Nashville, and it was a message that certainly wasn't lost on Jennings. "[Buddy] had a dose of Nashville where they wouldn't let him sing it the way he heard it and wouldn't let him play his own guitar parts", Jennings wrote in his autobiography. "Can't do this, can't do that. 'Don't ever let people tell you you can't do something', he'd say, 'and never put limits on yourself.'"

There is of course a star-crossed aspect to Jennings' life, which lends to his career the hint of miraculous inevitability. At the last possible moment he offered his seat on a plane on a frigid night in Clear Lake, Iowa, to J.P. Richardson, the Big Bopper.

Shortly after midnight on February 3, 1959 that small plane took a nosedive into the frozen badlands outside Mason City, Iowa. Holly, Richie Valens and the Big Bopper were gone and Jennings was left behind to pick up the pieces and roll on.

"I remember the last time I saw Buddy", Jennings said last year. "He had me go get us some hot dogs. He was leaning back against the wall in a cane-bottom chair and he was laughing at me. He said, 'So you're not going with us tonight on the plane, huh? Well, I hope your ol' bus freezes up. It's 40-below out there and you're gonna get awful cold.' So I said, 'Well, I hope your ol' plane crashes.'

"I was so afraid for many years that somebody was going to find out I said that. Somehow I blamed myself. Compounding that was the guilty feeling that I was still alive. I hadn't contributed anything to the world at that time compared to Buddy. Why would he die and not me? It took a long time to figure that out, and it brought about some big changes in my life—the way I thought about things".

In the 70s Jennings came into his own with songs like "Luckenbach, Texas (Back to the Basics of Love)", "I've Always Been Crazy", "I Don't Want to Get Over You" and "Waymore's Blues". His music (and his collaborations with Willie Nelson, who was also breaking loose from the shackles of Nashville) gave grit and substance to American music at a time when rock had flatlined into the likes of Journey and REO Speedwagon. The elemental spirit of rock and roll thrived in Jennings' country music; the sound was at once old and new. The Outlaws (which featured Jennings, Nelson, Tompall Glaser and Jennings' fourth and last wife, Jessi Colter) made the so-called country-rock being offered up by groups such as The Eagles sound processed and puerile by comparison. Next to Waylon Jennings, the perfectionist posings of Don Henley seem like Donny Osmond.

Jennings embodied that strange alchemy of American music, a music that was both popular and uncompromising; a sound that paid allegiance to Hank Williams, Son House and Buddy Holly and yet was unmistakably original. "I've always felt that blues, rock and roll and country are just about a beat apart", Jennings said. In his music, at times, they blended into one.

I had the undeserved fortune to meet Waylon Jennings in the summer of 1978, when he came to Indianapolis to play at a fundraiser for Senator Birch Bayh, the perennially embattled Democrat. I was working as gofer for the Bayh campaign, shuttling bigwigs around in a rented black Lincoln. God knows how he got hooked into doing a gig for Bayh. Most likely it was as a favor to Bayh's charismatic and brilliant wife, Marvella, who was to die of breast cancer a few years later.

I was supposed to drive Jennings from the concert to his hotel, about a mile away. But he wasn't quite ready to endure an entire night in downtown Indianapolis. He wanted to drive around. After a while, he turned to me, grinned and said, "Man, what are you doing working for these assholes?"

"Huh? We don't want the Republicans to take over the country again, do we?"

"Not a dime's worth of difference between them." He was right of course. But I'm a slow learner and it took me another decade to figure that out on my own.

Jennings pulled a cassette from the pocket of his black vest. "Stick this in that machine", he said.

It was a country blues, featuring a guitar as clear as a bell and a voice as ragged as a crosscut saw. "Oh the Rocky Mountains, they's a mean and terrible place".

At that time, it was my misfortune to know less about music than I did about politics. "Who is that?"

He shook his head in amazement, convinced he was talking with an imbecile. "That's Sam Hopkins, son. Now just kick this damn Lincoln into gear and drive".

As we rolled through the night, Jennings sat next to me, tapping his booted foot to the beat, working his way through a fifth of George Dickle, Tennessee's finest sipping bourbon.

We drove 30 miles west of the city on Route 40, the old National Road, into the heart of the heartland. "This'll be fine", he said. "Pull down that gravel road there".

I stopped the car in what was little more than a tractor lane, hemmed in by 12-foot-tall walls of sweet corn.

"What are we doing?"

"Come on out here and join me, Hoss", Jennings growled. "Let's take a piss in this cornFields and watch those damn meteors. Now don't they look just like the rebel angels falling down from the heavens".

Overhead the Perseid meteor shower was in full bloom—one meteor after another slashed across the August night.

To this day I've rarely missed a chance to escape from the city lights in August and watch those rebel angels fall from the sky, with my favorite bluesman, Lightnin' Hopkins, providing the soundtrack. Thanks for that, Waylon, and for everything else.

Dave Marsh

Mr. Big Stuff, Alan Lomax: Great White Hunter or Thief, Plagiarist and Bigot?

Seeing Alan Lomax's obituary on the front page of the New York Times irked the hell out of me. Harry Smith syndrome all over again—the Great White "Discoverer" as the axis of cultural genesis. Lomax, wrote Jon Pareles, "advocated what he called 'cultural equity: the right of every culture to have equal time on the air and equal time in the classroom'".

He did?

In 1993, when Lomax published *The Land Where the Blues Began*, his memoir of blues research in the deep South, Peter Bochan invited him to do a WBAI interview. Bochan ventured to Lomax that Elvis Presley stood as a great product of the Southern folk cultures. Lomax firmly denied this, and said that Bochan couldn't even know that Presley had listened as a boy to Sister Rosetta Tharpe's gospel radio show because "You weren't there". He said this so persistently and adamantly—with all the stupid "folklorist" purism that ruined the folk music revival that Bochan went home and intercut Lomax's prissy voice and dumb assertions with excerpts from Beavis and Butthead. It aired that way.

Even sticking to the blues, Lomax cut a dubious figure. As a veteran blues observer wrote me, "Don't get too caught up in grieving for Alan Lomax. For every fine musical contribution that he made, there was an evil venal manipulation of copyright, publishing and ownership of the collected material".

The most notorious concerns "Goodnight, Irene". Lomax and his father recorded Huddie "Leadbelly" Ledbetter's song first, so when the song needed to be formally copyrighted because the Weavers were about to have a huge hit with it, representatives of the Ledbetter family approached him. Lomax agreed that this copyright should be established. He adamantly refused to take his name off the song, or to surrender income from it, even though Leadbelly's family was impoverished in the wake of his death two years earlier.

Lomax believed folk culture needed guidance from superior beings like himself. Lomax told Bochan what he believed: nothing in poor people's culture truly happened unless someone like him documented it. He hated rock and roll.

The nature of the expert mattered, too. Lomax's obit made the front page mainly because he "discovered" Son House and Muddy Waters. But in *Can't Be Satisfied,* his new Muddy Waters biography, Robert Gordon shows that Lomax's discoveries weren't the serendipitous events the mighty white hunter portrayed. Lomax was led to House and then Waters by the great Negro scholar, John Work III of Fisk University. Gordon even shows Lomax plagiarizing Work, and not on a minor point. In his book, Lomax offers precisely one sentence about Work. He eliminated Work from his second Mississippi trip. He also burned Muddy Waters for the $20 he promised for making the records.

Maybe the fact that Lomax served as a folk music "missionary" (to use Bob Dylan's term) offsets all this. Provided that it doesn't turn out that Lomax used and discarded ethnic workers worldwide the way he used Work, I guess there's a case to be made. But I do hope that people understand that when Pareles says that "Mr. Lomax wasn't interested in simply discovering stars", part of the meaning is that he didn't want them to get in the way of his selfimportance.

Sometime soon, we need to figure out why it is that, when it comes to cultures like those of Mississippi black people, we celebrate the milkman more than the milk. Meanwhile, every sentence that will be uttered about Lomax this week—including these—would be better used to describe the great musicians he recorded in the US, the Bahamas and elsewhere. Gordon's book serves as a good corrective.

JEFFREY ST. CLAIR

The Story of Death Row Records

On August 7, 2001, Marion "Suge" Knight, the 350-pound boss of Death Row Records, walked out of prison after serving five years on charges stemming from a 1992 assault. About the time Knight regained his freedom, a new documentary film, *Welcome to Death Row,* about the rise and fall of his company, was making the rounds looking for a distributor to show it in theaters.

Five months later, *Welcome to Death Row* still hasn't had much of a public airing and the dozen or so artists who spoke on camera are feeling intimidated. Some have received death threats. Others fear for their careers.

The story told by *Welcome to Death Row* is a cautionary tale about the grimy realities of the entertainment industry, one that has made billions exploiting the talents of songwriters and musicians. It's a story of mercenary lawyers, drug gangs and unremitting harassment by police and the FBI. By the end, although the label generated more than $400 million in sales, its top star was dead, its business manager was in jail and all the money was gone, most of it filched by white businessmen.

Compton didn't give birth to rap, but the music that came off the streets of Los Angeles in the late 1980s took the genre to a new level, artistically and politically. The leading forces of this new militant sound included rappers Eazy E, Ice Cube, MC Ren and Dr. Dre. The polyrhythmic beats and explicit lyrics, about drugs, sex, the violence of the streets and police brutality, were way beyond what any radio stations were willing to put on the air. But it didn't matter. The records sold hundreds of thousands of copies anyway and drew the squawks of such sentinels of public morality as Tipper Gore, William Bennett and Joe Lieberman.

The records sold and made millions for the record labels, but that didn't mean the artists got paid. A small group of rappers from Compton, led by Dr. Dre and his partner DOC, wanted to break out of this cycle of exploitation, form their own label and keep control over their songs and masters.

Dre sought out Dick Griffey, a black LA businessman and owner of SOLAR records, which had recorded numerous local R&B groups. Griffey offered Dre and his fellow artists, including Snoop Doggy Dog, office space and a studio in Hollywood. "The major labels will never understand street music", Griffey says. "But rap proved to be our CNN, our 60 Minutes, our Dateline".

Now Suge Knight enters the mix. Knight met Dr. Dre while he was working as a bodyguard for Bobby Brown. Knight was a college graduate, also smart, imposing and had done the near impossible: extracted royalty money owed to black rappers from record labels and white artists (notably Vanilla Ice, who claimed that Knight had threatened to toss him off a hotel balcony unless he paid his client points on a record). Knight became part of Dre's team and helped to found Death Row Records, handling the fledgling label's business end.

Dre and his cohorts soon went to work in Griffey's studio creating what would become one of the most important albums of the Nineties, *The Chronic*. But while they had their own label, they didn't have much money or a way to distribute their records. That's when two other key players arrive on the scene: Michael Harris and David Kenner. In the 1980s, Harris, also known as Harry-O, was one of LA's biggest cocaine dealers. But he'd also dabbled in legitimate businesses. He'd been one of the first blacks to produce a Broadway show, *Chocolate*, starring Denzel Washington. But Harry-O had fallen on hard times. He'd been busted on conspiracy to commit murder, also on drug trafficking charges and was serving a long prison sentence.

Harry-O's attorney was David Kenner, a former prosecutor with a taste for the Hollywood scene. Harry-O said to Kenner, who was working to get him out of prison on probation, that he was interested in investing some money in an entertainment venture. He told Kenner that he had heard about Death Row Records and asked him to contact Suge Knight. According to Harris, Kenner brought Knight to meet him in prison, where they cut a deal. Harris would invest $1.5 million in Death Row for a 50 percent stake in the company. Kenner would become the lawyer for Death Row and its parent company, Godfather Entertainment.

The infusion of cash from Harris made Death Row a player. They decided to have a kick-off party for the label at Chasen's, a famous Old Hollywood restaurant. The invitations, which went out to some of the top executives in the music world, were printed to resemble subpoenas. It was an augury of things to come. Because at that very party David Kenner told a television interviewer that Harry-O had been a founder of the label—a statement that soon caught the attention of the FBI, which desperately wanted to connect the rap label to drug money.

Shortly after the rollout party, Dr. Dre completed work on *The Chronic*. Everyone who heard the tapes knew it was groundbreaking work. But when Sony was offered a chance to distribute the record, it refused, cowering under the storm stirred up by the likes of Tipper Gore over the explicit lyrics and militant politics of rap music. BMI also refused to distribute it. Finally, Knight took the album to Interscope Records, an LA-based outfit run by Ted Fields (the heir of the Marshall Fields department store fortune) and rock producer Jimmy Iovine. Interscope was about to go under at the time and Iovine, in particular, recognized on the basis of *The Chronic* demos that making a deal with Death Row might offer a glorious reprieve.

Interscope bet right. *The Chronic* went multi-platinum and unveiled one of rap's biggest new stars, Snoop Dogg. His first album for Death Row, *Doggie Style*, also went double-platinum. As did Death Row's next four albums. Within a year, Death Row was raking in more than $150 million in sales a year. And it had also lured into its stable Tupac Shakur, rap's biggest name. Shakur was in jail in New York City at the time and Suge Knight was the only one willing to bail him out. Shakur returned the favor by signing with Death Row and churning out a string of best-selling albums.

But behind the scenes all was not well. For starters, although Death Row was selling millions of records Michael Harris and his wife, Lydia, who later served as an executive producer of the film, weren't seeing any money. They'd turned over all the business dealings to their attorney, David Kenner. When Suge Knight publicly disavowed Harris and any link to his money, the Harrises realized that they had been betrayed by both Knight and their own lawyer.

Meanwhile, the political attacks on rap music continued to escalate, with Bob Dole and Dan Quayle both making Time/Warner's stake in Interscope a campaign issue. Enter C. Dolores Tucker, the prudish marm of the NAACP. *Welcome to Death Row* claims that Tucker attempted to parlay attacks on rap into a cushy deal with Time/Warner which would involve her overseeing an $80 million label, acting as censor of lyrical content. Apparently, Tucker convinced Michael Fuchs, head of Time/Warner's music division, that she could swing Suge Knight on this deal. A meeting was arranged at Dionne Warwick's mansion. Knight stood them up. Tucker went away empty handed and Time/Warner ended up selling Interscope back to Iovine and Fields.

But for all the money that was changing hands (some $400 million), only a trickle was making its way back to the artists. Even Dr. Dre, the creative force behind the label, wasn't getting his share and found it impossible to record in the Death Row studios, which had become clotted with gang members and

Knight's thuggish entourage. Snoop Dogg described the situation at the studio as "everybody being in a chokehold". Ultimately, Dre left Death Row Records. It was the beginning of the end.

The fateful day was September 7, 1996, when Tupac Shakur, under police and FBI surveillance, was gunned down in Las Vegas, with Suge Knight at his side. Knight was wounded and Shakur later died of his bullet wounds. Earlier that evening Knight had gotten into a scuffle with a man in the lobby of a casino. The fight was captured on videotape. The tape was used to charge Knight with a parole violation. Knight turned to David Kenner. This time Kenner had little to work with, and perhaps less motivation. Knight ended up getting hit with a nine-year sentence. Many Death Row employees think that Kenner didn't put forth much of a defense.

"Telling the story of Death Row records presented many unique challenges for anyone with the temerity to try", says Leigh Savidge, the film's director. "The people close to this story generally fall into one of two categories: those who make out like bandits, aren't talking and want the story to simply fade away; and those who were misused, threatened and are simply relieved to have survived the experience".

The making of the film *Welcome to Death Row* was also of considerable interest to the FBI, which was looking to go after the financial backers of Death Row, whom they suspected of being tied to drug traffickers. "At the time when a lot of the initial interviews were done, the government was investigating Death Row", says Savidge. "There was grave, grave concern. [The interviewees] had been approached by the FBI [which was] looking to get [them] to say things about Death Row. In a sense, to connect Death Row to drug money. It was a tremendous amount of fear we faced in getting people to talk when we first started off".

There were also threats from people close to Suge Knight. Many of the rappers who agreed to be interviewed by Savidge, including artists as established as Snoop Dogg, got threats. "There are things that flash before you. I'm not somebody who sits at home at night and racks up fear about what's going to happen to me", Savidge said. "That's either a good thing or not a good thing, but nothing is gonna stop me from telling this story and showing it to people and letting people get a sense of perspective on what happened".

In the end, the story of Death Row Records isn't so different from many other stories of black artists and entrepreneurs who run into the subtle racism of Hollywood and the merciless profit-hunger of the entertainment industry, from its CEOs and producers to the lawyers. Most of the money from this incredibly successful label was made by two white men, Ted Fields and Jimmy Iovine. Many of the artists ended up broke, in jail or dead.

"They just don't want us legal", says rapper Rick James.

As for Suge Knight, he's looking to reconstruct his crumbled empire on the backs of those who helped him build it: "I'm still gonna make my money no matter what. I don't care who put out a record, who did what. If there is an artist on Death Row, my kids [are] still gonna eat off that. Death Row artists got Death Row babies, they got Death Row wives. They got everything they got because of Suge Knight and Death Row".

SUSAN MARTINEZ

By the Hand of the Father

I WAS THE FIRST BABY DELIVERED IN SPANISH IN Bakersfield, California, by Dr. Ramirez at Greater Bakersfield Memorial Hospital. My father recorded the event on reel-to-reel tape, and he played it for me once. Actually, he played it for me several times, but I could only bear to listen to it once, the sound of my first song followed by his sobs of happiness, then he and Dr. Ramirez congratulating each other as if they'd done all the work.

Dr. Ramirez was Venezuelan but had been raised in Massachusetts, in English, with his mother's family. He wanted to find his Hispanic heritage and therefore started with language, by taking a night school course. My father, Chicano, taught him to speak, read, and write Spanish, and Dr. Ramirez in turn coached my white mother through pregnancy with such revolutionary ideas as preparing juice and instant milk with fluoridated water from the drug store, so that I would have strong teeth. My birth was his first step in providing health care to Spanish-speaking people in Bakersfield.

I told my mom, when we talked about the details of this, that he'd delivered the right kid. She hadn't thought of it that way, but that has always been the struggle between us: she sees my Hispanic heritage as a novelty, not central to my soul. Our struggle crosses the bounds of generation, race and geography.

My parents divorced 5 years after my birth and I was raised in New Jersey, in English, with my mom's side of the family—not unlike Dr. Ramirez. Thousands of miles from me, my father was a champion of bilingual education, but at my school no one could pronounce my last name, not even my high school Spanish teacher.

This is the Cliff Notes of my life; and there is a longer version but the soundtrack to my story is already composed and arrived in the mail on a CD last week. "By the Hand of the Father" is the music and selected stories from the theater-work created by Alejandro Escovedo in collaboration with playwrights Theresa Chavez, Eric Gutierrez and Rose Portillo. The play and music explore the relationships between immigrant fathers and their children, but the CD could also be the sonic companion to my journey as a woman staking a claim where race and culture are defined—and undefined—by the migration of time, boundaries, and blood.

"By the Hand of the Father" is not just about the border, and I don't mean any disservice by saying that, because the lyrics and imagery are tangible and fragrant, among the most exquisite poetry I have ever heard. "On the border of a new age, I have a foot in each century. But when time was measured differently and borders had another meaning, my father had a foot in each country, where the mud on each boot caked the same and the dirt sifted the same through each hand and the earth had but one scent". This is the music of contradiction and resolve, of carrying twice the story instead of clutching a history half-lost. It is a landscape populated by guitars and fathers who bury their sons; by violins and lovers swept up in Italian waltzes at the Aragon Ballroom; by the mourning of a cello as a daughter wonders what makes her father's hand suddenly strike. It is the man who cries after a lifetime of marriage that he wasn't a saint but he stayed. These are the songs of defending your identity, even to your own parents. I am not the first child in my father's family brought into the world in Spanish, more likely I was the last; nor am I the first of a wave of Mexican-Americans: my father's family has lived in the same area of the West, where the nation's border has migrated, not just the people. Mom bristles when I remind her that though her side of the family settled New England, dad's side was here first. When my great-great-grandfather traveled west to find gold, he cut through my other great-great-grandfather's sheep pasture and silver mine to get there.

"We met at a point in space and passed off a genetic code, a hand to hand return to earth. Two separate bodies, two separate minds under one roof. And when you leave this earth we will return to that point for just a moment, our two bodies becoming one continuous line till we float away from each other, two bright signals across a bright universe transmitting a message in pure silence".

My father died 15 years ago and it is too late to ask him questions I did not know to ask when I was young. He cannot tell me his stories one more time; it is up to me to remember them as best I can and pass them to the next generation in all of their pain and beauty, his cries of "my heaven, my blue-eyed heaven" when I took my first breath just part of a continuous line with whatever I say next.

JEFFREY ST. CLAIR
Ken Burns Doesn't Really Like Music

KEN BURNS' INTERMINABLE DOCUMENTARY JAZZ STARTS with a wrong premise and degenerates from there. Burns heralds jazz as the great American contribution to world music and sets it up as a kind of roadmap to racial relations across the twentieth century. But surely that distinction belongs to the blues, the music born on the plantations of the Mississippi Delta. Indeed, though Burns underplays this, jazz sprang from the blues. So did R&B, rock and roll, funk and hip hop.

But Burns is a classicist, who is offended by the rawer sounds of the blues, its political dimension and inescapable class dynamic. Instead, Burns fixates on a particular kind of jazz music that appeals to his PBS sensibility: the Swing Era. It's a genre of jazz that enables Burns to throw around such phrases as "Ellington is our Mozart". He sees jazz as an art form in the most culturally elitist sense, as being a museum piece, beautiful but dead, to be savored like a stroll through a gallery of paintings by the Pre-Raphaelite Brotherhood.

His film rolls through no less than 19 hours over seven episodes: beginning in the brothels of New Orleans and ending with the career of saxophonist Dexter Gordon. But in the end it doesn't cover all that much ground. The film fixates on three figures: Louis Armstrong, Duke Ellington and the young Miles Davis. There are sidetrips and footnotes to account for Sidney Bechet, Billie Holiday, Bix Beiderbecke, Count Basie, Charlie Parker, Thelonius Monk and John Coltrane.

But the arc of his narrative is the rise and fall of jazz. For Burns, jazz reached its apogee with Armstrong and Ellington and its denouement with Davis' 1959 recording, *Kind of Blue.* For

Burns and company it's been all downhill since then: he sees the avant guarde recordings of Coltrane, Ornette Coleman and Cecil Taylor and the growth of the fusion movement as a form of artistic degeneracy. When asked to name his top ten jazz songs, Burns didn't include a single piece after 1958. His film packs in everything that's been produced since *Kind of Blue* (40 years' worth of music) into a single griping episode. Even *Kind of Blue*—the most explicated jazz session in history—gets shoddy treatment from Burns in the film, who scarcely mentions pianist Bill Evans, the man who gave the record its revolutionary modal sound.

This is typical of the Burns method. His films all construct a pantheon of heroes and anti-heroes, little manufactured dramas of good and evil. Armstrong and Ellington are gods to be worshipped (despite their flirtations with Hollywood glitz), but Davis and Coltrane (both at root blues musicians to our ears) are fallen idols—Coltrane into the exquisite abstractions of *Giant Steps* and *A Love Supreme* and Miles into the funk and fusion of *Bitches Brew*, *On the Corner* and his amazing *A Tribute to Jack Johnson*. Coleman, the sonic architect of the Free Jazz movement, is anathema.

It's easy to see why. Burns boasts that his American trilogy—*The Civil War*, *Baseball* and *Jazz*—is at bottom a history of racial relations. But it's not a history so much as a fantasy meant for the white suburban audiences who watch his movies. For Burns, it's a story of a seamless movement toward integration: from slavery to emancipation, segregation to integration, animus to harmony. For every black hero, there is a white counterpart: Frederick Douglas/Lincoln, Jackie Robinson/Branch Rickey, Louis Armstrong/Tommy Dorsey. In other words, a feel-good narrative of white patronage and understanding.

This, in part, explains why Burns recoils from the fact that Davis, Coltrane, Coleman and their descendents have taken jazz not toward a soft, white-friendly swing sound but deeper into the urban black experience. When Davis went electric, it was as significant a move as Dylan coming out with a rock-and-roll band (and not just any band, but the Hawks). Despite the fact that *Bitches Brew* went on to be one of the best-selling jazz albums of all time, Davis is still being slammed. Burns includes a quote in his film deprecating Davis's excursions into fusion as a "denaturing" of jazz.

The Burns style, drilled into viewers over his previous films, is irritating and as condescending as any Masterpiece Theatre production of a minor novel by Trollope: episodic, monotonous, edgeless. By now his technique is as predictable as the plot of an episode of *Friends*: the zoom shot on a still photo, followed by a slow pan, a pull back, then a portentous pause—all the while a monotonous voice-over explains the obvious at length.

The series is narrated by a troika of neocons: Wynton Marsalis, the favorite trumpeter of the Lincoln Center patrons; writer Albert Murray, who chastised the militant elements of the civil rights and anti-war movements with his pal Ralph Ellison; and Stanley Crouch, the Ward Connerly of music critics. This trio plays the part that Shelby Foote did for Burns' *Civil War* epic,—a sentimental, morbid and revisionist take on what Foote, an unrepentant Southern romanticist, wistfully referred to as the war between the states.

Instead of interviewing cutting edge jazz musicians, Burns sought out Marsalis, a trumpeter who is stuck in the past. "When Marsalis was 19 he was a fine trumpeter", says Pierre Sprey, president of Mapleshade Records, a jazz and blues label, "because he was getting his ass kicked every night in Art Blakey's band and that's when he played the best jazz of his life. Fame struck and he left Blakey's band too soon. Then all his early classical training came back in force and his jazz grew boring. There's no doubt he was, and is, a good classical player, but his jazz education got cut short and it shows".

Crouch brings similar baggage to the table. "Crouch started out as a modern jazz drummer", says a veteran of the New York jazz scene. "But he wasn't very good. And finally he was booted from a lot of the avant garde sessions. He's had a vendetta ever since".

The excessive emphasis in the series on Louis Armstrong, often featuring inferior work, no doubt stems from the fact that Gary Giddins, another consultant for the series, wrote a book on Armstrong.

Burns' parting shot is the story of Dexter Gordon, a tenor saxophonist whose life is more compelling than his playing. Typically Burns transforms Gordon's life into a morality play, a condensation of his entire film: born in LA, Gordon mastered the Parker/bebop method and when it passed him by, he battled depression and heroin addiction, fled to Copenhagen, and finally returned to the US in the late 1970s, enjoying a brief renaissance in high-priced jazz clubs in New York and DC, starred in Bernard Tavernier's tribute to bebop *'Round Midnight* and died in 1990.

How different Burns' film would have been if, instead of Gordon, he had trained his camera on Sonny Rollins, who, like Coltrane, learned much from Gordon but ultimately surpassed him. Of course, Rollins is still alive and still making strikingly innovative music. His latest album, *This Is What I Do*, is one of his best. But this would have undermined the Burns/Marsalis/Crouch thesis that the avant garde and Afrocentric strains, which began about the same time Gordon left the States, killed jazz.

After enduring *Jazz* in its entirety, there's only one conclusion to be reached: Burns doesn't really like music. In the 19 hours of film, with one exception (an Aqrmstrong piece),he lets no song play to completion, or anywhere near completion. Yet there is a constant chatter riding on top of the music. It's annoying and instructive, as if Burns himself were both bored of the entire project and simultaneously hypnotized by the sound of his own words interpreting what he won't allow us to hear. Who else would have his own soundtrack play over Thelonius Monk?

This may be the ultimate indictment of Burns' *Jazz*: the compulsion to verbalize what is essentially a nonverbal art form. It's also insulting; he assumes that the music itself, if allowed to be heard and felt, wouldn't be able, largely on its own volition, to move and educate those who (unlike Burns) are willing to open their ears and really listen. In a film supposedly about music, the music itself has been relegated to the background, soundtrack for trite observations on culture and neo-Spenglerian notions about the arc of American cap-H History. In that sense, Burns and his cohorts don't even demonstrate faith in the power of the Swing Era music they offer up as the apex of jazz.

There are some great documentaries on popular music. Three very different ones come to mind: Bert Stern's beautiful *Jazz on a Summer's Day*, which integrates jazz, swing, avant guard, gospel and rock and roll into one event, Robert Mugge's *Deep Blues*, a gorgeously shot and recorded road movie about the blues musicians of the Mississippi Delta, and Jean-Luc Godard's *One+One*, which documents the recording of the Rolling Stones "Sympathy for the Devil". All are vibrant films that let the music and musicians do the talking. But Ken Burns learned nothing from any of them. Watching his *Jazz* is equivalent to listening to a coroner speak into a dictaphone as he dissects a corpse.

JEFFREY ST. CLAIR AND ALEXANDER COCKBURN

Did the CIA Poison Paul Robeson?

AUL ROBESON, THE BLACK ACTOR, SINGER AND POLITICAL radical, may have been a victim of the late CIA chemist Sidney Gottlieb's MK-ULTRA program. In the spring of 1961, Robeson planned to visit Havana to meet with Fidel Castro and Che Guevara. The trip never came off because Robeson fell ill in Moscow, where he had gone to give several lectures and concerts. At the time it was reported that Robeson had suffered a heart attack. But in fact Robeson had slashed his wrists in a suicide attempt after suffering hallucinations and severe depression. The symptoms came on following a surprise party thrown for him at his Moscow hotel.

Robeson's son, Paul Robeson Jr., has investigated his father's illness for more than 30 years. He believes that his father was slipped a synthetic hallucinogen called BZ by US intelligence operatives at the party in Moscow. The party was hosted by anti-Soviet dissidents funded by the CIA.

Robeson Jr. visited his father in the hospital the day after the suicide attempt. Robeson told his son that he felt extreme paranoia and thought that the walls of the room were moving. He said he had locked himself in his bedroom and was overcome by a powerful sense of emptiness and depression before he tried to take his own life.

Robeson left Moscow for London, where he was admitted to The Priory hospital. There he was turned over to psychiatrists who tortured him with 54 electro-shock treatments. At the time, electro-shock, in combination with psychoactive drugs, was a favored technique of CIA behavior modification. It turned out that the doctors treating Robeson in London and, later, in New York were CIA contractors.

The timing of Robeson's trip to Cuba was certainly a crucial factor. Three weeks after the Moscow party, the CIA launched its disastrous invasion of Cuba at the Bay of Pigs. It's impossible to overstate Robeson's stature at the time and his threat to the America government as a black radical. Through the 1950s Robeson commanded worldwide attention and esteem. He was the Nelson Mandela and Muhammad Ali of his time. He spoke more than twenty languages, including Russian, Chinese and several African languages. Robeson was also on close terms with Nehru, Jomo Kenyatta and other Third World leaders. His embrace of Castro in Havana would have seriously undermined US efforts to overthrow the new Cuban government.

Another pressing concern for the US government at the time was Robeson's announced intentions to return to the United States and assume a leading role in the emerging civil rights movement. Like the family of Martin Luther King Jr., Robeson had been under official surveillance for decades. As early as 1935, British intelligence had been looking at Robeson's activities. In 1943, the Office of Strategic Services, World War II predecessor to the CIA, opened a file on him. In 1947, Robeson was nearly killed in a car crash. The driver's side front wheel of the car had been monkey-wrenched. In the 1950s, Robeson was targeted by Senator Joseph McCarthy's anticommunist hearings. The campaign effectively sabotaged his acting and singing career in the States.

Robeson never fully recovered from the drugging and the follow-up treatments from CIA-linked doctors and shrinks. He died in 1977. Robeson, Jr. has been pushing the US to release classified documents regarding his father. He has already unearthed some damning material, including an FBI "status of health" report on Robeson created in April of 1961. "The fact that such a file was opened at all is sinister in itself", Robeson recently told the London *Sunday Times*. "It indicates a degree of prior knowledge that something was about to happen to him".

Robeson's case has parallels to the fate of another black man who was slipped CIA-concocted hallucinogens, Sgt. James Thornwell. Thornwell was a US Army sergeant working in a NATO office in Orleans, France, in 1961 (the same year Robeson was drugged), when he came under suspicion of having stolen documents. Thornwell, who maintained his innocence, was interrogated, hypnotized and harassed by US intelligence officers.

When he persisted in proclaiming his innocence, Thornwell was secretly given LSD for several days by his interrogators, during which time he was forced to undergo aggressive questioning, replete with racial slurs and threats. At one point, the CIA men threatened, in the words of a subsequent Army enquiry, "to extend the [hallucinatory] state indefinitely, even to a point of permanent insanity". The agents apparently consummated their promise. Thornwell experienced an irreversible mental crisis. He eventually committed suicide at his Maryland home. There was never any evidence that he had anything to do with the missing NATO papers.

Art and Architecture

VICENTE NAVARRO

The Jackboot of Dada: Salvador Dali, Fascist

THE YEAR 2004, THE CENTENARY OF DALI'S BIRTH, HAS been proclaimed "the year of Dali" in many countries. Led by the Spanish establishment, with the King at the helm, there has been an international mobilization in the artistic community to pay homage to Dali. But this movement has been silent on a rather crucial item of Dali's biography: his active and belligerent support for Spain's fascist regime, one of the most repressive dictatorial regimes in Europe during the twentieth century.

For every political assassination carried out by Mussolini's fascist regime, there were 10,000 such assassinations by the Franco regime. More than 200,000 people were killed or died in concentration camps between 1939 (when Franco defeated the Spanish Republic, with the military assistance of Hitler and Mussolini) and 1945 (the end of World War II). And 30,000 people remain desaparecidos in Spain; no one knows where their bodies are. The Aznar government (Bush's strongest ally in continental Europe) has ignored the instructions of the UN Human Rights Agency to help families find the bodies of their loved ones. And the Spanish Supreme Court, appointed by the Aznar government, has even refused to change the legal status of those who, assassinated by the Franco regime because of their struggle for liberty and freedom, remain "criminals".

Now the Spanish establishment, with the assistance of the Catalan establishment, wants to mobilize international support for their painter, Dali, portraying him as a "rebel," an "anti-establishment figure" who stood up to the dominant forces of art. They compare Dali with Picasso. A minor literary figure in

Catalonia, Baltasar Porcel (chairman of the Dali year commission), has even said that if Picasso, "who was a Stalinist", can receive international acclaim, then Dali, who admittedly supported fascism in Spain, should receive his own homage. Drawing this equivalency between Dali and Picasso is profoundly offensive to all those who remember Picasso's active support for the democratic forces of Spain and who regard his "Guernica" (painted at the request of the Spanish republican government) as an international symbol of the fight against fascism and the Franco regime.

Dali supported the fascist coup by Franco; he applauded the brutal repression by that regime, to the point of congratulating the dictator for his actions aimed "at clearing Spain of destructive forces" (Dali's words). He sent telegrams to Franco praising him for signing death warrants for political prisoners. The brutality of Franco's regime lasted to his last day. The year he died, 1975, he signed the death sentences of four political prisoners. Dali sent Franco a telegram congratulating him. He had to leave his refuge in Port Lligat because the local people wanted to lynch him. He declared himself an admirer of the founder of the fascist party, Jose Antonio Primo de Rivera. He used fascist terminology and discourse, presenting himself as a devout servant of the Spanish Church and its teaching—which at that time was celebrating Queen Isabella for having the foresight to expel the Jews from Spain, and which had explicitly referred to Hitler's program to exterminate the Jews as the best solution to the Jewish question. Fully aware of the fate of those who were persecuted by Franco's Gestapo, Dali denounced Luis Buñuel and many others, causing them enormous pain and suffering.

None of that is recorded in the official Dali biography, and few people outside Spain know of it. It is difficult to find a more despicable person than Dali. He never changed his opinions. Only when the dictatorship was ending, collapsing under the weight of its enormous corruption, did he become an ardent defender of the monarchy. And when things did not come out in this way, he died.

Dali also visited the US frequently. He referred to Cardinal Spellman as one of the greatest Americans. And while in the US, he named names to the FBI of all the friends he had betrayed. In 1942, he used all his influence to have Buñuel fired from the Museum of Modern Art in New York, where Buñuel worked after having to leave Spain following Franco's victory. Dali denounced Buñuel as a communist and an atheist, and it seems that under pressure from the Archbishop of New York, Buñuel had to leave for Mexico, where he remained for most of his life. In his frequent visits to New York, Dali made a point of praying in St. Patrick's Cathedral for the health of Franco, announcing at many press conferences his unconditional loyalty to Franco's regime.

Quite a record, yet mostly unknown or ignored by his many fans in the art world.

Vanessa Jones

Max Dupain, Olive Cotton and the Aboriginal Tent Embassy

'D E-MAILED AN OLD HIGH SCHOOL FRIEND. WE USED TO share final year art classes. I told him of a photography exhibition. One of his favorite old Australian photographers, Max Dupain. He used to like him a lot. I told him how I liked Olive Cotton's photo of the photographer himself (her husband at the time), "Max After Surfing",(1939).

One of the few images, when I first saw it, I'd call drop-dead-gorgeous. Probably because it was a woman's eye view of desire, which I hadn't often seen in visual history, or in society. Aretha Franklin and Bessie Smith express much of this in their music, but where else was it? I hadn't known of this seductive viewpoint of Olive Cotton's at school. Cotton wasn't part of the school's or the wider community's art knowledge the way Dupain was. Wonder why!

I'd heard of her and her work only when doing an art school essay—Cotton's photo "Teacup Ballet" (1935), had been an option in a choice of essay topics. I chose a comparative essay assignment, looking at "Teacup Ballet"and Margaret Preston's oil painting "Implement Blue" (1927), which had been included by lecturers Jennifer Turpin and Bruce Adams. Comparative art theory essays were never my interest, as I didn't believe that artists made their work for people to sit down and write complicated essays about. But I appreciated the introduction to Olive Cotton. It was the late 1980s, when Cotton was over 70 years old, before her photography enjoyed wider exposure in Australia.

The old school friend wrote of being overseas, far from the sea. And in the middle of summer, missing the beach. He told me how he'd hung up Max Dupain's iconic beach photo

"Sunbaker" (1937). The image summed up so much of what he missed, about the sea and Australia. The friend had educated himself as far as he could in Australia, in our open-access, low fees uni system, which is under attack by the current government. He was in a faraway land, but the photo exhibition of Dupain's was nearby.

It motivated me to go, the remembering of him, leafing through a Dupain photo book, in late adolescence. Life lived through reproductions. Rarely seeing the real thing. So, I went. With my son. Put some apples and a plastic knife and a box of crackers in the car and set off for the National Portrait Gallery at the Old Parliament House. We parked. I thought ahead, and asked my son, "Would you like some apple now?"

He saw the lawn. The lake. I saw the Aboriginal Tent Embassy. The newly burnt-out shell of the Tent Embassy's Information Cenet. "Arsonists" had attacked it under a month ago. The Tent Embassy was started in 1972, and since then it has symbolized and expressed Aboriginal people's fight for sovereignty. Aboriginal Australians are now approximately 1.1 percent of the population and did not receive the vote and access to social benefits until 1967. The Tent Embassy is a living monument to Aboriginal resistance and had been listed on the register of the national estate as a protest site of heritage value. Previous to its life at the Tent Embassy , the site-shed was a permanent protest installation outside the South African Embassy when that country was run under the apartheid regime.

I hadn't crossed that green lawn before. It seemed a no-go zone. I'd met a camera film guy at a refugee rally a year or so ago, who'd been slowly making a doco of the Aboriginal Tent Embassy. It seemed an unwritten Anglo code that non-Aboriginals didn't venture down there, or shouldn't go there, to those tents on the lawn with a fire smoking, with cars around and washing hanging. You should believe in God, Queen and country, and not much else.

We walked over the road, to the grass and steps. My son, keenly carrying the lunch box, tripped on the steps. An Aboriginal guy came over. Helped him up. "Do you mind if we eat here?" I started slicing my apple on the lunch box lid and chatted about what was happening. My son observed the burnt-out nature of the site-shed, which was the Information Center. A few Canadian journalists were sitting farther away, with some Aboriginal people.

"Cold down here, isn't it?" I said, as the wind seemed to run up from the War Memorial, over the lake. He said, "It was a three-dog night last night." I laughed. I hadn't heard that in a while. Aboriginal people sleep at the Tent Embassy. A three-dog night means he needed three dogs to keep him warm. Fur cover. An old outback drover saying, when men slept under the stars. I knew how they felt. I'd slept near the full-blowing gas heater. Three hours away were the Snowy Mountains ski fields, in full winter flight, at top prices. I asked if they do interviews. "Come back tomorrow. We've got some Canadians now, and we've just had some Norwegians."

The fire was burning. The old bush humpy, or "gunya", a traditional Aboriginal dome-shaped sleeping shelter, of tree branches woven with leaves, was standing with the War Memorial in view behind it. There were painted signs on and around the burnt-out Information Center: "Tent Embassy Information Center—Open to Public." "Sacred Sites. World Heritage." "Aboriginal Tent Embassy." Someone had put up sculpted metal razor wire around the burnt-out building, to show unity with Amnesty International. It also tied in with the locking up of refugees behind razor wire in our desert. Another sign read, "Native wisdom, Respect Culture, Sovereignty".

There was one sign there, decoratively painted and signed "Bunja 03", which read, from top to bottom, in 13 lines: "Infiltrate, Annihilate, Incarcerate, Indoctrinate, I DID NOT GO AWAY. Assimilate, Educate, Graduate, Self Determinate. I WILL

NOT GO AWAY. Pluralism, Multiculturalism, HOW ABOUT SOVEREIGNTY." That last sign seemed to sum up so much Australia's 215-year Aboriginal-Anglo history.

I'd learnt some things about Aboriginal culture from my father, who'd taught in a remote area of the Northern Territory, in northern Australia, for three years. At Beswick Creek, south of Katherine. Ten miles off the highway. He has a collection of Aboriginal paintings from that time, traded for dressmaking cloth and tobacco with the painter Charlie Lamjarrett. Lamjarrett was the Tribal Elder/ the Head Man of the Djoun tribe. It was better for artists to trade their art for goods, more useful than cash. I'd watched those images all my childhood. Turtles. Kangaroos. Snakes. On tree bark. Pigments. Blues. Reds. Yellow Ochres. As kids, he'd tell us stories of going hunting with the kids, shooting kangaroos, bush turkeys, goannas, lizards. He once shot a pelican and then they'd go and cook it up and eat it. The kids loved the pelican taste.

The government sent up supplies of tinned food—fruit, flour, tea, sugar. These Western types of food were later blamed for the prevalence of diabetes within Aboriginal communities. These foods were foreign, before, to these communities. The kids would go and fish at the waterhole. There would be fresh water crocodiles. The aim of the settlement, the government policy, was to assimilate the children into white ways. To teach them to work within white society. Many Aboriginals have been critical of government assimilation policy. Dad said that the biggest problem was for the kids to actually get a job after school. This is still an issue in Australia, and he pointed out that the town of Moree, in north-western N.S.W. is a contemporary example of the way in which communities are trying to deal with it. The documentary *Message From Moree* recently discussed these issues.

At Beswick Creek in the early Sixties, there was no alcohol, and thus no alcohol-related problems. Beswick Creek employed half a dozen white people, including the superintendent and his wife. Aboriginal men worked the cattle and learnt horse riding, for the white cattle station. There'd be a bullock slaughtered once a week for the Aboriginal people. The kids ate in the canteen to "have a decent lunch". They had a power generator lighting plant, and showed films. There was a garden to produce settlement fresh vegies. A church minister would come once a month—Brother Hamish. It was close to Arnhem Land. The Aboriginals would settle at Beswick, and then go off to Arnhem Land. Apparently they were free to move as they wished, to go hunting when they wanted. He'd taught the actor David Gulpilil, who has acted in the films *Walkabout, Storm Boy, The Last Wave, Tracker,* to name a few. When I saw *Storm Boy* as a kid, I was proud of the connection my Dad had had to this actor.

Dad used to take the bark paintings into his history classes at an urban high school, to show the boys. He'd also regularly taken us out to La Perouse in Sydney, in an old purple Valiant station wagon, to walk around and see the snake man. Station wagon Valiants in the late 1970s were nicknamed "wog chariots"—racist slang used by Anglos to people of Mediterranean origin, based on the old "worthy oriental gentleman" acronym. "Kingswood Country", an Aussie suburban comedy, used the phrase "wog chariot" in the late Seventies, in reference to the car driven by the comedy's Italian son-in-law "Bruno" and to many migrant families, in general, who drove Valiants.

Now Valiant wagons of 1967 vintage are quite chic, with their wind-down back windows, but back then they were more pragmatic. Dad had told me later that migrants were proud of these adequate cars. They were good for families with more than two kids, although Volvos were more middle-class-Anglo desirable. My family drove our Valiant all the way out to La Perouse often. A purple one at that.

The film *Vacant Posession,* written and directed by Margo Nash, shows this La Perouse region, the film being set at Botany

Bay. where Captain James Cook arrived with the first English boat people. One of the interesting themes of that film is its exploration of the taboo of Anglo women falling in love with Aboriginal guys. Of crossing that unwritten line. The story told of pregnancy, a fight with the young woman's father, the Aboriginal lover's subsequent detention and death. A forbidden desire. A broken culture.

I think many towns in regional areas of Australia had their own story of these deaths, as well as urban areas. Often suicides, of quiet young Aboriginal guys. Perhaps in love with white girls. Perhaps for other reasons. Not always in detention. Sometimes just the relationship. All too complex and painful. Once the line had been crossed. It was quiet, and rarely mentioned, but the sadness stayed, for many years, in the silent faces of the mothers and the girls who had been loved. And, others girls learnt, by watching, to avoid that pain. The names of the boy, the girl, and the boy's mother never vanishes. Remembering seeing them in the town, cuddling. Somehow stays in the memory. You knew that if your eye could see this, that it was better to transfer that site of desire to non-Aboriginal men. It wasn't safe, socially. (The government's aim was for the Aboriginal population to decrease, not to increase). But you couldn't repress this desire. It'd perhaps be like being gay—something you couldn't and didn't want to run away from, but it had the same taboo. So, you learnt to keep that desire, for your own survival, but seek its expression/connection elsewhere.

Yet, transferring that desire to a non-Australian man means risking putting a lot of racial clutter on him when you try to live within Australian society, and the man can end up feeling boxed in and revolted by the culture. Your own involuntary, internalized values of that culture can sit uneasily here too.

Looking at the bush humpy, or "gunya", at the Tent Embassy, which seemed to sit out of place with the permanence of the over-constructed War Memorial and the symmetry of Canberra behind it, I wanted a camera. The burnt-out site-shed painted with images and texts. The Aboriginal flag near it. A vacant plastic chair. Old Parliament House behind it. Well painted, white. It seemed strange, to go to a photography exhibition when outside, there were photos to be taken. History to be recorded while apple slices were eaten.

Inside Old Parliament House were exquisite black-and-white portraits by Max Dupain, of distinguished artists and unknown Australians. Their framed front glass, in the deep grey areas of the photos, reflecting the viewer's own portrait.

I remembered reading about Max Dupain saying that the skills of a photographer were in being able to take photos in your own environment i.e. of a magnolia or such. It was somehow as important, or more important, than travelling to far off, exotic locations in search of the alluring. Like Naguib Mahfouz living in Cairo and writing Cairo stories. Or Olive Cotton living out at Cowra and doing photography around there. Dupain had taken photos of Australian artists such as Lloyd Rees and Russell Drysdale in their studios. As a child at school, while lining up, I used to lean against a worn-out Drysdale poster of his painting "Moody's Pub" (1941). Drysdale had been a painter who went to Outback/regional Australia and recorded his European perspective of non-urban, human oriented landscapes, which included varying depictions of Aboriginal Australia. Seeing Dupain's photo portrait of the artist and former Art Gallery of N.S.W Director Hal Missingham, reminded me of Missingham's photographic books *Close Focus* or *Design Focus*, photographic studies of detail. The idea of detail has always interested me. Its intimacy. Its domesticity. Its power. How detail can be overlooked, yet any whole experience is usually made up of many details and fragments. Think of Paul Cox's film *Innocence*. All those details of memory, time, smell, music, place, touch and emotional experience. There were also many portraits of dancers, a couple of the writer Patrick White, one of the soprano opera singer Dame Joan Sutherland, architects. Musicians including Yehudi Menuhin. Conductors. Also, there were anonymous photos, amongst which was the portrait of a young boy "Smiling Boy at Glebe" (1939). The eyes, or the smile struck me. Something about his young face.

Aboriginal Australia is one of the hardest realities to face and write about, without being a patronizing white twit. Maybe it's not so hard, with some effort, but it is a difficult, living, breathing complexity, which is hard to face and easier to avoid. Where does one try to start from? Where to commence? I think it's better to leave the white critics aside. Better to read or hear Aboriginal people's own stories. Talk to Aboriginal people on your own. (Just as Olive Cotton had done, by placing her eye behind the camera at Max.) Visit the Tent Embassy, sit down by the campfire. Listen, hear the stories, and have your winter jacket come home smoke saturated. And when your kids ask you where you've been, as they smell that smoke within the canvas, just say, "Oh, just sitting by a campfire, listening to some Aboriginal people talk about their life", and already at 6 years, one says, "But there aren't many Aboriginal people anywhere".

A few days after seeing the photo show, I drove back to the Tent Embassy. This time, knowing why I was going there. I wanted to ask the name of the guy I'd been speaking with on that first unplanned visit, but no one could remember. "Probably it was Uncle Neil. What did he look like?" Medium build, I said. Perhaps a moustache or beard. "How old was he? How dark was he? Really dark or not?" At my hesitation to answer, we all laughed shyly a little. There was a chance now to sit down by the campfire, and listen. I didn't own a mobile tape recorder so I'd just brought pen and paper. Two other Aboriginal men turned up, strangers. Were offered a seat. I sat down. Listened to some talk about the Embassy. The arson attack. It turned out that three of the men around the fire had been adopted into white families at a young age. The men were in their 30s. It amazed me how they just slipped into each other's company—strangers, but somehow not strangers. Asking if one knew the other's relatives in the region where they'd come from. They'd establish shared connections, links to family and friends, and then keep talking. Opening up about the pain of adoption early in the chat. The different men spoke of being well cared for in their adoptive homes. The visiting men spoke of experiencoo in juvonilo dotontion oontoro, of thoft, of doing the Harry Holt (bolting off). The least pained of the adopted men seemed to be those who'd always known they were Aboriginal. Not so hidden. Two of the men were caring for relatives' children. I thought the kids were their own. But they both said, "Oh, no they're my sister's kids—giving the Mum and Dad a break to sort things out/ have some time together." Or they were a brother's kids. As a parent I could understand that. Their strength in the extended family reminded me of the social fabric of Egyptian society, which I'd experienced in Cairo. Something adoption would (and did) threaten in Aboriginal communities. Some of the men spoke of the affect of alcohol on family breakdowns in general, and their decisions to delete it from their lives.

Ivan Sen's film *Beneath Clouds* dealt with issues of Aboriginal youth in detention centers and the anger these young men carried within them. The music group Tiddas sings about deaths in custody in the song "Malcolm Smith". A song about a boy who steals a bike, gets locked up and dies in custody. The magistrate Pat O'Shane, herself Aboriginal, is aware of the frequent times Aboriginal youths are brought before court for offensive language. The artist Lin Onus did the sculpture "Fruit Bats" (1991) — 100 bats hanging upside down on an archetypal Australian Hills Hoist clothes line. Wonder what that's all about? Many young guys end up inside, having done little to warrant it. Perhaps they stole a packet of textas and something else. After doing something else minor.

Later, another man came over. He sat down, and some Timorese women came over, who'd been in Australia for less than two years. One Timorese lady came over, came up close and didn't stand back. She crouched down by the fire, and held out her hands to the campfire grate. "We cook like that, back home, on the fire, like that", she motioned to the black kettle and saucepan on the grate. The Aboriginal man who'd come over, Damien Eade, welcomed them, and started talking, explaining to the women the buildings. "One building, the one over there, was an East Timor Embassy. The one with the snake on it. That one, the one that got burnt out, was used before outside the South African Embassy, and was used as an information center, in the anti apartheid struggle, to share information. In our country, we have to have an Embassy. A Tent Embassy. In our own country. We still have problems in this country, we have people here living in Third World conditions. We sleep here like white people did when the boats came 215 years ago. We'd like to govern our own country, like you East Timorese want to govern your own country, without the fighting. You have the UN telling you how to run your government and your lives. When people come here, they should have respect for our way of doing things, like how in East Timor, they should respect your sovereignty. We have the West Papua flag here, and other flags from around the world, from other indigenous nations, in solidarity with them. They try and come and make us put out our campfire and we want to keep our campfire burning; it's the oldest form of energy. If they let us manage our land, as we did before 1788, there wouldn't be these problems like the firestorm (in Canberra in January 2003).... We want the chance to rule our country, so our kids can have a proper country." Then, Damien sang a welcome song for the Timorese ladies, and said to them to bring their flag, that they'll fly it, near the West Papua flag. He gets paid nothing for this singing, and story, but people who drop by are welcome to leave a gold coin near the steps.

Damien explained to me, "As sovereign people we have always acknowledged, recognized, welcomed other sovereign people in this sacred land since time immemorial, (from the beginning). Always was, always will be yolngu, ngar, nungah, murrie, koori koories (Aboriginal) land. We are refugees in our own country. And we didn't lock up other boat people who came into this country"—i.e., the British, referring to the mandatory detention of asylum seekers in Australia, especially over the past two years.

Damien and I spoke of refugees coming here as boat people, taking that huge risk in unpredictable boats, escaping oppressive regimes. Why when they came here, Damien wondered, why didn't they see this government as equally oppressive as the ones they'd left behind? I said I'd heard people in the migrant community express that frustration, but once you get here and start struggling to provide for yourself, learn English and study to improve your work prospects, it's hard to give all that up and return home. Yet other immigrants I'd met were simply happy with the money they could make, and a perceived political freedom.

Damien also questioned the loyalty of migrants to Australia, including British migrants, who could often hold dual citizenship. Where exactly was the loyalty? They could leave and run at any unsuitable time. Especially when Aboriginal people usually had just one citizenship, and had only recently got the vote. And he questioned the ease with which foreign nationals could buy Australian land.

Tent Embassy resident Darren Bloomfield warmed up stew in a saucepan on the fire, another man later grilled a chop on the open grill. One man warmed up toast, scraping off the burnt bits. Washing was hung up between two trees, on a line. Pots of dishwashing liquid were around basins for washing up. Kids were running around and jumping around inside cars or under trees, with all the formality of Old Parliament House behind them. Some men spoke of pinstriped blacks in well-paid jobs, too cozy to remember the real struggles. How money compromised the bravest of men. They told me that the new Parliament House land site is a traditional sacred birth site for Aboriginal women, and how important sacred land is for them. I said that where my children were born seemed like a sacred site, but that the N.S.W Carr government had sold the Royal Hospital for Women's old Paddington land site in Sydney, and the land was redeveloped.

I'd never really understood why Aboriginal people slept at the Tent Embassy. Were they guarding the makeshift buildings, my Anglo property-centric mind asked, like a security guard is paid to protect property? Most Australians work their entire lives to pay off their own home. People make sure mortgage payments are met, or all else is lost, including social inclusion, stability and respect. It is a national obsession. There are many lifestyle programs on TV about renovating houses to make money, house auctioning programs, backyard improvement programs galore. People learn to identify greatly with the house they live in, or aspire to live in, the area they live in, and the worth of their home. Increasing house prices are making this even more of an issue, with there being talk of banks permanently owning part of the property, so people can get a foot into the expensive urban real estate market, and the banks would keep a good part of the profit on sale. All this will tie up people's time more, and people will have less time to think about issues important to their lives or their nation, or their world. Less time to spend with their immediate or extended families. Or do what they want in their lives.

A shortage in urban housing should inspire the increased building of well designed public housing, to make sure people have stability, dignity and a decent shelter, not just motivate banks to come up with profitable schemes which capitalize on people's desperation for shelter. But adequate supply of public housing would take the plug out of the real estate market, and this would not help those who make a profit out of the boom, which includes businesses but also governments who collect large amounts of stamp duty. The most threatening thing to governments and big business about an adequate supply of decent public housing is that it would empower people, and allow them time. It would also lower the price of housing in general, taking out the desperation factor.

As seductive as a big profit is, coming after you sell a renovated house, allowing people to accumulate wealth quickly instead of slaving away at a job for years, the boom will make housing largely unattainable for current and future generations. It might help your family now, but how will your kids and others of their generation catch the market? As the old saying goes, shirtsleeves to shirtsleeves in three generations.

I knew that the Aboriginal people at the Tent Embassy were there to make a point, to protest, and did not want to be removed. That it was an act of defiance. Did the Aboriginal people at the Tent Embassy like being together and hanging out together, despite the cold and, to me, the simple provisions? One man agreed that it was better to be there than in a lonely flat watching TV. But, as a culture, we weren't supposed to talk about loneliness and suicide. (The film *Ken Park*, which has been banned in Australia for adults to see, deals with suicide and self-asphyxiation. The film critic Margaret Pomeranz was one of a group calling itself "Free Cinema", which attempted to start a public screening of the film on July 3rd 2003, but police stopped the screening.)

In an article in *The Canberra Times* by Kirsten Lawson on July 5, 2003, Lawson quoted Neil Simpson discussing why he has spent 31 years of his life, on and off, at the Tent Embassy. "We went from being classed as vermin, but here now we have a political voice. We will maintain this site as it is, simply because a lot of our uncles, sisters and mothers and aunts and children have to live on the fringes of our society. A lot of us have nice places to go but we choose to live here and suffer as our people has."

The men were not there to guard the buildings. This idea seemed odd to them. They were there to bring attention to their political cause, to keep their ideals alive, of sovereignty, and they were there to share information about their concerns and hoped to be there for a lot longer. The now burnt-out Information Center was a place for storing information, which was the value. The building itself in its original condition was not exactly the value, but its political-resistance significance, artwork, national heritage value and its capacity to contribute to helping share the information on their ideals were. Just as if your own home were destroyed in a fire, and you got an insurance check, but a lot more was lost than just materials. Family photos, family heritage, personal treasure. The men didn't speak of wanting a nice government building, in a nice quiet isolated location, to have for an embassy. And this probably would not further their cause. Especially in a country like Australia, where there is such limited media freedom, such tight concentration of ownership, getting tighter. A quiet location for an Embassy would make them hidden, as the government wants it all. These Aboriginal men want their own Embassy, on their own terms, and they seemed to deeply want to have it accessible and open to people. Communication, sharing and access were the main priorities. Modern comforts were compromised, and were put as last priorities. Perhaps three dogs are better than a full-blown, bill arriving, gas heater. It seemed these "discomforts" and "compromises" were the price they paid for their struggle. Like Mandela in prison all those years.

Perhaps the significance of the Tent Embassy and its burnt-out Information Center was like Aboriginal bark paintings- the bark being temporal, yet the spoken and visual history of story-telling ensured the story was passed onto the next generations, and not forgotten. The painted surface not expected to last forever, in traditional outdoor environments. Although rock and cave images have lasted, tree bark rarely does, except perhaps in galleries. The stories and political struggle are significant, and of great importance, and it is their content that is meant to be passed on. Access and sharing of the bark paintings, to the told story, and to the Tent Embassy, are of high importance.

After doing some of this writing, and having a siesta, I got up. And on the white wardrobe door, I saw a printed page stuck up. My husband had been cleaning up his papers, and had found an exhibition print out 1995. An Olive Cotton photography show I'd been to at the Josef Lebovic Gallery in Paddington. There it was: her photo "Max After Surfing". Alongside "Teacup Ballet". Placed there, in my own bedroom.

ALEXANDER COCKBURN

Freud's House

I POSTPONED MY PILGRIMAGE TO SIGMUND FREUD'S HOUSE almost to the end of a week's stay in Vienna. Friends had told me there really was not very much to see, beyond the rather bland geographical and architectural circumstances in which psychoanalysis was conceived and in which the founder of that movement had lived for almost half a century, from September 1891 to June 1938, when he and his family went into exile in London to escape the Nazis.

Freud lived at Berggasse 19—to use the Austrian style of address—in a middle-class district half an hour's walk northwest from the center of town. It was a Sunday afternoon, sunny and sedate. Almost nothing was stirring as I rounded the corner into Berggasse, thinking to pay a few moments of homage before turning south again in search of the Café Central, a place favored by Freud as well as by other saints of the modern movement. My father used to recall meeting Ezra Pound there in the late 1920s. The poet would wag his red beard at him and announce that the café had, by dint of his—Pound's—presence, become the center of the cultural universe.

I never got to the Café Central that day. From the moment I saw the blue plastic swimming pool across the road from No. 19 and, next to it, the curious arrangement of the diving equipment in the window of No. 18, I realized that Freud's old block was speaking to me in a language translated by its most famous resident. It is scarcely surprising but gratifying all the same that the street where he lived should be so delightful an illustration of Freud's view of the unconscious, and of the symbolism he instilled in our mental guidebooks of the way in which the unconscious expresses itself in everyday life,. As unwitting tribute to the power of Freud's name, Berggasse is hard to beat.

But I should start with No. 19 itself, for unless the Freud family had moved there in 1891 I very much doubt that the window of the handbag store at No. 17 would look quite the way it does now. The house was built in the 1870s, Renaissance style in its lower level with upper floors decorated in the detail of the classical revival.

In the late summer of 1891 Freud and his wife, Martha, were preparing to move from the apartment on Marie Theriesonsstrasse where they had lived for the first five years of their marriage and where Martha Freud had given birth to their first three children. The neighborhood was the best in Vienna but the rent was high, and Freud, 35 and far from success, could not afford it. He and Martha planned their move carefully, searching for a new home of adequate size, appropriate for a consulting doctor and near decent schools for the children.

In the middle of these plans Freud went for a walk after he had completed his house calls and suddenly found himself looking at a "For Rent" sign. He felt an immediate urge to investigate further, concluded that the apartment on offer was just what he wanted and signed the lease forthwith. He returned with Martha that evening to display their new home. She was aghast, and reasonably so. Berggasse 19 was in a shabby neighborhood, right next to Porzellangasse and not far west of the Tandelmarket—or flea market. It was precisely the locale a consulting physician would avoid. The Alsergrund district in which Berggasse was located was, furthermore, heavily anti-Semitic in complexion, being densely inhabited by German nationalists (and, years later, National Socialists). The apartment itself—No. 5, on the mezzanine, or second floor—was not nearly large enough, and Freud would have to take an extra suite of rooms for professional purposes.

What led Freud into his impulsive and irrational decision, stoically accepted by Martha? He provides a clue in a letter he wrote in 1927. There he recounted a luncheon party he had enjoyed in 1881. In the company of his friend Heinrich Braun he had visited the apartment of Victor Adler, a major star in the student life of Vienna at that time and subsequently the prime force in the Austrian Social Democratic Party. The contrast between Adler and Freud was sharp. Like Freud, but outranking him, Adler was working in the laboratory of Theodor Meynert. But unlike Freud, Adler was happily married and already the father of a young son. Freud, professionally isolated, could not afford to marry Martha.

The lunch party which Freud left with melancholic envy in 1891 was held in Adler's apartment, No. 6, on the mezzanine, or second floor, of Berggasse 19. A decade later the "For Rent" sign led Freud back into the house that had been such a vision of fulfillment. No. 5, across from the Adlers' old home at No. 6, became the Freud family's private quarters. Freud took three rooms on the first floor for his professional work and it was there, in his early books and psychoanalytic sessions, that he set his print indelibly on the twentieth century. In 1907 he took over No. 6 for his work. Nine years later he was able to say that his study had been the seedbed of a homicide. In 1916 Victor Adler's son assassinated Count Stürgkh, the Austrian prime minister who had led the world into the calamity of the First World War after the assassination of the Archduke Franz Ferdinand. The Adler boy was pardoned in 1919, but for years afterward Freud could tell visitors that his study had been the nursery of a murderer and—looking back to that lunch in 1881—that "the future assassin of Austria was then a blond, curly-headed, pretty little boy"—a recollection which no doubt gave him considerable ironic satisfaction, since in that same study he had spent so many hours of his life ruminating on the parricidal fantasies of little boys, some of whom were probably as blond and pretty as young Adler.

This was the house countless visitors sought out for 47 years. Analysands would enter the large double doors off the street (which, after 10 PM., would have to be unlocked by a concierge). Ahead of them they would see etched glass doors leading to a garden and a statue of a girl with a pitcher. Freud's doctor concluded, wrongly, that the statue was of Aphrodite and that Freud had got the idea of the Oedipus Complex from gazing at it. Until 1907 they would turn right, climb four bare stone steps and enter Freud's offices. After 1907 they would—and if in a state of psycho-neurotic tension, probably count them—climb six and then thirteen more stone steps before doubling back up fourteen more before gazing at the door of No. 5 to their left and No. 6 to their right. It was a closed option that destiny was offering them, since both doors led to Freud, but No. 6 had his consulting hour for new patients, 3-4, written on it.

They would have to wait in a room with four indifferent allegorical prints, facing a set of double doors. Those leaving a session would exit by another route into the foyer. The "Wolfman," analyzed by Freud for many years in two separate treatments, wrote that "I can remember, as though I saw them today, his two adjoining studies, with the door open between them and with their windows opening onto a little courtyard. There was always a feeling of sacred peace and quiet here. The rooms themselves must have been a surprise to many patients, for they in no way reminded one of a doctor's office, but rather of an archaeologist's study."

Shelf after shelf, case after case, held Freud's large collection of antiquities, many of them forgeries foisted on him by dealers. They would surround the patient as he lay on the couch, which extended along the inner wall. Light would strike the right side of his face from the window across the room, which gave onto the inner courtyard. There was plenty to stimulate a reverie. On the wall just above the patient's face was a replica of Ingres's picture of Oedipus interviewing the Sphinx. Beyond his (or more likely her, since two-thirds of Freud's published cases concerned women) feet an old Austrian stove glowed with primal warmth and to its right another set of double doors, left open, revealed the desk and chair in Freud's study—the archetypal paternal sanctum, zone of punishment and gratification as so well evoked by the poet H.D. in her marvelous account of her analysis by Freud.

Behind the patient's head but often intruding into his view would be Freud, voluble, puffing on one of his small cigars, occasionally looking up to direct the analysand's attention to a statue or figurine illustrating one of his points. "She is perfect", said Freud meaningfully to H.D., as he showed her a bronze statue of Pallas Athene. "She is perfect, only she has lost her spear."

A witness to the sessions would be Jofi, one of the chows to whom Princess Marie Bonaparte introduced Freud and to which he became passionately attached. Some patients claimed that Freud knew the 53-minute session was over when Jofi got up, yawned or scratched.

These rooms were photographed by Edmund Engelman the month before the 82-year-old Freud, along with Martha and Anna, left for London. A Nazi swastika hung over the front doorway and storm troopers had already forced their way in, looking for plunder and departing with money. International pressure on the Nazis had permitted the Freuds to ship out all their belongings. Evidence of Freud's lifelong sojourn in a city he once said he hated "almost personally" became harder to find. All trace of Freud vanished from Berggasse. In the mid-1930s Freud had rejected as "nonsensical" the suggestion of the City Council that Berggasse be changed to "Freudgasse." Only in 1953 did newcomers to the block and admirers of Freud get the news, in the form of a plaque on No. 19 fixed there by the World

Federation of Mental Health, that "from 1891 to 1938, in this house, lived and worked Professor Sigmund Freud, creator and founder of Psychoanalysis". In 1968 the Sigmund Freud Society was founded, with the intention of reopening Freud's quarters— vacant once more—to the public. And reopened they were, in 1971, furnished with some of Freud's collection and furniture (though not the couch, which remains in London) and blow-ups of the Engelman photographs to show visitors the way things had been.

And so Freud returned, at least in memory, to Berggasse, so too did the shop windows change in response—unconscious, no doubt—to his aura, and to the knowledge, visible after 1953 to every new resident, that Dr. Freud, a man who had notoriously said that there was more in man's instincts and desires than met the eye, and that a fair amount of it had to do with sex and death.

So let us take a walk along Freud's block at least as it presented itself to me that day, some years ago. On the first floor of No. 19, right where the First Vienna Food Coop used to be in Freud's time, was the northern front of a store purveying aquatic equipment. Little white clouds, which we may reasonably take to symbolize the fantasy bubbles of dream and reverie, were painted along the top of the window. Inside the window loomed the prow of a boat, set to cross the sea of the unconscious or even Lethe itself. Propped against the boat, instrument of impaling, tool for anchoring in the sea of unknowing, was one of three separate anchors displayed along the block.

The day I was there a large blue plastic swimming pool was perched on a flatbed truck outside the other half of the aquatic enterprise, at No. 18 directly across the street. In the eastward of the windows, offering a magnificent "Freudian display" were pictures of hearts and fish—the latter have always been symbols of man's coarser urges in the dream lexicon—along with much equipment, in the form of sinuous white hoses and vacuum devices, to clean out the bottom of pools. The western window contained a diorama that is brusquely direct: three white oxygen diving cylinders, propped almost against an electric battery, point up to a circular life belt hanging high in the window behind the words "swimming pool center". As I gazed at this display with considerable pleasure I could see the doorway of Freud's house reflected in the glass.

Right next to No. 19, heading along the Berggasse (literally, "mountain street"), which rises steeply up toward the west, is the store that once housed the butchering establishment of Siegmund Kornmehl, now a store selling women's handbags and men's belts. Whoever arranged it had put the dark bags—including one that resembled a doctor's valise—at the bottom next to the belts. One pretty little pink bag hung in the center of the window and above it are suspended white ones. Students of Freud will at once recall his celebrated analysis of the case of Dora, published in 1905. As the 18-year-old woman recounted her troubles with Herr K and her father, while repressing her true feelings, Freud noticed that "she wore at her waist...a small reticule [or handbag].... As she lay on the sofa and talked, she kept playing with it—opening it, putting a finger into it, shutting it again, and so on. I looked on for some time, and then explained to her the nature of a sympathetic act.... He that [has] eyes to see and ears to hear may convince himself that no mortal can keep a secret. If his lips are silent he chatters with his finger tips; betrayal oozes out of him at every pore..."

Betrayal of unconscious preoccupations continued to ooze out of Berggasse as we moved west. A Lotto shop advertised the gamble that is life, the stacked odds endemic in Freud's dark view of human destiny. A cleaning establishment gave way to a curiously energetic display of women's underwear (bargain prices attached) and a nightdress lunging down diagonally at a quilted dressing gown. Next were the first of a set of windows displaying pairs of women, with one model's left hand gesturing in a languid motion of introduction at her neighbor's midriff.

Directly across Liechtensteinstrasse, as Berggasse continues to the rise toward the Votivkirche another women's clothing store echoed the theme.

Across the road from where the Vienna Institute for Psychoanalysis was once quartered at No. 7 there was a frightening bookstore window display arranged by someone who apparently loathed Freud. Right next to three copies of a book with Freud on its cover were three copies of a book displaying a picture of a woman and—separately—of a jaw. Above were seven copies of a book about food and adjacent two nurses uniforms and a stethoscope. The symbolism seemed tastelessly clear. In 1921 Freud underwent the first of many operations for cancer of the jaw—operations that were repeated intermittently for the rest of his life and that often left him in agony. He had to wear a prosthetic device and often ate with considerable difficulty.

I headed back down the south side of Berggasse and there, halfway down the block on the other side of the street from Freud's house, came upon what was undoubtedly the centerpiece of Berggasse's unconscious tribute to the force of Freud's memory. The single window display of this little furniture store displayed the following: at the back, a pair of curtains slightly parted, on the wall to the right a hanger, at center right a velvet-colored stool, next to the picture of a blue couch and armchair. At left another picture of a fishing line and metal fish lure with hook was propped against the wall. Between this picture and the stool was a small black vase containing a posy of flowers.

As I read the display, the curtains evoked the theater of the human drama, from whose mysteries Freud drew away the veil. Before it stood the stool or backless, castrated couch above which was the empty hanger representing a Freud no longer with us. The picture at the bottom of the enormous couch, juxtaposed to the fishing line and hook reaching down into the unconscious, represented Freud at his prime. The vase of flowers was the final graveyard tribute. Overwhelmed by this sight I suddenly heard the slow clatter of a horse's hooves and, reflected suddenly in the window, what seemed to be the shape of a hearse. I turned to see the black-jacketed coachman driving two tourists along. As the twilight thickened the horse ambled past No. 19 and I heard the man's voice say Freud's name with a laugh that contained a timbre of unease, as if in fear of a man who knew too much.

JEFFREY ST. CLAIR

Flesh and Its Discontents:
The Paintings of Lucian Freud

THERE IS A RED CHAIR IN AN INDISTINCT ROOM. IT stands alone. Hundreds of naked bodies have sat here or sprawled across it. Now its arms are frayed. The upholstery is stained black by contact with human skin. The painter is Lucian Freud. The chair is a fixture in his Paddington studio. It reappears over and over again in his paintings. Once the chair was a mere prop. Now it is the subject of a portrait. A nude of orts, stripped of its usual human cover yet evoking the same sense of tired isolation found in Freud's other paintings.

Lucian Freud has a thing about chairs and couches. So did his grandfather, Sigmund Freud. Sigmund probed the mind. Lucian is obsessed by the body. His interest in chairs and couches and beds derives from their proximity to the flesh, which is his unyielding concern as an artist.

Freud was born in Berlin in 1922. His father, Ernst, the second son of Sigmund Freud, was an acclaimed architect and amateur painter, who loved Hokusai, Durer and Degas. His mother, Lucie, was a well-educated daughter of a grain merchant. Both were Jews.

Lucian Freud grew up under the tightening grip of the Nazis. According to his mother, Freud's first word was "alliene"—"leave me alone." This initial utterance would become an apt motto for much of his work.

It was a circumscribed and closely watched childhood. There were occasional visits to Vienna to visit his grandfather, where he played with Freud's collection of Egyptian statues and laughed at cartoons. Freud was suffering from cancer of the jaw and young Lucian remembers the hole in his cheek. But by 1932, with Hitler now chancellor, the situation in Berlin had become intolerable for Jews, and Ernst Freud, with the help of Marie Bonaparte, spirited the family away to London. Freud's early Max Beckman-like painting, "The Refugees", documents the paranoid existence of middle-class European Jews on the run from murderous thugs. Sigmund Freud would hold out in Berlin until 1938, when he left for Hampstead.

Lucian recalls visiting Freud in London, where they would laugh over the cartoons of Wilhelm Busch and Punch's Fougasse. Freud also gave Lucian a print of Breughel's "Seasons: Hunters in the Snow". But Lucian mainly remembers his grandfather taking him to see horses and secretly slipping him money.

In the 1940s, Lucian Freud endured the Blitz and the V-1 and V-2 rocket strikes on London. Fires, bomb craters and dead bodies were common sights in his late teens and early 20s. In the summer of 1944, his block was hit by a V-1 rocket, shattering his window, while one of his best early paintings, "The Painter's Room", sat unfinished on the easel. "The Painter's Room" is a surrealist effort featuring a room with a couch, a potted palm tree and a zebra with blood-red stripes sticking its head through the window. The painting survived unscathed. But the brush with death seems to have jolted Freud. He moved away from stylized surrealism, owing much to the Italian Giorgio De Chirico, toward an extraordinary series on Kitty Garman, his first wife.

These paintings, which Freud says were influenced by his study of Ingres, are drained of color, the faces overwhelmed by large brooding eyes, the jaws clinched. The paintings are charged with an inexplicable tension. In "Girl With a Kitten", a young woman with a baleful look grips a kitten by the throat. There's no hint of violent intentions in the woman's face, but the kitten seems on the verge of being strangled.

Two years later Freud painted "Girl with Roses". The pose is nearly identical. Again Kitty Garman is the model. The same strange look haunts her face, this time with her lips slightly parted. Now she is tightly griping a long-stemmed rose, spiked with thorns. Our concern has shifted from the object being held to the woman herself.

Another painting from this period is the strangely unsettling "Interior in Paddington". A man is standing in a room, near a sickly palm tree growing from a cracked terra cotta pot. He is wearing a raincoat and thick glasses. His skin has a green cast to it, as unhealthy as the tree. He holds an unlit cigarette in his left hand; it dangles like a penis. His right hand is tightly balled into a fist. Outside the barred window is a young boy crouching against the wall of an alley.

Taken together, these postwar portraits present the troubled faces of the children of an empire that has slipped away: inward-looking, unsure, anxious. As such, they are perhaps an unsettling preview of the faces of American youth.

Two works from Freud's early career stand out. One is called "Dead Heron", a painting worthy of the great Morris Graves, who did a series of paintings of dead birds in the 1940s and 1950s. But where Graves' birds seem like totemic creatures, Freud's painting is an clinical study of the process of death and decay at work, the structure of the awesome bird crumpling into the canvas. But it is also a study of beauty. The outstretched wings are given a cubist treatment that almost puts them into motion. Call it the aesthetics of organic decay, a theme that Freud will return to again and again with his human subjects.

Another early work that is particularly striking is his 1952 sketch of the English painter Francis Bacon. Using an economy of sharp lines, Freud captures Bacon's demonic leer. He could be beckoning someone in a back alley, his leather pants partially unzipped, his legs crossed provocatively, his shirt held open by unseen hands. A solicitation to danger.

Freud fell under Bacon's spell. He painted him again later in the year—a small, Vermeer-like close up of Bacon's face, painted on a glowing surface of copper. This compact masterpiece was stolen in 1984, when on loan from the Tate Gallery for an exhibition in Berlin. Bacon returned the favor by painting Freud, dressed in suit and tie, entering a dark room. The face on Lucian Freud's body, however, is not Freud's. It's Franz Kafka, Freud's favorite writer.

Freud and Bacon were close friends for more than 25 years. Bacon played the role of mentor. But eventually the prodigy surpassed the master. Bacon resented it. Bacon's grotesques are shocking, but superficial. They have the quality of bad dreams or hallucinations. You know they'll pass. You shiver and walk on. They don't get under the skin the way Lucian Freud's comparatively realistic paintings do. The more you look at Freud's post-sixtiess work the more disturbing it becomes.

To be painted by Lucian Freud is to be subjected to a kind of aesthetic autopsy. His portraits are as unsparing as Goya's. But unlike Goya, who savaged the ruling class even as he pocketed their commissions, Freud largely paints his most intimate acquaintances: friends, family, lovers and fellow artists.

But Freud is equally unforgiving of his body. In "Reflection (Self-Portrait)" , Freud's grizzled face is shown in a grim and threatening profile, suggesting Gauguin's devilish self-portrait. In "Painter Working" from 1993, Freud depicts himself standing nude in a dark room. It is an old man's body. He is wearing curious, unlaced boots and nothing more. In his left hand he holds a palette. In his right hand, a palette knife, slightly raised, as if it were a switchblade.

These paintings aren't nudes. Freud paints naked people. Nothing is hidden. Imperfections are relished, almost fetishized. The painter gives no quarter.

The flesh is raw, the skin achingly pale, the extremities often a scrubbed pink. The models are English and Irish mostly. Bodies deprived of sunlight look as if they were grown in these curtained rooms. In a sense, they were. The setting for nearly all of the paintings is his studio, as evidenced by the spatterings of paint on the floor and wall, the repetition of the same chair and bed, the same narrow window and its shade.

If light is the language of painting, then skin is the text of Lucian Freud. He obsessively paints each fold of flesh, traces each scar, zit, bluish vein. He paints booze-reddened faces with an enthusiasm not seen since Franz Hals.

Many of the figures are asleep, exposed, vulnerable. You can't help feeling that they have in some way become Freud's victims. The painter is a voyeur and he transfers this sensation to the viewer of the paintings. There is a slight sense of guilt in viewing Freud's work, as if you are an intruder in a private space. In one portrait of a nude woman sleeping, there is the shadow of a head on the floor. It is surely meant to be Freud's. But it also becomes the viewer's.

This painting is part of a series called "Naked Girl Asleep". Each of these paintings reimagines what is arguably the most erotic painting in western art, Gustave Courbet's "L'Origine du Monde". Courbet's canvas shows a naked reclining woman, legs spread, vulva exposed. The painting was eventually acquired by the neo-Freudian Jacques Lacan, the obscure philosopher of desire, who kept it hidden behind a wooden sliding door.

Freud's version drains away Courbet's eroticism. The woman may be sleeping. Her eyes are closed. But her pose seems too uncomfortable. There is the sense that she may be dead. Here Eros has been supplanted by Thanatos.

There are also portraits of naked couples. Men and women. Women and women. Men and men. They lie on beds and couches. Across futons on the floor. Their legs and arms slide around each other. But, with a precious few exceptions, these are portraits of post-coital ennui, suggesting a loneliness and alienation more pervasive than any Antonioni film.

The most acclaimed group portrait is his 2000 painting "After Cezanne". There is a futon on the floor with a crumpled seat. A chair is tipped on its side. The floor is stained with paint.

Against the wall is an empty bookcase. A naked woman is holding a platter with two cups of tea. She is staring at the floor, as she strides across the room. A naked man is laying on the futon, his elbow propped on a dirty stair-tread. There is a look of despondency on his face. A woman sits next to him, her fleshy back to the viewer. She places a consoling hand on his shoulder. The scene is at once humane and profoundly disturbing.

The same male subject appears on another large canvas by Freud called "Freddy Standing". It is night. A longhaired man is standing naked in the corner of a yellow room. There is a window, with the shade partially drawn. In the reflection of the glass, there is a glimpse of Freud, brush in hand. Freddy's body is emaciated. His hands are limp. His feet seem to almost levitate off the floor. Strangely, his body casts a shadow on each wall, as if it were swaying. Although there's no rope, I wipe away the impression that Freddie isn't so much standing as hanging.

Is Lucian Freud a Freudian? His technique is certainly anal. He compulsively wipes his brush clean after every stroke and throws the rags on the floor of his studio. In the late 1970s, these stained rags began showing up in his paintings. The 1992 portrait of the art critic Bruce Bernard shows him standing alone in a dark room, his hands stuffed into the pockets of his gray pants. There is a stern, almost constipated look on his face. Behind him is a pile of soiled rags.

There is another painting called "Standing by Rags", featuring a naked blond woman leaning against a pile of rags flecked with paint. But now the paint takes on the appearance of blood. The woman's eyes are closed, her body limp. One arm is raised unnaturally. She looks for all the world like the pose in Annibale Carracci's "Dead Christ". The rags could be her winding sheet.

Indeed, many of Freud's paintings seem to re-enact the mortification of the saints or the disposition of Christ, recalling Correggio and Caravaggio. In "Two Men in the Studio", a pale-skinned man stands on a futon, his arms raised above his head, hands crossed. He is St. Sebastian, stripped of the arrows and the flesh wounds.

Aside from these subtle echoes of other paintings, there are no narratives to Freud's canvasses. These are captured moments, clipped of context. "I don't paint people the way they are, but the way they happen to be", Freud says.

These are bodies languishing in a kind of isolation tank. The room is as anonymous as the one in *Last Tango in Paris* (which opens with a painting by Bacon, though Freud may have been the better choice for the mood of Bertolucci's film.). Even when shown in groups charged with Freudian possibilities, there's little communication between them. Fathers and daughters, mothers and sons, lovers after sex. None look at each other. Indeed, they scarcely recognize each other's presence. The only obvious hint of real affection is reserved for animals.

In 1970, Freud's father died. His mother drifted into a deep, incapacitating depression. Freud and his mother had never gotten along. He found her overbearing, excessively maternal. She was made uncomfortable by much of his work. But he brought her up to his studio and painted her day after day for the next decade. "I started painting her because she had lost interest in me", said Freud. "I couldn't have if she'd been interested. She barely noticed but I had to overcome avoiding her."

Lucie Freud sat for her son for more than 2,000 sessions, continuing until her death in 1980. Even then, Freud couldn't stop sketching. His last drawing of her is an eerie image of her face only moments after her death, the skin pulled back tight, her mouth a small black cave. Though far from sentimental, the paintings of his aging mother are the most humane works Lucian Freud has produced to date. And the sessions themselves proved to be a more beneficial form of therapy than Sigmund Freud ever achieved with his retinue of bourgeois patients. His mother pulled out of her depression, and she and Freud reestablished a cordial and productive relationship.

In 1990, Freud stumbled across a powerful new subject, the 300-pound performance artist Leigh Bowery. He met Bowery in a line at a play and immediately noticed the giant's immense legs and feet, which were shoved into a pair of clogs. "His calves went down to his feet, almost avoiding the issue of ankles altogether," Freud said.

Bowery is a corpulent colossus, with a prodigious penis, which Lucian Freud reproduces in extravagant detail, each vein rendered like a river. Bowery seated is one of Freud's masterpieces. Here is the red chair again, barely visible beneath Bowery's bulk. He is a bald mountain of flesh, as imposing as that first shocking glimpse of Brando in *Apocalypse Now*. There's something vaguely Egyptian about the work, like one of the hulking scribes from the court of Ahmen-hotep.

The large canvas barely seems able to contain him. And for the first time, Freud paints a figure who looks the painter directly in the eye, challenging him. Unlike the somatic figures in most of Freud's work, the portrait of Bowery presents a self-assured and slightly menacing presence. He is the first of Freud's nudes to convey the sense that he knows how much his portrait may unnerve many viewers.

Yet, even Bowery seems vulnerable, rendered down to a fragile casing of flesh. As I stared up at this huge human mound I couldn't help thinking what a mess a Daisy Cutter would make of this even this monumental body. Surely this is a subtle theme of his work. You search Freud's painting in vain for technological artifacts: there are no telephones, TVs, computers, electrical cords, cars, or lamps. There is just bodies, a chair, a bed, a couch. Like an elided note in a Miles Davis solo, the missing machines assume an added menace in Freud's work. The room serves as a sanctuary, a momentary refuge from the truly obscene horrors that swirl outside. This then is Freud's existentialist Eden: a dingy garret in Paddington with a small dog and potted plants for company.

Like his grandfather, Lucian Freud argues that biology is destiny. But Lucian goes further than the old man. Biology isn't just destiny. It's apparently all there is left to cling to in an age of fleshless bureaucracies and killer machines.

Alexander Cockburn

The Rich and Their Castles in Spain, Part I: Mizner in Florida

I N January 1918, shortly before the end of the worst carnage in the history of the world, one more refugee from suffering alighted at Palm Beach. On the threshold of middle age, physically debilitated and at a low spiritual ebb, his only prospect seemed to be the grave. Life grew in allurement under the Florida sun. His strength returned and to fill in the spaces of his idle days he built his host a Chinese pagoda and put a stuffed alligator on top of it to defy good taste. Then the two of them decided to build a hospital for the veterans returning from the Western Front. The veterans, as it turned out, had to take their shell shock elsewhere. The hospital became the Everglades Club, and with its construction was launched one of the most exhilarating architectural spasms in the history of the country.

That Paris Singer, one of the many sons and ample heirs to the sewing machine fortune, should have invited Addison Mizner to Palm Beach was one of those lucky strokes of patronage with which the world is occasionally blessed. At 45 Mizner was a society architect of modest achievement, and if he had died in the damp New York winter of 1918 his name would scarcely feature in the history books, unless as a brother of the scoundrelly Wilson. Ten years later he was the most famous architect in the United States. Reviewing a magnificent folio of his work in *International Studio,* Curtis Patterson compared him to Bramante and Michelangelo, exclaiming: "Against the at times tawdry and gingerbread meretriciousness of the pre-Mizner Palm Beach background the solidity and opulence of the Mizner architectural scheme stand out with a definiteness which, to an almost justifiable degree, is comparable to that of the Acropolis and St. Peters against their background."

Within that decade Mizner's output was extraordinary. He came to a resort of melancholy architectural aspect burdened with bleak New England farm houses, Middle West Queen Anne Saratoga frame and the ineluctable modality of the shingle. Skilled labor was not available, and the outer limits of the contractors' vision were bounded by the Florida pine trees which were their major resource. Such tiles as were commercially available had a tin-like sheen and were, as Mizner put it, the color of a slaughterhouse floor. Within four short years Mizner had a loyal workforce and a small industrial complex turning out tiles, wrought iron, carved wood, vases, dressed stone. Clients would leave Palm Beach at the end of the season and return, nine or ten months later, to find immense palaces awaiting them, stuffed with antiquities that Mizner had acquired on a mid-summer boating trip to Europe.

It is always humbling to review the output of an artist when circumstances have at last conspired to release his creativity, and this is true of Mizner no less than of Nash. In 1923 Mizner completed 17 projects, which included houses for Anthony Drexel Biddle, Joseph Cosden, Angier Duke, Edward Shearson, Dr. Preston Pope Satterwhite, Rodman Wannamaker and George Luke Mesker. He built in that year also a house for himself and additions to that of Henry Phipps, along with the Gulfstream Golf Club. But to study that list is also to perceive the sadness of Mizner's subsequent eclipse. Six of those buildings have been demolished. Playa Riente, the exuberant Xanadu rushed up to dignify the social ambitions of the parvenu Cosdens and bought by Mrs. Horace Dodge in 1925, was razed by the same lady in 1957, victim of her anger at the size of her local tax bill and the town's refusal to allow her to rezone her property. Year after year the wrecker's ball has swung, and the toadstool condo sprouted from the rubble of Mizner's spacious reveries.

The reveries contrived by Mizner were of a history that neither Florida nor his clients had ever hoped to enter, and that is why his success was so immediate once he arrived at Palm Beach. By the start of the 1880s, Florida was still an unpleasing swamp, barely recovered from the Seminole wars and ravaged by yellow fever. The beachcombing inhabitants of Palm Beach prospered mainly upon the misfortunes of mariners until at last Henry Flagler, carving his way south from St. Augustine in search of decent winter sun for the tourists in his hotels, built the Poinciana. In this unpleasing wooden structure a thousand guests negotiated the staid pleasures of the season.

To the immediate heirs or actual amassers of the great American fortunes, involuntarily secluded by war from the Riviera and other European resorts, Mizner offered the warm south's answer to Newport. "The transition of art has become my greatest enjoyment", he once remarked in one of the most succinct expressions of his aesthetic philosophy. "Most modern architects have spent their lives carrying out a period to the last letter and producing a characterless copybook effect. My ambition has been to take the reverse stand—to make a building look traditional and as though it had fought its way from a small, unimportant structure to a great rambling house that took centuries of different needs and ups and downs of wealth to accomplish. I sometimes start a house with a Romanesque corner, pretend that it has fallen into disrepair and been added to in the Gothic spirit when suddenly the great wealth of the new world has poured in and the owner has added a very rich Renaissance tradition."

Mizner's central inspiration was always Spanish architecture, a taste derived from his childhood trips to Central America and nourished later as a student in Salamanca, but he did not disdain invitations from other portions of European architectural history to round out what Alva Johnston famously called his Bastard-Spanish-Moorish-Romanesque-Gothic-Renaissance-

Bull-Market-Damn-The-Expensestyle. In a single evening guests could pass in an evening from the Venetian Gothic of Casa de Leoni, Leonard Thomas's house, to the festive Spanish garrison of The Towers, built for William Wood. As Johnston put it so well: "His Palm Beach was a Graustark located on the old Spanish invasion route, where the Christians and Moslems fought it out in the Dark Ages. The town lots and subdivisions of Palm Beach and Boca Raton formed the gory background of the Charlemagne epics.... If the Florida boom had not collapsed, Addison would eventually have summed up a thousand years of Spanish history in one Boca Raton castle."

He was eclectic but not unnatural, unlike his innumerable imitators who have done more to desecrate the name of Spain than any since the Inquisition. Mizner was an impresario of history but an impresario with discrimination and taste, and even if it is impossible to look at Dr. Satterwhite's cathedral dining chamber without laughing—the guests did complain that it was "not altogether cheerful as a place to dine"—one does so in the knowledge that if at times Mizner went too far he went too far in the right direction. Just as his fellow creators in Hollywood were learning to describe epic history on celluloid, so he learned to invent the past. His workmen would stamp up and down the fresh concrete stairs in their hobnail boots to simulate the dent of Saracen boot and spur; they would lash the furniture from his factory with chains, the better to impart the censure of time; they would spray walls and ceilings with condensed milk from a flit gun, then rub it down with steel wool, thus tactfully miming the grime of a fourteenth-century banqueting hall. Skilled craftsmen would quit as Mizner knocked corners off their carvings and swung his hammer at an ingenue balustrade. His brother Wilson would blaze away at the furniture in the antiquing factory with an air rifle to inject the appropriate wormholes, shouting instructions to his friends: "Don't shoot straight at it. Shoot from the side! Remember, a worm always charges at a piece of furniture from the side!"

His customers were in on the conspiracy. His brochures advertised openly enough that the Salamanca paneling in their dining rooms were pressed from Woodite, a Mizner compound guaranteed to resist the damp of the hurricane season. As they paced their cloisters and loggias, munched yellow tail in a souvenir of the cathedral at Burgos and clambered up spiral staircases to their sixteenth-century beds, they were not dupes but accomplices in the manufacture of these castles in Spain.

Through 1925 and 1926 the great Florida land boom surged to its climax. In the summer of 1925 the population of Florida swelled, as 2 million rushed south to get rich. Policemen threw aside their uniforms and became real estate speculators instead. Mizner and his associates dreamed up the grandest development of all, at Boca Raton. He threw up the Cloister and the administration buildings and spun out an entire Spanish town on paper with his own castle secure behind its moat and drawbridge. Then, in November 1925 T. Coleman du Pont, Jesse Livermore and other major backers and board members of the Mizner Development Corporation got scared of the wild ecstasies of the boosters and resigned, expressing their disquiet in a letter to the *New York Times.* It spelled the end of the boom and the end of Mizner's pre-eminence, along with his own financial ruin. He survived on the indulgence of friends, designed a few more notable buildings, published a partial memoir in 1932 and died in 1933, at the age of 61.

Until 1979 an admirer of Mizner had few resources available with which to disinter the achievements of this remarkable man. Stylistically in eclipse, his work was best commemorated in the folio volume of rotogravure photographs by Frank Geisler published with the sponsorship of Mizner's friends in 1928, under the title *The Florida Architecture of Addison Mizner,* with an intelligent and entertaining appreciation by his friend Ida Tarbell, muckraker of the early Rockefellers and the Standard Oil

Company. For those who wish access to great Mizner houses now demolished—Stotesbury's El Mirasol, Phipps's Casa Bendita, Cosden's Playa Riente—Geisler's large photographs are still the best means of transportation. In the early 1940s Alva Johnston published a series of articles in *The New Yorker* on Addison and his brother Wilson, and his researches were published in book form under the title *The Legendary Mizners* in 1953. This is a wonderfully funny book, in which the Mizners come vibrantly alive. Too vibrantly, in the opinion of Addison Mizner's more scholarly admirers, since Johnston related with gusto many of Mizner's self-deprecating jests about his architectural conduct: how he forgot to put stairs inside Casa Nana, which he was building for George Rasmussen, and had to add them on to the exterior at the last minute; how he shouted "building first, plan afterward" to one intrusive client; how he was ignorant of the elements of his profession. Thus was born the Mizner of Palm Beach folklore, an amiable adventurer, hustling up his structures the far side of the great International Style divide.

Rescue operations began with the 1979 exhibition organized by the Norton Gallery of Art in cooperation with other museums in Palm Beach. The Norton Gallery's curator, Christina Orr published an excellent introduction to *Mizner, Architect of Dream and Realities.* Then in the eighties came *Mizner's Florida,* by Donald Curl, in the admirable series put out by the Architectural History Foundation and the MIT Press. Professor Curl completed the work commenced by Ms. Orr. He discusses all Mizner's known buildings and projects, disentangles legend from reality in his picaresque career, distinguished the essential elements of his style and provides plans of the major houses. The book contains the excellent photographs of Craig Kuhner. The only regret an admirer of Mizner could have is that the book contains no color reproductions. As Ms. Orr's little book makes clear, the architect was a dazzling colorist whose most famous chromatic inventions—Mizner Blue and Mizner Yellow—were no accident of the palette.

The Mizner enthusiast now has all the essential tools for appreciation, from Curl's precise delineation of his achievements to Johnston's book, which is still essential in bringing these times to life. However much Orr and Curl may not relish the imputations, Mizner was an adventurer, a buccaneer with an eye to the main chance and the instincts and energy to seize that main chance when finally it hove into view.

The soundest judgement Addison's father, Lansing, seems to have had was to back Benjamin Harrison's presidential ambitions from the earliest hour. Harrison took office in 1889, and Mizner Sr. was soon elevated from the family home in Benicia, near San Francisco, to become US plenipotentiary to the Central American republics. His own diplomatic career was maladroit, but it contained the single achievement of taking his son Addison to Guatemala, where Spanish architecture took the boy for its own. A year as a student in Guatemala was followed by a three-year sojourn in the architectural offices of Willis Polk, noted proponent of the Spanish Mission style. Mizner learned here the elements of his profession before departing on a peripatetic course which took him from gold prospecting in the Yukon to some adventuring in the South Seas. When the heiress he had been planning to marry urged him to a sounder style of life he went to Guatemala to plant coffee. He lingered to buy up antiquities from Antigua's crumbling churches and while purchasing an entire monastery for $600 heard that his intended bride had launched herself from an upper window of the Waldorf Astoria. He thereupon relinquished dreams of a fortune in coffee and set up in New York, fully capitalized with his Guatemalan treasures, architectural ambition and charm enough to breach the battlements of New York society.

He stayed 15 years, had some success as an architect but lost his great chance when Mrs. O.H.P. Belmont, formerly Alva

Vanderbilt, rejected his design for her chateau at Sands Point. The most enduring achievement of these years were probably his vast architectural scrapbook, in which he compiled the sketches, postcards, part designs, historical details which enabled him to change the face of Palm Beach in half a decade. When Paris Singer invited his penniless and infirm friend to Palm Beach at the end of 1918, Mizner—facing suddenly a challenge greater than the treasure troves of Antigua or the Yukon—was able to plunge into these scrapbooks for the facades, patios, stairways, orangeries, towers, fenestrations and kindred effects that made the Everglades Club the sensation of 1918. Within weeks of its completion came a commission from Mrs. Eva Stotesbury, prima mobile of the local scene, to build El Mirasol, and Mizner was on his way.

In spinning his dream houses, Mizner kept a firm grasp of essentials. Florida, he never forgot, "is as flat as a pancake. You must build with a strong skyline to give your building character. You must get effects with changes in level of a few feet. The landscape gives you no help." His clients went to Florida to enjoy the sun and the air. So Mizner turned, as he put it, the fortified Spanish house of real history inside out. The windows became large. Loggias and cloisters helped blur the transition from interior to exterior and helped circulate the cooling breezes. His buildings almost invariably extended round an interior patio, with entrance points to the public rooms on two sides to the living room, loggia, library, dining room. His facades were flat, gathering the eye, as Ms. Orr points out, at a strong focal point, like entry steps or a spiral stairway. A more personal scale—cloister or stairway—would then launch the visitor back into the grand scale of a vast entry hall. His living room would be large, with high-beamed, paneled or coffered ceilings. Curl emphasizes his use of the local pecky cypress, whose imperfections, the despair of builders, imparted the requisite sense of antiquity. His sense of color was masterly, as can be gathered from his lyrical description of the cream on the stucco exterior of the Cosden houses which became shaded with the rising and setting of the sun, reflecting the brilliant white light in a delicate amber, pink, saffron and old wine. Ida Tarbell, reeling from the drive between Miami and Palm Beach during the land boom ("Never had I seen so continuous a stretch of benevolent devastation"), stressed the soothing calm of a Mizner house and added that "there was an extraordinary practical sense in his houses—places for things—all sorts of things. No woman was left without ample shelves for her slippers and shoes, even if they ran into the hundred or more pairs—and every house was planned with the kitchen on the north east corner. The prevailing wind was south west."

Mizner was a great dramatist of space and perspective, and that is why his eclecticism generally produced such harmonious results. He could work up his sketches from his scrap books, have them converted by his staff into blueprints and then rework them with enormous self-assurance and speed because he was absolutely at ease with the history he loved, with the environment he adorned and with the clients he served. The allure of great resort architecture—whether the masterpiece of the Brighton Pavilion or the streamlined little Hohauser hotels of south Miami Beach—has been escape from the mundane, the imagination on holiday. With his castles in Spain this genial prophet of the post-modern certainly offered such a vacation, at least for passengers who could afford to travel first class.

JEFFREY ST. CLAIR
Brett Weston: A Natural Eye

O N HIS 80TH BIRTHDAY, BRETT WESTON FED 60 YEARS'
worth of his negatives into the large fireplace in his
home on the Big Island of Hawai'i. Some of the negatives didn't burn immediately. So Weston doused them with
kerosene. Yes, he was something of a pyro. Over the course of
that evening in 1991, flames consumed the raw material of one
of the greatest photographic legacies in the history of the
medium.

Unlike Franz Kafka, who ordered his writings destroyed,
Weston hadn't been struck by a sudden insecurity about the
validity of his art. Quite the opposite. Weston simply didn't trust
anyone else to develop his prints.

"Printing is a very personal thing", Weston said. "My negatives are a bitch to produce. I wouldn't want to develop anyone
else's prints and wouldn't want anyone else developing mine."

There was another, more personal reason Weston burned his
negatives. When his father, Edward Weston, died, he left his
prints to Brett and his negatives to Brett's younger brother, Cole,
a landscape photographer with considerably less talent than
Brett. In the 1960s, Cole began rapidly pumping out Edward
Weston prints and selling them for thousands of dollars apiece.
He made a fortune, but Brett considered it an exploitation of his
father's work. He also griped that Cole's prints didn't live up to
his father's work.

In fact, Brett Weston did develop another artist's prints: his
father's. Stricken by Parkinson's disease in the 1950s, Edward
Weston, who along with Edward Steiglitz had laid the theoreti-
cal foundations in the US for the acceptance of photography as
an art form, was too ill to develop his own prints after an English

patron offered to pay for a portfolio of his body of work. Weston selected 800 images and Brett, by then a seasoned and innovative photographer in his own right, developed the prints. The result is widely viewed as one of the century's master works.

EDWARD WESTON IS CREDITED WITH FATHERING THE MOVEMENT known as Western straight photography: no staging, no contrived lighting, no cropping, no enlargement, no touch ups. Weston began his career as a portrait photographer in Glendale, California, taking photos of starlets, families and bankers. His early creative work was in the lushly romantic "pictorialist" style popular at the turn of the century: soft-focus, sentimental settings, atmospheric lighting.

In 1923, Weston left Glendale and his studio, running off to Mexico with Tina Modotti, the fiery Italian actress, who, under Weston's tutelage, would become a photographer of the highest order. He abandoned Brett and his mother, Flora Chandler, who would soon divorce Weston.

In Mexico City, Weston's art underwent a dramatic transformation. His series of nude photographs of Modotti, lounging on a rooftop or on a sand dune, are images of stunning clarity, essays in lines and tones of the human form: sensuous and realistic at the same time.

Meanwhile, back in LA Brett was acting out. He became belligerent with his mother, skipped school, and ran with a tough crowd. When Weston returned from his first trip to Mexico in 1924, he said that he found Brett on the verge of a life of delinquency.

This seems to have been something of an exaggeration on Weston's part. Brett may have been ditching algebra, but he was becoming an accomplished amateur naturalist. He spent much of his time collecting butterflies and meticulously preserving them and recording them by species and location, as he would later catalog his vast collection of prints and negatives. Not exactly Brando in *The Wild One.*

A few months later, Weston took Brett back to Mexico City with him. He enrolled Brett in a sixth grade class in an English language school. He lasted two weeks before quitting. It was the end of Brett Weston's formal education.

The real learning took place in the Weston house over the course of that year in Mexico City. At the center of the household was Modotti, Weston's lover and apprentice, his muse and political tutor. Then there was the trio of great Mexican painters who were regular guests: Diego Rivera, Jose Orozco and David Alfero Siquieros. D.H. Lawrence also came and went while working on his novel on life in Mexico, *The Plumed Serpent.* Over dinner and on outings to the coast and the mountains, intense debates erupted over politics and art, arguments fueled by prodigious consumption of tequila.

Soon after Brett arrived in Mexico, Edward Weston gave his son a Graflex camera, launching his life as a photographer. His first shots were of stems of lilies and an image of the tin roofs of houses that has the disjointed composition of a Cezanne painting. Brett's first photos were unmistakably modern: crisp, unadorned, devoid of sentimentality. They show the influence of Rivera and Orozco as much as any other photographer.

Later, Weston confessed that painters, especially the Mexican muralists, exerted more of an influence on his work than did other photographers. He expressed little admiration for the photographs of Edward Steichen, Paul Strand and Steiglitz.

Soon the teenager was schooling his father. Brett's most important early contribution to the advancement of Edward Weston's work was to convince him to shift from platinum/palladium prints to the silver gelatin prints that marked the best work of both Westons. Brett also introduced his father on the erotic possibilities of vegetables, as seen in the remarkable 1930 photograph by Edward Weston titled "Pepper No. 30." Brett later boasted of having devoured the subject.

By 1926 the Westons were back in Glendale, and Brett began working in his father's studio, learning the rudiments of photography by developing negatives and doing enlargements for Weston's commercial and portrait work. Brett himself took dozens of photos every week of flowers, shells, cars, buildings, hands and feet, broken windows, the San Bernadino Mountains. His photos received their first public showing at an exhibition at UCLA in 1927, along with a series taken by his father. He was 16. Two years later, Brett's photos were shown at the Film und Foto exhibition, sponsored by the Bauhaus group, in Stuttgart, Germany.

By 1930, the Westons had moved from Glendale to Carmel, where they would be at the center of a community of artists for the remainder of their lives. Edward Weston's small studio attracted other photographers, such as Imogen Cunningham and Ansel Adams, as well as writers and musicians seeking to have Weston take their portrait: Robinson Jeffers, ee cummings and Stravinsky.

Brett lived frugally for most of his life, eking out a living as a photographer without resorting to portraits, commercial work or magazine commissions. "I didn't mind whoring," Weston said. "I just wasn't very good at it."

Broke in LA in the 1930s, he ended up house-sitting in a new Hollywood home designed by Frank Lloyd Wright ("stunning structure, but it leaked"). He tried his hand at working as a cinematographer on a movie set. The results weren't satisfying for either the studio or Brett.

A few years later, Orozco, whom Brett had idolized from his days in Mexico City, showed up in southern California and hired Brett to assist the painter in his "Prometheus" mural at Pomona College in Claremont.

Weston's work from this time represents a robust Western expressionism, livelier than Ansel Adams' austere work and more attuned to the parallel modernist movements in painting and sculpture. He photographed a delicate series of faceless nudes dominated by twisting legs and hands, close-ups of tide pools and shells, and an erotic barrel cactus that looks like it is sprouting dozens of spiky breasts.

He received his first solo exhibition in 1932 at the DeYoung Museum in San Francisco, which was soon followed by a joint showing with the members of the f/64 Group, including Adams, Cunningham, Willard Van Dyke and Sonia Noskowiak. Brett's close-up of a hand and ear was so admired by Russian director Sergei Eisenstein that he swiped it off the gallery wall.

But Weston didn't consider himself part of this collective or of any photographic movement per se. Indeed, he maintained a lifelong rivalry with Adams, who was one of the first West Coast photographers to make a fortune. Adams poured much of his money into building a palatial house and large darkroom made of redwood in Carmel near Weston's small, self-made adobe. "You spent more on your darkroom than my father did on his entire house, Ansel, but you're pictures aren't nearly as good", Brett told Adams. "You cut down an entire redwood forest to build your house and they still let you stay on the board of the Sierra Club?"

Unlike his father who wrote compulsively, Brett was not a theoretician and perhaps that explains the reason he is less known despite being in many ways the superior artist. Edward was loquacious, a gifted self-promoter. Brett was a loner, reticent and uncomfortable speaking about his art.

"My father was driven and so am I," Weston said. "You're ruthless. You brush off your friends and women. He was much kinder than me. I don't verbalize well and I don't socialize much. Too time consuming. And I'm not a good salesman of my work. I love people, but they can be a drain. Some are stimulating; some are leeches. So I seek people on my own terms. Most artists are loners. I guess they have to be."

In 1935, Brett caught a break. He was hired as the supervisor of the photographic section of the Federal Arts Project. He trained and managed more than 20 photographers. This position, and a short-lived job as a sculptor for the Public Works Art Project, eased him through the Depression.

He was drafted into the Army in 1942 and went through basic training twice. Later he was sent to the Signal Corps before finally being assigned to a position as an Army photographer, where he had to be retrained. For two years, he was stationed in Long Island under Lieut. Arthur Rothstein, formerly the head of the photographic project for the Farm Security Administration, where he had supervised the work of Walker Evans and Dorothea Lange. Rothstein assigned Weston to photograph New York City. The images Weston came back with, taken with an 11 x 14 camera loaned to him by the Frick Museum, are original and startling explorations of a cityscape. In "Manhattan Courtyard", a frail, leafless tree with a knot of thin branches stretches upward toward an unseen light in a canyon of buildings. The image is strikingly similar to a photo he would take 25 years later in the heart of Glen Canyon, where a cottonwood tree stands alone before the sheer wall of the canyon. In "Sutton Place", Weston captures a dark, winter afternoon at a brick apartment complex encased in vines of ivy. His photo "47th Street" is a study of rooflines and staircases that is as disorienting as any work by M.C. Escher.

But Weston was primarily a photographer of the West, and he relished his transfer from New York to El Paso in 1945. On his way, Brett passed through Tularosa Basin and the great dunes of White Sands National Monument (and the missile testing range that engulfs it) and promptly went AWOL. He stopped his truck, got a room at local hotel, phoned the Army base to say that he had been felled by the flu and spent the next few days photographing the wind-sculpted dunes, cactus, yucca and the ser-rated peaks of the nearby Sierra Blanca mountains.

He would return to White Sands many times over the coming decades. Indeed, Weston tended to migrate in his Chevy truck with camper to the same landscapes year after year: Death Valley, White Sands, Oceano Dunes, Baja, southeast Alaska, coastal Oregon, the Owens Valley, the Big Island of Hawai'i and, of course, the tide pools, headlands and beaches of Pt. Lobos and Big Sur just down Highway 1 from his home in Carmel Highlands.

Weston's photos from the 1950s and 60s, whether of shiny black strands of kelp or a close-up of the cracked ice of the Mendenhall Glacier, had a luminescent quality to them, which he later described as "glowacious.".

IN 1969, WESTON TRAVELED TO EUGENE, OREGON TO GIVE A talk at the university. There he met Art Wright, a grad student in photojournalism, who had long been an admirer of Weston's art. At the time, Wright was kicking around ideas for his thesis project. On a whim, he asked Weston at a party if he would allow Wright to make a film documenting the photographer at work. Weston, an intensely private man, surprised Wright by enthusi-astically agreeing to the project.

"I liked the pure simplicity of Brett's vision", says Wright. "There was nothing ostentatious about his life or his work. I was in awe of his photographs."

At the time, Wright was living on a commune outside of Eugene, paying $30 a month rent and looking for a way to live outside the system, as Weston had done. "One of the things on my mind at the time was how to lead a creative and exciting life and not work for the Man", says Wright. "Brett Weston lived a frugal life, but without compromise."

A few days later Wright accompanied Weston to the Oregon Dunes National Seashore near Reedsport. It was a trial run to see if Brett could tolerate working while Wright filmed him with his buzzing 16-mm camera. The two men hit it off and remained friends for the next 20 years.

The sharp black-and-white footage Wright filmed of Weston setting up a shot inside the ruins of an old wigwam burner at an abandoned timber mill site and trudging across the dunes with his Rolleiflex became the opening sequence of his extraordinary film, *Brett Weston: Photographer.*

Wright's wife, Janet, a librarian and artist, had located a grant program run by the National Endowment for the Humanities that was offering $1,500 for projects dealing with "the land". Wright pitched his project on Weston and got the grant. Of course, that paltry sum wasn't nearly enough to finance the film. Wright had to max out his and Janet's credit cards to purchase film stock and gas.

A few weeks after the Oregon outing, Wright joined Weston and two of his friends for a trip across California and Nevada. The film follows Weston as he explores some of his favorite photographic haunts: the Alabama Hills, Death Valley, Lake Isabella, a truck graveyard in Goldfield, Nevada, and the Owens Valley under the shadow of the Sierras.

Weston isn't really a nature photographer. He isn't interested in Ansel Adams-esque landscapes or in documenting threatened wild places like Eliot Porter. He was obsessed with capturing the intricacies and rhythms of form, light and shadow. Weston is as fascinated by close-ups of the exfoliating bark of a bristlecone pine or the spikes of a Joshua Tree as he is with the visual poetry of peeling paint on the side-panel of a rusted out truck.

"There are a million choices for each shot", Weston tells Wright. "At its simplest, photography is very complex. So I try to keep it simple and focus on things I can master."

How do you know when you have something, Wright asks.

"I have an orgasm, Art", Weston chuckles. "You just know it. There's a flash of inspiration. Like with certain women. You feel marvelous and just take off."

There were many women in Weston's life and four wives. Even so, except for the stunning series of underwater nudes, shot in the black tile pool at his home in the Carmel Highlands, his body of work does not offer many images of women. But many of his images are highly erotic, especially the sinuous lines of the dunes at Oceano or on the Oregon coast, the wet tangles of kelp in tide pool, the flesh of a barrel cactus, the thigh-like humps of sandstone in the Alabama Hills in the California desert.

He tells Wright that he has been photographing Point Lobos for going on 40 years but still finds it fresh. "Point Lobos is always changing", Weston says. "I've lived and photographed there nearly all my life, but even in the last few years I've done some of my best work there."

Wright's film is one of the most detailed and intimate document, of a working photographer ever made. He follows Weston from scouting locations, to setting up shots, to the tedious work in his small darkroom in Carmel.

Brett Weston got up each morning before dawn, whether he was in the field or working at home in the dark room. In his last decades he would awaken even earlier. It wasn't unusual for him to be working in the darkroom by 2 AM. He would work for four or five hours straight, dipping the print paper into the toxic amidol developing chemical that turned the fingernails on his left hand black.

In Wright's film, a weary Weston emerges from the darkroom after five hours of developing prints. "I come up for air at 9 or 10 in the morning," he tells Wright. "It's a great drain on one's vitality. You have to be disciplined. Without discipline there's very little art. It's hard work and sheer brutal, drudgery, like writing literature." According to Wright, Weston's small, spartan house had a lot of bookshelves. "He loved Louis Lamour."

Wright films the photographer preparing dozens of prints in preparation for the first comprehensive exhibition of his work at the Friends of Photography gallery in Carmel. Here the short film reaches its conclusion, with dozens of people, hippies, working stiffs and art snobs, mulling through the exhibition of photos, many of which were taken during the trip with Wright.

"I enjoy the reaction of ordinary people who are not art patrons", says Weston. "I like some guy or gal with an honest admiration for a photo, a carpenter or bricklayer, instead of some pseudosophisticated museum director from the art world who thinks he knows it all."

Wright's film on Weston came out in 1972 under the title, *Brett Weston: Man of the Land.* "It was a silly title", Wright says, "but we had to call it that to fulfill the grant".

A year and a half and later he released a tighter version called simply *Brett Weston: Photographer.* At the time, photography was just beginning to be viewed as a fine art in the university system. Wright rented out his film to schools and universities for the next 15 years, introducing Weston to a new generation of photographers and artists. Weston and Wright remained close for the next 20 years, until Brett's death in Kona, Hawai'i in 1993.

A couple of years ago, retired from his job as a cameraman at a local Portland TV station, Wright put himself to work transferring his film on Weston to DVD. He also got permission from the Weston archive to include 800 of Brett's photos on the DVD. In its current format, Wright's film is as close as we get to a biographical and critical study of Brett Weston's career. He is perhaps the most important American artist who is yet to be the subject of a full-length biography. Shot in stark black-and-white, Wright's film is, in its way, as beautiful to look at as a Weston print. And then there is Weston's voice, gruff and serious as a rattlesnake one moment and impish and jesting the next.

With the notable exception of the series on the doomed Glen Canyon, Weston's photography can't be considered in any way overtly political. But it's clear where his allegiances are. As he drives across the Sierras and up the Owens Valley, lashing out to Wright about the new interstate highways and rash of housing developments in Tahoe and Sacramento he reveals himself to be a kind of western anarchist, not all that different from Edward Abbey.

"There's no tremendous change in people", laments Weston. "But the machines have changed. And that's the monkeywrench for the whole goddamn mess."

AFTER WRIGHT'S FILM CAME OUT, WESTON'S CAREER BEGAN TO take off. In the mid-1970s, art photography became a chic form of investment. The prices for Weston's prints soared from a couple hundred dollars to over a thousand. He came into money for the first time in his life.

In the 1970s, Art Wright bought a print of Weston's famous "Ear and Hand" photo for $75. The photo hangs in Wright's house with the canceled check to Weston taped to the back of the frame. Today that same print sells for $30,000.

For a short time, Weston, who had always been a kind of one-man band, framing his prints and selling them himself, even hired a manager to sell his prints to rich patrons and corporations.

He built a house on the big island of Hawai'i, where he made some of his most astonishing photographs. Much of the money went into cars, an obsession that began early on, when he manned the wheel on his father's expeditions. Edward never learned to drive. By the 1980s, the old Chevy trucks had been replaced by new Corvettes. Two of them. According to Wilson, Weston's first Corvette was a stick shift, which he had a hard time handling after a bite by a poisonous spider impaired his right arm. So he bought an identical Corvette with an automatic transmission. He refused to let anyone else drive him around or drive his cars.

In his last years, Brett was slowed by a bad heart. It was hard for him to lug his camera up the slopes of Mauna Loa, so increasingly he devoted himself to printing, churning out thousands of prints from his negatives. In a final editing of his oeuvre, Weston destroyed many of his prints. "An artist must eliminate, I've destroyed prints by the thousands."

Then there was the final inferno in 1992, a year before he died, when he pitched all of his negatives into the huge fireplace, one of the few on Big Island.

When he died, he left 10,000 prints to the Brett Weston Trust. Brett believed that the prints would be sold off gradually for the financial benefit of his sole daughter, Erica.

Instead, an investment banker snatched up the entire lot for a few million dollars. The Weston photographic legacy, which he had fought so hard to preserve on his own terms, is now locked in a vault in the basement of a bank in Oklahoma City.

By incinerating his negatives, Brett Weston assured that the value of each remaining print would skyrocket to the lofty levels that they could only be owned by the rich elites and art snobs that whom he had despised all his life. Even Weston might have seen the irony in that final development.

ALEXANDER COCKBURN

The Rich and Their Castles in Spain, Part II: Hearst and Morgan in California

THE YEAR ITS DESTINY WAS ALTERED FOREVER, 1919, Camp Hill—part of the old Mexican land grant bought by William Randolph Hearst's father, George, in 1865—was just one more surge in the Santa Lucia coastal range, empty and windswept, spotted with manzanita, oak and greasewood. By 1947, the year Hearst and Marion Davies finally left, Le Cuestra Encantada, the Enchanted Hill, had become the most singular individual exploit of domestic architecture in the country. Amid the hostile passions Hearst provoked while he was alive, and shadowed by the doppelgänger of Welles's Xanadu, the Enchanted Hill was long seen as an outcrop of California kitsch, Camp Gothick on Camp Hill, vulgarity on a titanic scale. Now, amid shifting tastes, Hearst's castle can be seen for what it is—as powerful an expression of the American soul as the Brooklyn Bridge, Rockefeller Center or the Ford plant on the Rouge River, and all the more striking because the dream was given concrete form by one indomitable woman, Julia Morgan.

Morgan was, along with his mother, Phoebe, and Marion Davies, one of the most important women in Hearst's life. When the Enchanted Hill became the property of the state of California and was opened to the public on June 2, 1958, plaques at the foot and top of the hill mentioned both Hearst and his mother; Morgan was ignored. Of the hundreds of thousands of visitors who pour through the castle each year, only a fraction can know her name, yet if La Cuestra Encantada is the story of a dream arduously achieved, it was Morgan rather than Hearst who prevailed over the more formidable odds.

She wanted to be an architect when the profession was unheard-of for a woman and when architecture was not even an official part of the curriculum of the University of California, Berkeley. One of the first women there to graduate in engineering, Morgan went on to storm the Ecole des Beaux-Arts in Paris. She was the first woman in the world to study architecture there, and four years later won her certificate. By 1950 she had opened her own architectural practice, and by sheer force of personality commanded the respect of the clients, draftsmen, contractors and artisans with whom she had to deal.

Morgan died six years after Hearst, at the age of 85, and although their joint endeavor at San Simeon will be the work for which she will be most famously remembered, it was only a fraction of her output; by the time she closed her office in 1951 she had completed almost 800 projects, mostly in the Bay Area—many of them unrecorded, since she ordered her files be burned upon her death. It is hard to imagine another person surviving such a partnership with Hearst. And if Morgan and Hearst were right for each other, the time and place were propitious for both. They were both nourished by that fortunate constellation of architects who began work in San Francisco in the 1890s and who, out of an academic and eclectic tradition, helped create a regional style and distinctive cultural disposition.

Of these, the most influential on the life of Julia Morgan was Bernard Maybeck. Son of a profoundly idealistic German cabinetmaker, he had studied at the Ecole des Beaux-Arts in the early 1880s before returning to the United States. It was Maybeck who urged upon Julia the importance of studying at the Beaux-Arts, Maybeck who encouraged her through all the obstacles thrown against this plan, and finally Maybeck who introduced her to the Hearst family.

In 1895 Phoebe Apperson Hearst, as diminutive as Julia and equally as determined, approached Martin Kellogg, the president of the University of California, Berkeley, and discussed the prospects of a memorial building for her husband, George. Mrs. Hearst was already a lavish philanthropic donor to education, and Kellogg made haste to introduce her to Maybeck. It was not long before Phoebe had approved his design for a memorial building and responded alertly to his enthusiastic introduction of Morgan. Hardly had Maybeck done so than Phoebe was offering her financial assistance. Although the financial help was declined, Phoebe Hearst's patronage was helpful to Morgan as she began her career as an architect. The late Sara Holmes Boutelle, author of the definitive life of Morgan, traced the influential network of California women who gained for Morgan the commissions that helped establish her reputation; they range from Mills College campus, through the YWCA headquarters at Asilomar in Pacific Grove, to other YWCAs as far afield as Hawai'i, to the scores of private houses and club buildings around Berkeley and San Francisco.

No less effective than her patronage of Morgan, through the ownership of two houses, was Phoebe's influence on the architectural ambitions of her son. From Maybeck she commissioned in 1902 the country estate of Wyntoon, set amid the Siskiyou forests of northeast California on the McLoud River. Drawing on his own predilections and also his Beaux-Arts grounding in expressive form and appropriate materials, Maybeck realized a Gothic dream, which he lyrically described in 1904 in *The Architectural Review:*

> Imagine the clear...foam of the river in the foreground roaring ceaselessly, and...at the dawn of day, an enchanted castle.... The dark height of the room, the unobstructed archways...the tapestries, the little flicker of the fire...and you satiated, tired, and inspired by the day's trip among...aged pines, rocks, cascades, great trunks of trees fallen years ago,— a dishevelled harmony,—here you can reach all that is within you.

In Alameda County, 250 miles south of Wyntoon, lay another property belonging to Mrs. Hearst on which, in 1895, her son decided to raise an edifice "totally different in every way from the ordinary country home". He commissioned A.C. Schweinfurth— along with Maybeck, Willis Polk and Ernest Coxhead, one of the Bay Area's innovative architects—to build the resoundingly named Hacienda del Pozo de Verona, described by the architect as "provincial Spanish Renaissance". Hearst thought of everything except the elementary task of informing his mother that he was making his first foray into architectural eclecticism on her land. Phoebe was in Europe when she was apprised of this surreptitious endeavor. She hastened west and expropriated the expropriator. Desiring to make the Hacienda into a home for herself, she commissioned Morgan to remodel it.

Here, in 1902, as her mentor Maybeck labored on Wyntoon, Julia Morgan met William Randolph Hearst for the first time, thus rounding out the encounter of persons and of architectural ambitions that would engender San Simeon. Seventeen years later, within weeks of the death of the mother he adored, Hearst was urging Morgan toward a grandiose fusion of the spirit of the Hacienda and of Wyntoon. Even as his relationship with one determined woman was severed, his association with another truly began, with a torrent of telegrams and letters from Hearst to Morgan, which persisted throughout their relationship and to which she assiduously responded down the years. They agreed fairly quickly about the basic plan for La Cuestra Encantada: the Casa Grande or "ranch house", as Hearst rather affectedly called it, fronted on the Pacific side of the hill by the smaller Italianate villas—Casa del Mar, Casa del Monte and Casa del Sol. On October 25, from his newspaper offices in New York, Hearst wrote Morgan:

> In plan A the sitting room ran parallel with the front line. I
> have made it run perpendicular...and have partially shut off

the sides of the old sitting room with bookcases about 4' in height.

This detailed flow continued from wherever Hearst found himself. A month later he wrote:

Dear Miss Morgan,

I have just bought a very stunning tapestry screen or panel, 9' 4" high and 13' 6" wide. It occurs to me that this might be placed at the north side of the sitting room in my little house (Casa del Mar) where we now have the fireplace.... In that case we could put fireplaces at the east and west ends of the library recesses, where we now have windows. I had suggested putting bookcases there.

Nor was Hearst's desire to tamper and to change quelled when plans had been rendered as architecture. Time and again fireplaces were ripped out, relocated, then ripped out again and put back where they started. Morgan later said that demolition formed a good part of the project.

By December 1919, Hearst was holding forth in two long letters written on the thirtieth and thirty-first about the Spanish Baroque and urging Morgan to see Allan Dwan's film *Soldiers of Fortune,* which had some scenes set in the San Diego Panama-California International Exposition in 1915: "I understand the San Diego expo stuff is largely repros from Mexico and Latin America." Then, after ruminating that the Mission style of California was too "primitive" and that of Mexico "so elaborate as to be objectionable", Hearst pondered: "The alternative is to build...in the Renaissance style of southern Spain. We picked out the tower of the church of Ronda.... The Renaissance of North Spain seems to me very hard, while the Renaissance of southern Spain is much softer, more graceful."

But who was leading whom? A week later Morgan was edging Hearst away from the Churriguersque effects associated with Hearst's preference:

> I question whether this style of decoration would not seem
> too heavy and too clumsy on our buildings.... We have a
> comparatively small group and it would seem to me that they
> should charm by their detail rather than overwhelm by more
> or less clumsy exuberance.... I believe we could get
> something really beautiful by using the combination of the
> Ronda Tower and the Seville doorway with your Virgin over it
> and San Simeon and San Christopher on either side.

Day after day, month after month, the work crept forward.
The bungalows were completed by 1922, the central section of
Casa Grande by 1927. Never fewer than twenty-five men, and
often five times that number, toiled on the Hill. During the
Depression it was the largest private construction project in
California. Hearst's agents fanned across Europe, shock troops
in the service of his rabid collecting. Most assiduous were
Arthur and Mildred Staplay Bynes, expert at skills of conjuring
whole suites from Iberian palaces and maneuvering them past
Spanish custom officials. Not once but twice the couple, over
roars of outrage from Spanish villagers, managed to deconstruct
whole cloisters stone by stone and shipped them to the States,
where one still lies in a rude tumble of rocks.

Year after year, never letting the rest of her practice decline
for a moment, Julia Morgan pushed the enterprise along.
Designs for everything—from the Hill's water supply to the five-
mile drive (both major engineering undertakings) to the tile-
work—flowed from her drafting table. With the contractors she
organized argosies of small ships carrying building supplies
from San Francisco to San Simeon. Three out of four weekends
she would step into a sleeping berth on the San Francisco-Los
Angeles express and work at her drawing board until 3 in the
morning, when she disembarked at San Luis Obispo. Then Steve
Zegar, the local taxi driver, would take her through the dawn for
a few hours north to San Simeon. Saturday and Sunday she
would work with Hearst when he was there or with the superintendent of construction and the master craftsmen on the site.

Many of them—Ed Trinkeller the ironworker, Camille Solon the muralist, Jules Suppo the woodcarver—devoted much of their working lives to the project. On Sunday evening Zegar would drive her back down to San Luis Obispo, and she would get back on the midnight train to San Francisco and be in her office in the Merchants Exchange on Monday morning. According to Sara Holmes Boutelle, Morgan's invoices show that between 1919 and 1942 she made that journey 518 times. In a practice almost unheard of at the time, she divided profits among her staff and kept only a small percentage for herself. She had little money when she died, and as for her funeral, she had asked to be "tucked away without any fuss". She lived entirely for her work, never married and seems to have developed no significant personal attachments. She worked up to 16 hours a day, often seven days a week. A mastoidectomy in the mid-1920s impaired balance, but this never prevented her from clambering up and down scaffolding, often sustained for days by nothing more than Hershey bars.

And Hearst? As San Simeon grew toward the sky, he was also building the Beach House for Marion Davies in Santa Monica, acquiring St. Donats in Wales, buying a Long Island mansion for his wife, expanding Wyntoon, running his repellent empire stealthily toward near-ruin, which in 1937 finally halted construction on the Enchanted Hill as salvage work on Hearst's affairs began. He was 74 by that time and the rituals of life at the ranch were firmly prescribed. P.G. Wodehouse sent an entertaining description to his friend Bill Townend in 1931:

> The ranch—ranch, my foot; it's a castle... Hearst collects
> everything, including animals, and has a zoo on the
> premises, and the specimens considered reasonably harmless
> are allowed to roam at large. You are apt to meet a bear or
> two before you get to the house, or an elephant, or even Sam
> Goldwyn. There are always at least fifty guests staying here....
> The train that takes guests away leaves after midnight, and
> the one that brings new guests arrives early in the morning,

so you have dinner with one lot of people and come down to breakfast next morning and find an entirely fresh crowd.... Meals take place in an enormous room...served at a long table, with Hearst sitting in the middle on one side and Marion Davies in the middle on the other. The longer you're there, the further you get from the middle. I sat on Marion's right the first night, and then found myself getting edged further and further away, till I got to the extreme end, when I thought it time to leave. Another day and I should have been feeding on the floor. You don't see Hearst till dinnertime.... He's a sinister old devil, not at all the sort I'd care to meet down a lonely alley on a dark night.

Dinner, the only compulsory event of the day, would come at 9 and then at 11 a film in the private chamber. Guests detected bringing alcohol onto the premises could find their bags packed the following morning, though Marion Davies was known to slip empty bottles of gin behind the commodes in her bedroom.

It was a strange experience to drive for an hour north along the Pacific shoreline, then climb 1,500 feet up the five-mile drive and find oneself in a refectory with a ceiling from a sixteenth century monastery, eating broiled honeycomb tripe (served, for example, for lunch on December 31, 1946) beneath the banners of Siena. Everywhere, in every room, a profusion of objects from almost every century and style. Volume one of the inventory of antiques on the Hill and in the warehouses below in San Simeon runs to 6,776 items, and here one can see precisely the prices, far from reckless in many cases, that Hearst or his agents had paid. High up in the Celestial Suite, an architectural afterthought on top of the towers, there are two Geromes of Napoleon in Egypt, and one can see from the inventory that Hearst bought one from Knoedler in 1898 for $900 and the other for the same price from the same gallery fifteen years later. Although his frenzied collecting may have skewed the art prices of two continents, the most Hearst paid for anything on the Hill was $100,000, for a tapestry. For the whole of San Simeon, Hearst paid about $8 million. More than once Morgan, superintending the payroll at the site, complained that they were two months behind. She finally announced that she would yield to another architect to continue the project and by the mid-1920s Hearst forced himself to organize a regular system of transfers.

How does the Hill strike a visitor now? As Thomas R. Aidala points out in an admirable monograph, the experience of the main house is "hermetic and episodic", in that there is little sense of flow between the rooms on the main floor and even less sense of connection between the various floors.

Both Hearst and Morgan stated on more than one occasion that what they were really building was a museum of architecture of which Hearst was only an interim tenant. What gives the museum its emotional strength, rounding out the Gothic and Renaissance themes of the various casas, is the Neptune Pool on which construction commenced in 1927, after Gertrude Ederle, the cross-channel swimmer who happened to be staying at the Castle, remarked that the previous one was too small. The Neptune Pool, with its green and white Vermont marble, Italian temple facade, classical colonnade and Italian cypresses, subtly redefines the character of the Hill from obsession to dream, from the weight and religious frenzy of the Gothic and Spanish Baroque to the tranquil reason of antiquity. The pool and the five levels of terracing, the landscaped hills nearby on which Hearst's men planted over 6,000 trees, the wild beasts roaming, the mile of pergola ("the longest in captivity") embrace the Casa Grande as orders of nature soothing the orders of architecture massed on the Hill's crest.

Hearst would work through the night in his private office behind the third-floor Gothic study, reading his newspapers sent to San Simeon from all quarters of his empire. The wall of this office was largely glass, and the sun, which rose from behind the Santa Lucia Mountains, had earlier lit his properties across the continent, leaving this one till last. Behind him lay only the Pacific. San Simeon must have seemed to him to be the final résumé: the triumph of the New World, expressed as a triumph of art and architecture imported from the Old, down the centuries from the Athens of Phidias and Pericles.

Jeffrey St. Clair

Usonian Utopias:
Frank Lloyd Wright, Low-Cost
Housing and the FBI

F RANK LLOYD WRIGHT ONCE BOASTED THAT HE DIDN'T design his buildings to last for more than a century. It's not something you hear from many architects. But that doesn't mean Wright was being humble. Indeed, there's a hefty element of hubris to this admission. With Wright, you always get the sense that the conception, as realized in his beautiful drawings, was more important than the structures themselves.

Then again, it was true. While most of Wright's homes have stood up pretty well over the years, a few of his better designs began to crack and crumble soon after they were erected. Usually, this was a result of Wright trying to build on the cheap, often by using local sand as a source for the reinforced concrete that became a signature of his later buildings, such as La Miniatura, the house in the Hollywood Hills that looks like a compact Mayan temple. (Of course, it took the giant temples of Tikal 600 years to acquire the characteristics of a ruin and La Miniatura only a decade.)

It's also an idea that Wright swiped from the Japanese, whose traditional houses were temporal structures, built to last for only a few years. Characteristically, Wright didn't credit them, though he did admit to a fondness for Japanese art, especially the woodblock prints of Hiroshige and Hokusai.

More fundamentally, Wright held to the theory that a house should be designed to reflect the specific needs and personality of its occupants. It was a tenet of his notion of "organic architecture". According to this mode of thinking, there was no reason for a building to outlive its owners. Houses should be constructed to function well for 40 years or so and then torn down to make way for new structures for new owners.

This was a way to keep architecture moving forward, to keep on, as Wright said, "breaking out of the box". It was also an attitude that may have grown out of some of his personal peeves. Wright hated the English and described most of their architecture (Edwin Lutyens, the Walter Scott of English architecture, was a notable exception) as monuments to British imperialism. He so thoroughly despised the old Victorians that loomed near his house in Oak Park, Illinois, that he built a wall around his home and studio and designed that house's curious windows so that he wouldn't have to look at the hulking outlines of the older structures.

Even so, Wright spent most of his first 20 years as an architect drafting up homes as sturdy and immutable as anything conjured up by Antonio Palladio or Christopher Wren. The justly famous prairie designs of the early 1900s weren't houses so much as striking horizontal mansions for millionaires, equipped with parlors, music rooms and discreetly hidden quarters for servants.

These days, of course, the super-rich couldn't care less about Wright's houses, except as pictures in coffee table books, and they cringe at the prospect of actually living in them. Mega-square footage and techno-wiring are what count now. Wright's houses (even the big ones such as Hollyhock House and the Frank Thomas House) are too small to contain the accumulated trappings of today's millionaires. And they are downright impossible to redecorate, intentionally so, since Wright didn't trust anyone's taste over his own. Most of his houses didn't even have closets; where would all the shoes go? Plus people (often of the most noisome disposition) are always showing up at the door wanting a peek at the structure. Much better to buy up the land, then hold the house for ransom with a wrecking ball and wait for a buy-out.

That's exactly what happened to the Gordon House, the only structure Wright designed for construction in Oregon. Wright drafted plans for the house in 1957, and it was constructed on a bend in the Willamette River near Wilsonville in 1963, four years after his death, for Conrad and Evelyn Gordon. After the Gordons died, the house fell into disrepair following the predictable familial spat over whether or not to subdivide the homestead.

In 1999, the property was bought by David Smith for $1.1 million. Smith had no plans to live in the house, a T-shaped two-storied structure made of cinderblocks and Oregon cedar. Instead, he announced his intention to bulldoze it and build on its grave a sprawling mansion to rival the other executive monstrosities that line the Willamette River these days. Apparently, Smith and his wife, Carey, had no idea who Wright was and didn't much give a damn after they found out. They had good reason to be smug. Within the past couple of years, the Portland area (supposedly home to the most progressive zoning and historical preservation laws on the continent) has seen houses by three of its most notable local architects, John Yeon, Walter Gordon and Pietro Belluschi, destroyed, with barely a squawk of protest.

But Yeon—Oregon's version of California's Bernard Maybeck—doesn't' enjoy Wright's cult following and once word leaked about the Smiths' plans, an international crusade was launched to save the structure. It is a testament to the power of the Wright name and the influence of the Frank Lloyd Wright Building Conservancy that not one of the remaining 350 structures designed by Wright has been demolished in the last 12 years.

The Smiths offered to give the house to anyone who'd take it (they weren't keen to pay for the demolition), as long as it was removed it within 105 days or they'd flatten it themselves. Ultimately the Frank Lloyd Wright Building Conservancy and the Oregon Chapter of the Institute of American Architects stepped forward to claim the house. It was dismantled, moved to a botanical garden 30 miles away in the tourist town of Silverton and reassembled, under the supervision of architect Burton Goodrich, who apprenticed with Wright in the 1950s. The Smiths ended up with a nice tax deduction and a shiny new McMansion looming over the Willamette.

Wright would surely be bemused at the effort and expense that has gone into saving his buildings from the wrecking ball. After all, the Gordon House was one of his "low-cost" Usonian homes, built for less than $10,000. Relocating and restoring the house will end up costing more than $1.2 million. This is architecture as a kind of cultural fetish.

A half-century after his death, Frank Lloyd Wright remains something of a brand name. And it's been that way since nearly the beginning of his career. Brendan Gill, writing in *Many Masks: a Life of Frank Lloyd Wright*, suggests that many of Wright's clients didn't want a Wrightian solution to their architectural needs so much as they simply craved the Wright name attached to their house, thus inaugurating the birth of name-brand architecture. During the early days of Wright's fame, there's little doubt that his older contemporaries, Daniel "Uncle Dan" Burnham, John Wellborn Root and Louis Sullivan, were equally, if not more, accomplished. But, among his many other talents, Wright was a genius at the game of self-promotion. He was the first architect as celebrity.

Wright was both a utopian and a narcissist. He could jive talk his way through almost any crisis and there were many of them, usually of a financial nature. Wright was especially adept at snowing corporate titans, such as Herbert "Hib" Johnson, CEO of the Johnson Wax Company.

The Wright style with CEOs was unique, a full-frontal assault more than pandering. "He insulted me about everything," Johnson said of his first encounter with Wright. "And I insulted him. But he did a better job. I showed him pictures of the old office, and he said it was awful. He had a Lincoln-Zephyr, and I had one, it was the only thing we agreed on. On all other matters we were at each other's throats. If a guy can talk like that, he must have something."

Although they became close friends, Wright didn't trust Johnson to present his plans before the Johnson Wax board. Hib Johnson agreed to let Wright attend the meeting, but warned him: "Please, Frank, don't scold me in front of my own board of directors."

Like most narcissists, Wright was an unrepentant mamma's boy, coddled by a mother who told him he was a genius when he was 3 years old. Anna Lloyd-Jones Wright trained her son to be an architect almost from the crib, giving him the famous Freobel blocks that he continued to play with his entire life. Indeed, the floating planes of the Usonian designs seem directly traceable to simple structures made from wooden blocks that Wright would assemble in a matter of seconds on his desk to dazzle prospective clients.

The crypto-fascist Philip Johnson dismissed Wright as the greatest architect of the nineteenth Century. (Perhaps architects who build glass houses, particularly ones ripped off from Mies van der Rohe, shouldn't throw stones..) There's a certain grain of truth about this, though not, certainly, in the sense that Johnson, who embodied the direst strains of modernism (and postmodernism), meant to convey.

Wright was a utopian in the grand romantic tradition. He was grounded in Rousseau and often let slip that his favorite poets were Walt Whitman and the dreamy Samuel Taylor Coleridge. Along with fellow poet (and snitch) Robert Southey, Coleridge cooked up an idea for a utopian community in western Pennsylvania they called, somewhat clumsily for two poets capable of stunning lyricism, the Pantisocracy. They were going to pay for the land on the proceeds of a long poem chronicling the life and death of Robespierre. But the plan ultimately fell apart over violent disagreements between the two on sexual freedom (which Coleridge advocated) and slavery (which Coleridge abhorred). Interestingly, the Pantisocracy, charted out only on maps in Coleridge's house in Keswick, was to have been located not far from where Wright built his most famous house, Fallingwater.

Wright also pored over Robert Owen's experiments in socialist communities, most notably in New Harmony, Indiana, where, as fate would have it, Wright's rival Johnson later built his open-aired church shaped like death's cap mushroom. But the class divisions and authoritarianism of Owen's community proved anathema to Wright's innate egalitarianism. He was more drawn to the Modern Times commune in Brentwood on Long Island, established in 1851 by the American anarchist Josiah Warren. Among other things, Warren's community was organized on the principles of "no police" and "free love", earning it the unyielding animosity of the snobs of New England who referred to it as the "Sodom of the Pine Barrens".

The early half of the nineteenthth century was a time of incredible optimism and radicalism in the United States. In the 1840s, there were 100,000 people living in more than 150 socialist/utopian communities across the country. "Those towns stood for everything eccentric: for abolition, short skirts, whole-wheat bread, hypnotism, phonetic spelling, phrenology, free love and the common ownership of property,", wrote the journalist Helen Beal Woodward in a1945 article on utopian communities. The Civil War largely put an end to all that, but the utopian spirit continued to thrive after the war, particularly in the prairie states, through the rise of the populist parties and the Wisconsin progressives.

But it was good old Rousseau, perhaps more than anyone else who seems to have shaped Wright's thinking the most. In one of his notebooks, Wright highlighted this passage from

Emile: "Men are not made to be crowded together in ant hills, but scattered over the earth to till it." Throw in a free car (Wright preferred fast ones, such as Jaguars) and you've got the basis of Wright's utopian community, Broad Acre City.

Broad Acre City wasn't a design for a single community, as much as an organic zoning plan for the entire country: a kind of motor-age update of Jefferson's vision of rural America. Wright believed each American family should be entitled to an acre of land and a car. The property lines and building sites would conform to the contours of the landscape, not the rigid grid system proposed by Jefferson and his followers and enacted in gthe famous survey whose consequences can be seen from any planc flying over the plains states. There would also be a pattern of green spaces, community gardens, walking trails, parks and wildlands, concepts that he adapted from the English garden cities designed by William Morris. Wright's idea was that each town would be self-sufficient, with growth limited by available water supplies and arable land.

It wasn't until the 1910s that Wright began to think seriously about designing low-cost housing for working-class people. But World War I and then thc Dcprcssion intervened. Then followed a real dry spell. Between 1928 and 1935, only two structures designed by Wright (other than his own house and studio at Taliesin) were constructcd.

Then in 1935 Wright received a visit from Herbert Jacobs and his wife, Katherine. Jacobs was a columnist with the *Madison Capital Times,* the city's most progressive newspaper. He was an admirer of Wright's work and wanted the great man to design their house. The problem was Jacobs was far from wealthy. Wright had little else on his plate and agreed to design a house that would cost $5,500, including his customary 10 percent fee. He called the design Usonian.

What does Usonian mean? Who knows? Some suggest that Wright came up with the name during his first trip to Europe in

1910, when there was some discussion about referring to the USA as "Usona" in order to distinguish it from the new Union of South Africa. (It's easy to see how in those days, as for much of the century, the two nations could be confused.) Wright once said he took the name from Samuel Butler's utopian novel *Erewhon.* But no one's been able to track it down there. (I did a word search of the online edition of *Erewhon* and couldn't find it.) Most likely it was a joke.

Even so what Wright produced was little short of a revolution in American architecture: a beautiful structure, efficiently designed to sit on an odd (and cheap) lot, at a price affordable for lower-income families. But the Jacobs House, and the dozens of Usonian designs that would follow, did more than that. It was truly one of the first environmentally conscious designs, utilizing passive solar heating, natural cooling and lighting with his signature clerestory windows, native materials, radiant floor heating and L-shaped floorplan that anchored the house around a garden terrace.

The Jacobs house was an immediate hit in Madison, nearly as popular an attraction as the Johnson Wax Building, which was under construction at the same time further east, in Racine. On weekends so many people showed up at the door, the Jacobs began selling tickets to tour their new house. At 50 cents a pop, they quickly recaptured enough money to pay Wright's fee.

Over the next 30 years, Wright produced hundreds of Usonian designs, never wavering far from the original concept. "We can never make the living room big enough, the fireplace important enough, or the sense of relationship between exterior, interior and environment close enough, or get enough of these good things I've just mentioned", Wright wrote in a 1948 issue of *Architectural Forum.* "A Usonian house is always hungry for the ground, lives by it, becoming an integral feature of it."

The Usonian homes inspired great loyalty in their original owners. In 1975, John Sergeant did an inventory of the homes and found that over 50 percent were still owned by the original families, more than 35 years after construction. The same thing can't be said for Wright's larger projects. The beautiful Robey House, near the University of Chicago, was inhabited for less than a full year, while Fallingwater served as little more than a weekend retreat.

So what happened? Why didn't the Usonian design take off? Why are we left only with the barest elements of the design, the cookie-cutter ranch houses that came to dominate the lots of suburban America?

There's no simple explanation. But one thing is clear. Wright's plans to revolutionize the American residential living space ran afoul of interests of the federal government. Think about this: in his 70-year career Wright didn't win one contract for a federal building. Not even during the heyday of the New Deal.

It all came down to politics. Wright's politics were vastly more complicated and honorable than those embodied by Howard Roark, Ayn Rand's self-serving stand-in of Wright in her novel *The Fountainhead.* Sure there was a libertarian strain to Wright, which Rand seized on and distorted to her own perverse ends. But he also was drawn to the prairie populism espoused by the likes of the great Ignatius Donnelly. It's this version of Wright that makes an appearance in John dos Passos' *USA* trilogy.

Wright was a pacifist, and his outright opposition to war cost him government commissions, the great lifeline of the professional architect, especially during the Depression and World War II. It's no accident that Wright was down and out most of his career. The high points came at the beginning and the end. He made more than 50 percent of his designs after he turned 70, and these weren't hack work but some of the most innovative plans of any architect then working.

John Sergeant, in his excellent book on Wright's Usonian houses, argues that there's a mutual admiration between Wright and the Russian anarchist Peter Kropotkin. In 1899, Kropotkin moved to Chicago, living in the Hull House commune, set up by the radical social reformer Jane Addams, where Wright often lectured, reading his famous essay "The Arts and Crafts Machine".

But, in those crucial decades of the twenties and thirties, Wright's political views seemed to align most snugly with Wisconsin progressives, as personified by the LaFollettes. In fact, Philip LaFollette served as Wright's attorney and sat on the board of Wright's corporation.

None of this escaped the attention of the authorities. From World War I to his final days, Wright found himself the subject of a campaign of surveillance, harassment and intimidation by the federal government. In 1941, 26 members of Wright's Taliesin fellowship signed a petition objecting to the draft and calling the war effort futile and immoral. The draft board sent the letter to the FBI, where it immediately came to the attention of J. Edgar Hoover, who already loathed Wright.

Twice Hoover himself demanded that the Justice Department bring sedition charges against Wright. He was rebuffed both times by the attorney general, but, typically, that only drove Hoover to expand the surveillance and harassment by his goons.

But, as a review of Wright's FBI file reveals, the feds' interest in the architect extended far beyond his pacifism. Hoover's men recorded his dalliances with the Wobblies, his continuing attempts to combat the US government's dehumanization of the Japanese during and after the war, his rabble-rousing speeches on college campuses, his work for international socialists and Third World governments, including Iraq, and his rather unorthodox views on sexual relations (the feds noted that Wright seemed to have a particular obsession with Marlene Dietrich).

It could be more sinister than ironic, then, that Carter H. Manny, one of Wright's apprentices at Taliesin West during the years when the architect and his cohorts were under the most intense scrutiny by the feds, would go on to design the FBI headquarters (1963). The building, as conceived by Manny, exudes a bureaucratic brutalism that is far removed from anything that ever came off Wright's pen. Manny spent less than a year under the Master's tutelage, instead of the normal three. Some Wright devotees believe his tenure there had a more nefarious purpose.

The FBI wasn't the only federal agency giving Wright a hard time. Indeed, Hoover's snoops were only a minor irritant compared to the damage done him by the Federal Housing Authority, who routinely denied financing to Wright's projects. There's no surer way to crush the career of an architect, particularly one trying to revolutionize the housing of working class people, than to cut off his clients' access to mortgages.

The Federal Home Loan Association also refused to underwrite mortgages for Wright's houses, often citing Wright's signature flat roofs as a lending code violation. Here's a paragraph from one of the rejection letters: "The walls will not support the roof; floor heating is impractical; the unusual design makes subsequent sales a hazard." All bullshit, of course.

A disgusted Wright wrote in his autobiography that the federal government had "repudiated" his Usonian designs. In truth, it wasn't so much repudiation as flat-out sabotage. No paper trail has yet been discovered linking the FBI's harassment of Wright with the FHA's refusal to issue mortgages for his houses. But it has all the hallmarks of a Hoover black bag job.

There were other attacks on Wright. In 1926, the State Department even tried to get Wright's third wife, Olgivanna, deported as an undesirable alien. They were once again saved by the fast legal footwork of Phil LaFollette.

The IRS began harassing the architect in 1940, socking him with back taxes, penalties and interest dating back at least a decade. It was the kind of bill that can never be paid off, and it haunted Wright for the rest of his life. Even after he died, the agency kept after him. In 1959, the IRS audited the Wright Foundation, which was the main funding source for Wright's troublesome colleagues at Taliesin. The feds saw the Taliesin Fellowship as troublespot and wanted to extinguish it. It was after all a kind of commune, where the architecture students not only designed structures but grew their own food, milled timber and ran a private school (not to mention the rampant bed-hopping.) Eventually, the tax agency forced the foundation to sell off many of its most prized assets, including what remained of Wright's remarkable stash of Japanese prints, perhaps the best private collection in the United States, after two awful fires at Taliesin.

Wright's plans to put portions of his Broadacre City model into reality ran into other problems with federally connected lenders. Several of Wright's cooperative communities, including one in Michigan and another in Pennsylvania, came to nothing because banks refused to back the plan. The reason? Wright and his clients refused to include restrictions prohibiting houses from being owned by blacks and Jews.

KIMBERLY AND I VISITED THE GORDON HOUSE ON A HOT AND muggy June afternoon. Hot for Oregon anyway. The house is now the feature attraction of The Oregon Garden, which bills itself as a world-class botanical garden. It's nothing of the sort. Indeed, it's little more than a permanent dog-and-pony show for the chemical agricultural industry and the timber lobby. There are better gardens in any old neighborhood in Portland or Eugene than you'll find here.

It was close to 90 outside, but inside the house was cool, breezy, shaded by the jutting roofline. Wright detested air conditioning almost as much as he did contractors and academics. Even his home at Taliesen West, in the frying pan of Scottsdale,

Arizona, is kept livable by the use of natural features and architectural tricks .

The Gordon House, like most of the Usonian designs, is a collage of Wright's influences: Japan, Central America, the curves, angles and tones of the American landscape itself. It is a beautiful mix of visual puns and little ploys of light as subtle and deceptive as a painting by Wright's contemporary, Eduard Vuillard.

The shape of the house is fairly simple. Wright called it a polliwog design, a T shape with the kitchen and bedrooms massed in one section of the house, the living room jutting out like the tail of a tadpole.

Even the design was political, reflecting Wright's disdain for contractors, those middlemen of the construction trade who do so little work but pocket so much cash, consequently driving prices through the roof. Wright wanted to do away with them, particularly at the level of the American home. In fact, Wright wanted the Usonian houses to be so simple that they could largely (and ideally) be constructed by the owner of the house. The prefabricated home becomes an extension of the Emersonian tradition.

One of Wright's dictums for the Usonian designs was that the houses should "spring from the ground and into the light". By and large they do.

That's one of the most frustrating things about the migration of the Gordon House. It was originally designed to sit on a small bluff, with a view of the Willamette River to one side and the glacier-clad pyramid of Mt. Hood on the other. Each Usonian was different, fine-tuned to the site. The uprooted Gordon House seems alien , like a snow leopard I saw many years ago in the Cincinnati Zoo.

Once you take one step out of place, it's so much easier to take the next one. The restored Gordon House sits over a basement. Wright hated basements and they certainly weren't part of the Usonian plan, which used a concrete floor mat laid over gravel and hot-water pipes as a source of radiant heating. The addition of a basement (in order to serve as an office for the docents) destroys the very nature of the house.

So what remains is really little more than a shell, a kind of exoskeleton of Wright's original house. Instead of being a low-cost home, it's transformed into a mauled museum piece, a model home for the path not taken in American residential architecture. J. Edgar Hoover must be laughing as he roasts in Hell.

JEFFREY ST. CLAIR
The World Trade Towers:
An Architecture of Doom and Dread

THESE ARE DAYS OF LAMENTATION: FOR THE HORRIFYING toll of the innocent dead, for the near certain prospect of thousands more American and Middle Eastern-slated to die in the impending retaliatory strikes, and even for a weird kind of innocence and naïvete that seemed uniquely American, a naivete that persisted in the heart of the nation's most cynical city.

But one loss that mustn't be mourned are the Twin Towers themselves, those blinding prongs that rose up like a tuning fork above the Battery. You could say the World Trade Center was a singular atrocity—except there were two of them. As the architectural historian Francis Morrone wrote his 1998 *Architectural Guidebook to New York:* "The best thing about the view from the indoor and out observation decks of Two World Trade Center's that they are the only high vantage points in New York City from which the World Trade Center itself is not visible."

But now there's talk, serious talk from people like Hillary Clinton, Rudy Giuliani and the building's new owner, Larry Silverstein, of rebuilding both skyscrapers. This impulse must be resisted. Those buildings terrorized the skyline of Manhattan for too long. They combined ostentation and austerity with all the chilling precision of an economic package devised by the IMF.

The architect of the World Trade Center complex, Minuro Yamasaki, was morbidly afraid of heights. It shows in his work. Like the tycoon in Akira Kurosawa's wonderful film *High and Low,* Yamaski projected his own nightmares on all of us. His towers were more than blunt symbols of corporate power. They

233

were erections of dominion that injected a feeling of powerlessness in those who must encounter their airy permanence. His architecture does violence to the psyche as surely as those planes did violence to the human body. Yamaski said he wanted enough space around the base of the towers so onlookers could be "overwhelmed by their greatness".

Yamasaki, who died in 1986, saw himself as a field marshal of space, a kind of Japanese-American version of Philip Johnson, the avatar of the glass curtain skyscraper. Johnson's neo-fascist erections made him the favorite architect of Fed chairman Alan Greenspan, with whom he once debated the finer points of Martin Heidegger in the salon of Ayn Rand. Yamasaki is like Johnson, only duller. He was more ruthless in his desire to shave all aesthetic pleasure out of his cubes and tubes, to make them monuments to functionality.

The towers were meant to be impervious to the elements, as if they could not only defy space, wind and the colors of nature, but time as well. That was Yamasaki's biggest lie, a conceit as big as the ever-expanding bull market or the prospect of an impenetrable missile shield. But the lie was shattered in a matter of minutes, as first the load-bearing exo-skeleton quivered and buckled, then the joints melted in the inferno of the burning jet fuel, and finally one floor after another collapsed with all the finality of an Old Testament prophecy fulfilled.

Compare Yamasaki's structure to the great old spire just up the street and you can almost read the arc of corporate America. The Woolworth Building, Cass Gilbert's gothic confection, offers the city a kind of airy whimsy. Illusory, yes, but self-consciously fun. It doesn't demand your attention so much as it seduces it.

Yamasaki was a favorite of the new corporate order because, unlike Frank Lloyd Wright or the spendy Johnson, he built on the cheap. The WTC towers cost only $350 million. The early price tag on rebuilding the structures is put at $2.5 billion.

Also recall that the towers were for most of their life public buildings, owned by the city of New York. But there was little truly civic about them: they were cold, sterile, forbidding symbols of a government that had turned inward, that had begun to co-inhabit with the very corporations and financial houses it was charged with regulating.

Of course, the WTC buildings had their admirers, mainly a cadre of engineers and construction magnates dazzled by the logistics of erecting such behemoths in the bowels of one of the most gridlocked cities on Earth. With this in mind, it may not be coincidence that the towers became an obsession to Bin Laden, whose fortune derives from a family construction conglomerate that made billions building mega-projects for the Arab oil states.

It might be argued that the towers were an attractive nuisance, that they were, in a sense, standing there asking for it, inviting all comers to take a shot. Indeed, this very argument was made in an excellent book on the towers by Eric Darton, *Divided We Stand*. Darton argues that the buildings were inextricably linked to the terrorists who tried to bring them tumbling down in 1993.

"One kind of extremism, unfortunately, begets another, and when you raise up an icon like the WTC and fill it with vulnerable humanity, it's a pretty sure bet that someone will try to bring it down if they can", said Darton in a 1998 interview. "What emerges when you juxtapose mega-development with terrorism is a kind of unity of opposites. Both master-builders and terrorists consider everyday life at street level to be absolutely trivial. The former make their plans the rarefied air of executive boardrooms, while the latter carry out their schemes, quite literally, underground. Both master-builders and bombers adhere to single-minded cataclysmic visions—either the creation of a bright, corporate future; or a return to the 'fundamental' values of the past. Both visions are abstract projections of an ideal world which has nothing to do with the here-and-now."

The construction of the World Trade Center towers began with the destruction of a community, a community that the rich rulers of the city of New York, such as David Rockefeller and Robert Moses, considered a blight. It was a program of forced eviction and relocation that is not dissimilar to what is going on at the behest of American corporations in the Third World every day. The New York City Port Authority was used as the muscle to transform lower Manhattan from a community of people to a blinding canyon of corporate might. For an excellent documentation of the vicious history behind the construction of the WTC complex, I highly recommend *The Destruction of Lower Manhattan* by Danny Lyon.

Now the wreckage has a surreal cast to it, a kind of macabre beauty, like the best abstract expressionist paintings, or the smoldering end game of one of those self-destructing sculptures by Jean Tinguely. A friend of mine has spent much of the last week down in the ruins, helping the workers, giving comfort to the families of the wounded, the missing and the dead. "Of all the awful things about it, one of the worst is that there's no dirt, no earth, underneath a blown-up city, only more and more city" she told me. "I kept looking, but there's only gray ash, everywhere, on everything, but no dirt. The horrible illusion about skyscrapers is that they make you think you're close to somebody's idea of nature or God by being so high up in the sky, but you're as far away from that as you ever could be."

Now that the towers are gone, those blocks where they stood should be left as open space, graced by sunlight, so that, to paraphrase Yamasaki, people can appreciate the "greatness" of what was lost.

MAX PAGE AND SIGRID MILLER POLLIN
Proposal for a Landscape of Learning

GROUND ZERO WILL SOON BE RINGED BY OFFICE TOWERS, monuments to private capitalism. But down below, around the foundations of the Twin Towers, the public sphere should hold sway. New York should use the funds for a memorial to invest in what has always made New York great: not its private capital but its human capital. Instead of spending millions making a tourist destination and a resplendent front lawn for financial firms, we propose a totally different memorial idea: invest in New York's future by creating a public school for international education, a landscape of learning in the foundations of ground zero.

We want to defy the New York State Appeals Court's recent decision that an eighth-grade education is all that New York City's young people need. Instead, we propose to create a public school designed to house after-school, weekend and summer programs for New York City public school students to learn about the music, literature and art of other cultures, to debate world politics, and learn from one another about the people of their remarkably diverse city, what E.B. White called "the greatest human concentrate on earth, the poem whose magic is comprehensible to millions". Over the past three decades we have let that magic of New York—not the skyscrapers but the convulsive human life of the city—become weakened by an unerring focus on building the monuments to finance and world trade. Now that it is time to rebuild the World Trade Center site, it should also be the time to affirm a new faith in public life.

We have done this before. After World War II, the country didn't build a triumphant physical memorial to the soldiers lost in battle (only now, fifty years later, are we building a memorial on the Mall in Washington). Instead, Congress passed the GI Bill and invested hundreds of millions of dollars to give veterans access to education, loans and decent housing. That helped launch the greatest expansion of the middle class the country has ever seen. Their living success was perhaps the finest memorial the dead could have asked for.

So let us mark the anniversary of 9/11 by choosing to make New York's young people living memorials to those lost on September 11. The Austrian writer Robert Musil famously wrote that "there is nothing in this world as invisible as a monument". But the sounds of young New Yorkers of every hue and tongue, laughing and learning at ground zero, would hardly be invisible. And it would be impossible to forget. The school we propose will metaphorically take on the task of rebuilding ground zero, by "filling in" much of the four acre foundations of the former Trade Center site with a living memorial , a series of classrooms, meeting halls, rehearsal spaces, and art studios to educate New York's future, its school children.

We imagine two buses arriving at the same moment, one a school bus, dropping off 60 children with 60 different ethnic backgrounds, and a tour bus, bringing visitors who wish to remember those who perished on 9/11. Those honoring the past and those equipping themselves for the future will merge and walk alongside one another on bridges that take them over a chasm created by the slurry wall. They will enter onto a roof landscape made up of a flowing carpet of shorn grasses and colorful ground covers that change with the seasons. Scattered throughout the gardens are small sitting areas, that can serve as places for contemplation for the families of victims or gathering spaces for student discussions and performances. As visitors walk from the busy streets of Lower Manhattan to the core of the site, they will experience both beautiful urban gardens and glimpses of the school activities through courtyards, skylights and softly upturned roofs. We imagine this as a new Central

Park for Lower Manhattan, but one that merges the serene qualities of Olmsted's pastoral ideal with the kinetic activity of the public square.

The sloping paths will take visitors to an outdoor amphitheater designed to serve the needs of both visitors and students. Speeches on September 11 will be followed on September 12 with a concert of world music performed by New York City kids. In the morning students might sit to hear the words of a foreign diplomat, while in the afternoon family members of the victims of 9/11 could sit to contemplate the towers' foundations.

The square foundations of the Twin Towers will be lined with red granite linear memorial tablets.. Visitors can traverse a path around the two footprints and pause to sit in front of specific names from the tragedies of New York, Washington and Shanksville, which will be arranged alphabetically.

This journey to a tragic past will be inextricably bound up with the uplifting sight of the future. Having reached the formal memorial , the quiet pathways marking the foundations of the Twin Towers, visitors may realize that they have, in fact, just walked alongside the true memorial: the living, human building blocks of a future New York.

Ripley's World

HAVING ESTABLISHED THE BASIS OF HIS FORTUNE BY collecting bizarre facts, Robert Ripley began to collect countries. He had been an unhappy, bucktoothed child burdened with a stutter, the name Leroy and a mother widowed when he was 12. Travel seems to have been his way of stating that he never had a true home and was always on the lookout for a substitute for the earliest home of all. At the peak of his fame, at the end of the thirties, he liked to boast that he had visited 201 countries out of a possible 253. In the manner of globetrotters of that period he liked to be photographed in each country set against the appropriate fauna and flora, looking manly in tropical kilt and white and brown sports shoes.

Just to make sure that guests to his home in Mamaroneck got the point, he had miniature flags of his country collection in the bar, and a compass sunk into the floor of his sun porch, along with the directions and number of miles to all the many hundred places in the world more exotic than Mamaroneck or the small town in California where he was born.

With his wild and undiscriminating, childish curiosity, Ripley built up one of the great child's collections of all times. Most children have their tiny collection of bugs, coins, stamps and so forth. Ripley filled room after room in house after house, and when he ran out of space he stored the crates of his treasures in warehouses around the country.

Anything strange in all countries that met Ripley's maniacally acquisitive game was bought, parceled up and sent home. Humans were not exempt. When Ripley, in the course of his wanderings, met Wenseskeo Manuel in the Yucatan, who had survived both a firing squad and the coup de grâce, he hired him at $75 a week to display his bullet-riddled features in one of the Ripley "Odditoriums".

Ripley retained three or four people to scour the world in search of the bizarre for a collection that he finally valued at $2 million. Geoffrey Hellman, who visited him for a *New Yorker* profile, early in 1940, reported on the surreal atmosphere of the Mamaroneck household with its chastity belts, Aztec masks, 500 beer steins, the skeleton of a two-headed baby and photograph of himself with a woman leper, "the most horrible looking human being in the world". Over those and hundreds of other treasures brooded his equally odd housekeeper, Mrs. Almuth Dold, formerly the wife of a Russian baron, once in a Turkish harem as a guest and finely cultivated in the arts of graphology, astrology, palmistry, phrenology, numerology and tea leaves. Married to an efficiency engineer, she ran Ripley's house for him, acting as his hostess and, according to Hellman, "conversing easily with his guests in the barroom and at table".

Fanatical collectors are mostly a repressed lot, stumbling uneasily about in their unconscious. My personal favorite is the collector of antique chairs who came to believe that he had glass buttocks and didn't dare sit down, eventually dying of inanition. Ripley was no exception. He spent hours every day compulsively rearranging all the pieces of his collection, before pottering about the waterways of his estate in various outlandish forms of marine transport. The libido burst through his surface pudeur in some curious ways; for example, he insisted that a lady sword swallower in one of his "Odditoriums" should ingest not tempered steel but a neon tube at the end of an electric flex. He was, in sum, an eccentric, with all the appeal of those delightful and childish creatures, as I realized in the course of a visit to the Ripley Museum in St. Augustine, Florida.

Like many children in the dying years of the British Empire, I grew up surrounded by a collection of the Ripley genre. Curios and antiques assembled by the innumerable members of that empire filled the house and in the case of my grandmother's place, a few miles down the road in southern Ireland, these memorabilia were profuse enough to cram not only many display cases in the main house but also a small museum at the bottom of the wall garden.

My grandmother's father had been an Irish adventurer who settled into a successful and prosperous career as a colonial governor: from bleakly inauspicious beginnings administering Newfoundland, he had passed through government houses in the Bahamas, Jamaica and Ceylon before ending up as a governor of Hong Kong at the end of the nineteenth century. The display cases and museum were thus filled with the consequences of a thousand Victorian shopping expeditions, from Kingston through Kandy to Kowloon; carved figures, vases, baskets, scrolls, howdahs, palanquins, robes, a carved dug-out canoe, ivory, jade, mounds of imperial medals and—best of all for a child—a veritable army of spears, clubs, shields, swords, daggers and arrows whose tips were darkened with traces of what my grandmother said was curare.

No collection of this sort was complete without its shrunken head. The one in my grandmother's museum hung, out of my reach, from one of the museum's beams.

It was supposedly acquired by Great Uncle Maurice on one of his diamond-prospecting expeditions up the Orinoco. Great Uncle Maurice had been something of a black sheep—another essential perquisite of any family's imperial collection—and we thought it quite possible that he had done the processing himself, shrinking this trophy down to the size of a tan grapefruit with long black hair. Irish damp began to overwhelm the museum in the end and so most of its contents were crated up and sent off to scholarly institutions to languish in pedantic and well-labeled obscurity.

The appeal of the Ripley collection is that it immediately recreates that childlike view which is the dawn of curiosity.

There in the St. Augustine museum were the curio cabinets, the palanquin and, grinning amiably from its display case, the shrunken Javaro head. All around me were crowds of happy children, speculating just as I had done on shrinking techniques and the toxic properties of native South American poisons, peering at the waxwork figure in the entranceway of the buck-toothed Ripley in his middle years looking welcoming and avuncular: the sort of uncle every child should have, with his shrunken heads, his horde of bizarre facts and charming huckster's cry of "Believe It or Not!"

I cannot speak for the eight other Ripley Museums scattered across the North American continent, but for anyone in northern Florida, wishing a respite from Interstate 85 or Flagler's great Spanish-style Ponce de Leon Hotel in St. Augustine (first major structure in the US built with poured concrete), the Ripley Museum is well worth a visit, and if children are of the party, merits a major detour. The museum reminds us what the world was like before public television, the late Sir Kenneth Clark or universal college education. In the American pantheon Ripley should stand in the same corner of the wall as such great entertainers as H.P. Stanley, P.T. Barnum and Walt Disney: less serious than the first, less outrageous than the second and without the latter's degrading addiction to the cute. Of the time when newspapers had their star writers always traveling the world in search of strange tribes, places and customs, Ripley was Sancho Panza to Stanley's Quixote and while the latter sent sober dispatches from the darkness of Africa, Ripley, in a more frivolous era, would return—as he did from China in the thirties—with a small glass vial, now in the St. Augustine museum, labeled "The only unbroken object in the city of Chapei after the Japanese invasion—a bottle of Chinese mange cure!" Like any resourceful uncle, Ripley could make anything interesting, even a tiny glass bottle.

Ripley was born in Santa Rosa on Christmas Day, 1893. His father died when Robert was 12 and the boy helped support his mother by polishing gravestones. He was a talented illustrator and after a stint on some California papers, Ripley came east and got a job on the old *New York Globe* as a sports illustrator. Short of material one December day in 1918 he strung together some odd sporting achievements in an illustrated panel. A *Globe* editor titled it "Believe It or Not" and within a few months, responding to surging reader interest, Ripley's employers were asking him to do one a day.

True success came in 1928. Simon and Schuster published *Believe It or Not*, "a modern book of Wonders, Miracles, Freaks, Monstrosities and almost-Impossibilities, Written, Illustrated and Proved by Robert L. Ripley". The book ran swiftly through several reprints and William Randolph Hearst sent a simple telegraphic directive to his men in New York, "Hire Ripley."

Ripley's salary went from $10,000 to $100,000 forthwith, and within a few years he was a major journalistic institution. About 19 million newspapers carrying his feature were sold each day and he reached 90 million readers. After scanning the headlines people turned to Ripley. He received an average of a million letters a year and launched radio and television series (the Ripley cartoons and program of today are not, I should hasten to say, particularly satisfactory). By 1940 there were three Odditoriums and a number of Ripley trailer shows touring the country. Still immensely successful—though on the threshold of an era less sympathetic to his brand of journalistic showmanship—Ripley died in 1949.

He grins toothily from the picture in the pamphlet available at the museum, but Ripley, like many compulsive travelers and collectors, seems to have been a complex and inhibited character. He was married for a few years in the twenties to a Massachusetts beauty queen but thereafter remained single. He had many cars but could not drive. Slightly vulgar, he was the quintessential Innocent Abroad, forever amazed at the strangeness of the world, forever determined to contain it within the confines of pragmatic American common sense. The child who had polished gravestones had a taste for the macabre but not the occult, the incredible but not the false. He was a collector for the common man, with a marvelous ability to reduce space and time to the status of Collector's Item.

The first *Believe It or Not* book has more of Ripley's personality in it than later products. "In Lhassa, Tibet", Ripley wrote, "there is a man with a horn growing from his forehead to the extent of thirteen inches. The reflected glory of the golden sun bounces off K2 and Mount Everest on this curious promontory each morning as its bearer makes his obeisance to Gatama while turning a prayer wheel. The horned Kaffir of Africa, like the Horned One of the Himalayas, is still alive. I saw him in London several years ago. He seemed self-centered and satisfied, though black and a Christian."

As this last sentence suggests, Ripley lacked the Disney blandness. Although, as he said of himself, he made his living out of the proposition that truth is stranger than fiction, he did not feel it necessary to view all the world's truths with equal sympathy. Discussing the Hindu pilgrims at the Kali-Chat temple in Benares—"Sky-facers who hold their faces rigidly upward until unable to bend them back; UP-arm men, who hold up their arms in the same way until they wither away..."—he concluded sternly, "Most of the wretches that we see around the holy places of worship have no idea what their attitudes and symbols mean; all are intellectually degraded and some are mere fakers."

As collector for the common man, Ripley had a keen appreciation for time and effort, qualities he esteemed. One exhibit at the Ripley museum in St. Augustine is a table with a label noting that it was made of "11,000 separate pieces of wood from 29 different species of tree, by Klaus Finzar of Innsbruck".

Conventional museums would have stopped there, but Ripley adds the all-important news that the table was intended "as a wedding gift for his daughter who entered a convent and never had use for it. It took nine years to complete."

There are kindred monuments to such pertinacity throughout the museum: a tiny bottle painted on its ulterior surfaces by manicured fingernails, a railroad arc bridge made of "more than 3,100 ordinary tooth picks" by Joe Gross of Brooklyn, a vase 24 inches high wrought from the bladder of a camel. There are stamps covered with the entire Constitution of the United States and biblios the size of a fava bean.

Ripley knew the common man appreciated not only time and effort but also their expression as value. So he made a particular point of collecting bizarre types of money from around the world. Cases in the St. Augustine museum are filled with stones, shells, whales' teeth, beads, pictures, symbolic objects and notes of hand that have served through history as a means of exchange.

The rhythms of its eccentric accumulation throb from these samples of money, to the camel's bladder, to the Iron Maiden of Nuremberg, to the final Barnum-like touch of "The Bathtub Marshall". This last, found at the top floor of the museum, is a tribute to the curator's ingenuity in making good use of every square foot. Behind a glass partition is an antique bath with dripping tap. In the half-filled bath sits a uniformed figure and the label informs us that this is "The Bathtub Marshall... Marshall de Castellane (1788–1862), Governor of Lyons, France", who "had three uniforms and three sets of medals, one for bathing".

By all rights one of Ripley's most cherished possessions, the Chinese junk in which he sailed on inland Florida waters near his winter quarters at Palm Beach, should be anchored in St. Augustine's Matanzas Bay, off the Castille de San Marcos. Visitors to the museum would thus get in advance that intimation of the exotic Orient which Ripley found so alluring and which caused him, after his first trip to China, to sign his cartoons Rip-Li for a while. The Orient—outlandish and mysterious—lay at the very heart of his appeal, as the adventurous uncle who has knocked about the world, seen a thing or two and returned to tell the tale.

Sex

ALEXANDER COCKBURN
Love Button

I T WAS A STRONG WEEK FOR THE CLITORIS. NOT JUST HERE in the US, with Jerold Mackenzie's successful defense of his constitutional, non-harassing right to distribute pieces of paper with the word clitoris written on them. Phillip Hoare had just published his interesting book *Wilde's Last Stand: Decadence, Conspiracy and the First World War,* about a mad trial in England in 1918. It centered on allegations that the beastly Germans had prepared a book containing the names of 47,000 British men and women who had become habituated to Hunnish practices of sexual debauch, with the result that "the sexual peculiarities of members of the peerage were used as leverage to open fruitful fields of espionage", while "in lesbian ecstasy the most sacred secrets of state were betrayed". A member of Parliament, Noel Pemberton Billing then wrote an article called the "Cult of the Clitoris" in which he suggested that "several thousand of the first 47,000" would be found among those who had bought tickets to a production of Wilde's *Salome,* put on by J.T. Grein and featuring the actress Maude Allan. Grein and Allan sued Billing for this preposterous nonsense, which implied that they had fomented treachery.

The trial, presided over by Mr. Justice Darling, was a farce, in which female sexuality made an edgy appearance. In his amusing review of Hoare's book in *The Observer* Peter Parker cited the prosecuting counsel asking whether an orgasm was "some unnatural vice", while outside the courtroom a confused old buffer asked, "Who's this Greek chap Clitoris everyone was talking about?" (Don't get too uppity. Polls show 70 percent of all American men are either unaware of the clitoris or think it's a tourist destination in the Aegean.)

It seems the whole absurd affair was set up by the British military high command which feared that the government was planning peace talks with the Germans, and which therefore was eager to present upper-class society as infested with sex-crazed quislings of no moral account.

In fact English upper class society in London during World War I was a lot more outré than is commonly reckoned. For one thing, most of the eligible young men had been killed on the western front, so there most certainly was a big upswing in lesbian practices on grounds of simple supply and demand, as in New York today, where the male-female ratio has got entirely out of kilter. And beyond that, as always, wartime lowered the moral fences.

Meanwhile, in Argentina a novel called *The Discovery of the Clitoris* is now on its seventeenth week on the bestseller list. Against all the odds, the musty old professors administering a $28,000 literary prize offered by the richest woman in Argentina, gave it to this work of fiction, which argues that the clit was discovered in 1558 by a man called Columbus (no relation). The Argentinian billionairess is outraged, and has tried to compel the young fiction writer from associating her prize with his book. This has only increased the *succes de scandale,* and doubtless the book will soon be offered to an American audience.

SUSAN DAVIS

Eros Meets Civilization: Gershon Legman Confronts the Post Office

J UNE 6, 1950, IS A HOT DAY IN WASHINGTON, DC. Gershon Legman, folklorist, sex researcher, bibliographer, social critic, struggles in a wheelchair to a hearing room in the United States Post Office building. Earlier in the week Legman has broken his foot rescuing one of his wife's cats from the roof of their house in the Bronx, and the trip on the train from New York has been an ordeal. He has requested a hearing before J.C. Haynes, Senior Trial Examiner, Office of the Solicitor, United States Post Office Department, to contest a finding that he has been sending an obscene book through the mail.

Here we see Gershon Legman at the beginning of the middle of his varied and flamboyant career. He is 32, and according to his FBI file, he's five foot eight inches tall, and heavy, with blue eyes and dark brown hair. He's not wearing a suit, for he's famously poor. Any chance of financial stability is subverted by his love of collecting, studying and writing books.

This isn't, yet, Gershon Legman the acknowledged world expert on pornography and erotic folklore, self-taught in at least four languages. But he's getting started. He's not famous as a song, story and word collector, student of graffiti and master of the arcana of the obscene. He hasn't pulled together his enormous collection of bawdy ballads and songs, remnants of a singing world so long ignored in respectable folklore studies. In the future he will produce intricate intellectual detective stories, uncovering the identities of the authors of some of the ninedteenthth-century's most notorious dirty books. Over the next 25 years he will publish two volumes, deliriously annotated and cross-referenced, analyzing according to a Freudian schema his collection of thousands of dirty jokes. He will fire salvos at American scholars for their timidity about all things erotic. He will become legendary for his impatience with censorship and his irascibility with editors. Later in life, he will pass into oral tradition as an icon of anti-respectability, an uncontrollable scholarly volcano of sexual folklore.

But right now, all the books and articles, if not the personality, are works in progress. To date, he has attracted literary notice by editing for Jay Landesman, the hipster impresario, an irreverent small magazine, *Neurotica*, that delights some of the early Beats. He's had contributions from Marshall McLuhan, John Clellon Holmes, Leonard Bernstein, Judith Malina, William Steig and other young writers and artists. He's writing an encyclopedia of sex acts. He's fired off a devastating critique of Alfred Kinsey's report on male sexuality on the grounds that its research overly relied on the confessions of white Indiana University students. He's helped smuggle Henry Miller's *Tropic of Cancer* into the country for an unauthorized edition. Legman is a minor but not insignificant denizen of the fringes of New York's literary bohemia. His reputation spreads by word-of-mouth.

To keep body and soul together, Legman has conducted sex research for doctors, book-scouted for collectors of rare erotica, and written pornography to order for the wealthy. He's ghostwritten for the famous and churned out detective novels under pseudonyms. He's been a printer, a carpenter, even a house painter. Legman is Jewish, and although he grew up with immigrant parents in Scranton, Pennsylvania, his extended family remained in Europe. Most were killed in the war. In his spare moments and for his own future purposes, he's been compiling an extensive diary of his sexual and social life as a young man in literary New York on thousands of inconvenient 3 by 5 note cards. Decades later he will use the note cards to write *Peregrine Penis: An Autobiography Of Innocence.* In 2002 it remains mostly unpublished.

Today Legman is at a breaking point in his life; it's a day after which, even if he doesn't realize it now, nothing will be the same. The book he is here to defend from the Post Office is, at least in his own opinion, the most important one he will write. Looking back on *Love & Death: A Study in Censorship,* he will insist that it was his favorite work, in fact it was him. "Le text, c'est moi!" he will write with a flourish as he sends a copy to Ewing Baskette, a collector of banned books. But today's proceedings will force Legman to decide whether he can live in the United States, or if he must leave for good.

Also filing into the room along with Examiner Haynes are Mr. J. Melaugh, Jr., the lawyer for the Post Office, the hearing recorders, and Inspector Chester A. Battles of the New York district. A loyal postal employee for 28 years, Battles has been keeping a close eye on Legman, probably for more than a third of his own career. Battles has followed Legman's activities since early 1940, when the Post Office and police raided Jacob Brussel, one of Legman's many publisher employers. Brussel was arrested, his printer's plates, stock of books, pornography and pamphlets, and mailing lists seized and ordered destroyed in a special furnace the New York police keep for the purpose. Legman barely escaped arrest himself. Does Battles know that one of Jake's most objectionable publications, *Oragenitalism,* a treatise on cunnilingus, was written by Gershon under a French-sounding pseudonym? Thanks to the police raid, in 2002 the first edition is a very rare book, priced at about $7,000. In any case, Battles has shown up in the role of the government's main witness against Legman. They detest each other.

This is an ex parte, or one-sided administrative hearing, meaning that no formal legal charges have been filed, and few legal guidelines apply. No formal counter allegation or defense can be made. As the literary historian Jay Gertzman tells me, "Post Office cases could be argued by one party only, the Post Office, and hearings were held in-house". Because the Post Office has decided *Love & Death* is obscene, it has become "unmailable". The New York Post Office has either stopped accepting *Love & Death* in the mail, or it has blocked deliveries to Legman's address, or both. Legman has seen Battles to ask about the mail block, and has been told that he is entitled to a hearing in Washington. But, under the mid-twentieth th century regime of postal power, the same men who have decided *Love & Death* is obscene will hear Legman argue for its merit. They alone will make the final decision.

Even if Legman could afford one, a lawyer would only rail against the power of the Post Office to decree obscenity in an extra-legal proceeding. The letter summoning Legman to Washington accuses him of retailing "indecent, vulgar and obscene materials" in the mails under the Fraud, Fictitious Business and Lotteries statute. In 1950, this statute is the main tool the Post Office has against what it deems obscenity. There is a malevolent Star Chamber aspect to the hearing: Legman or any other petitioner may be subject to a kind of softening-up session, in which examiners try to see if they can discover anything more about his activities, to catch him in another crime.

Today, most Americans don't think much about the Post Office in connection with censorship. But from the 1870s until nearly 1970, postmasters shaped the practical and imaginative universe of Americans. Some of us still remember the Post Office rubber stamp "Report Obscene Mail to Your Postmaster" on our letters. In 1873, at the urging of self-appointed cultural purifier Anthony Comstock, Congress granted the Post Office Department near-absolute power to regulate material sent through the mails. The Comstock Act authorized the Postmaster General to ban any book, picture or letter, or any other material he found to be "obscene, lewd, lascivious or filthy" but notoriously failed to define obscenity, thus leaving applications of the charge to the postmaster. For many years this made the Post Office Department, along with the Customs Department and Hollywood's Hays Office (run by a former Postmaster General), a powerful arbiter of what Americans could see, read and buy. Into the 1950s and beyond, as Eisenhower's Postmaster General Arthur Summerfield boasted, the Post Office was "an apparatus that reache[d] into every home and business in America". Postmasters also wielded the power to root out political materials they deemed seditious or radical.

In 1950 "unmailable" was a capacious category. It could encompass information about reproduction, contraceptives and birth control; it ranged from marriage manuals to nude picture postcards, from cheap comics to stroke books. The definition of "obscene, lewd, lascivious or filthy" was expansive and variable because it was locally enforced. Comstockery reigned a long, dreary century.

Book dealers and publishers of all kinds, including pornographers, were dependent on the mails for advertising and distribution of their materials. From the 1930s, the Post Office had been going after the mail-order business of big-time pornographers, notably Samuel Roth, Jake Brussel and Benjamin Rebhuhn, all of whom went to prison for publishing obscenity and all of whom would be hailed later as courageous pioneers in the publication of experimental literature. Roth was responsible for publishing the first excerpts of James Joyce's *Ulysses* in the US. Using police raids, pretrial gossip in the press and scandal sheets, highly publicized federal prosecutions and long prison sentences, postmasters and attorneys general sought to put the fear of God into the smut mongers.

The general effect was less to stamp out smut than to keep pressure on the whole publishing industry, lest some inattentive editor at a respectable house let salacious trash like Edmund Wilson's *Memoirs of Hecate County* ("the best damn book I ever wrote") slip through the cracks. Small book dealers and entrepreneur publishers were also intimidated. As Legman often complained, censorship's major result was an atmosphere of stifling timidity around sexual expression in American letters.

Legman's mail block fell under the mail fraud statutes. Perhaps counterintuitively from today's perspective, Justice Learned Hand found in 1939 that pandering to sexual desire constituted a kind of fraud. Although his argument was complex and found some valid place for erotica, it boiled down to this: because American Puritanism viewed sexual acts as disgusting and feared their literary and photographic representation, arousal of sexual impulses amounted to an assault on the vulnerable. Mail-order advertisements for sexual literature were illegitimate for the same reason: one didn't know who might stumble across them or who might be aroused. To use the postal system to circulate erotic material was thus dangerous and deceptive. For example, flyers pitching anthropological treatises on sexual customs, or sociological studies of the intimate practices of married people, were highly suspect. The ads might arouse or delude and thus defraud the general reader. They might fall into the hands of children. Then there were the books themselves. Indeed, a great deal of phony anthropology was retailed. Exceptions were made if these treatises were aimed only at medical men or scholars, who would presumably know how to evaluate this or that custom in its proper ritual setting and not be aroused by its description. But this was window dressing for the basic intent to suppress all kinds of writings having to do with sex, as well as to ban frank erotica. One result was that publishers of marriage advice, sexual anthropology and erotica tried to find someone with "Dr". in front of his name to serve as an out-of-town distributor. Another result was that many kinds of scholars and even medical libraries had difficulty collecting the books they needed. Thus Legman's occupational niche as a go-between.

Obscenity could also be attacked under a fictitious name and business charge, another kind of fraud allegation leveled at Legman. Some mail-order book dealers were forced to use false names and addresses. Indeed, Legman knew this from his own research: the bibliographic tangles of late Renaissance pornography were created by just such necessity, and he had made sorting out mysteries of authorship and provenance an area of expertise. As he later wrote in *The Horn Book*, whether in the world of pulp or among the stylists of high-class erotica, no one was who they seemed. Authors rarely published from a traceable place, and the names of presses and dates of publication were completely unreliable. Publishers and dealers used changing addresses, as well as moving drop boxes, hiding places and the elegant false fronts memorably sketched by Raymond Chandler in *The Big Sleep*. Whenever postal inspectors closed in and threatened to shut down a business, the businessman simply moved and set up shop under a different name. The most successful pornographers were moving targets.

Finally, fraud could be committed when a mail order house offered erotica that turned out not to be very erotic. A packet of "spicy French photos" might be homemade snapshots of the dealer's sister posing demurely in her winter nightie.

Rather than resort to the law courts, the Post Office most often used its administrative sanction. After 1930 postmasters were increasingly likely to be castigated by judges for overreaching their powers. They could lose in court, but not often in their own administrative backyards, unless their victim, like Samuel Roth, was spoiling for a long and expensive challenge.

So here are the charges piled up against Gershon Legman: he is running a fraudulent business under a fictitious name, and under this cover he is using the United States mail to distribute an obscene book. Once the hearing is under way, it is discovered that there is nothing to the first two charges. "G. Legman", stigmatized as false, is Gershon Legman's favored pen name. (He has long since stopped using his legal name, George Alexander Legman. Gershon is his Jewish family name.) Under examination, he swears he is running a real press called Breaking Point from his home address—858 Hornaday Place in the Bronx—a real house that he rents and an address that still exists in 2002. The press is a legal business registered to G. Legman-Keith, a combination of Gershon's and his wife Beverley's last names. He has been advertising very real books, magazines and pamphlets of criticism for sale. He hopes and intends to keep doing so. He is proud of, and the Post Office is interested in the little magazine *Neurotica,* which he edits with Landesman. *Neurotica* and Landesman are under a simultaneous Post Office investigation in Connecticut because of an issue edited by Legman containing a column called "Degenerates' Corner". But the central issue on June 6, 1950, is the self-published *Love & Death,* a book that has been rejected by more than 50 publishers, mostly because Legman has refused to expurgate a single word. A postal spy using the name of "George Barnett" got hold of a red card, perhaps through the mail, perhaps tucked into the magazine. It is an advertisement for Legman's new book and it reads:

Published Sept. 12 [1949] *Love & Death* by G. Legman, A Study in Censorship: Murder-Mysteries. Comic Books. Bitch-heroines. Attacks on Women. 95 pp. paper bound. Retail price $1, Breaking Point, 858 Hornaday Pl. New York 60.

Around the card's border trails a tantalizing quote from Montaigne's "Notes on Virgil": "We Bravely Say Kill. Rob. Betray. But That Other We Dare Pronounce Only Between Clenched Teeth?"

It perfectly expresses Legman's theory of censorship in America.

When Barnett returned the card asking for more information, he was sending a "test letter". On receiving an order form, he mailed it with a money order for $1. Legman shipped a copy of *Love & Death* and Barnett proceeded to go over its contents. In the year running up to the hearing, Legman received test correspondence from many parts of the country. While working for Brussel he'd learned to recognize entrapment, even the familiar fake names. On one postcard, he scrawled "smells like a Post Office rat to me, but fill anyway". Isn't it peculiar, Legman points out in the hearing, that false names can be used to discover whether someone is using a false name?

Mr. Melaugh, lawyer for the Post Office, testifies that for all his odd social views, Legman appears to be an orderly and efficient businessman. Those who wrote for information about *Love & Death* received it promptly; when they sent in their money orders they got their books.

Legman affirms that he answered the entrapment letters and cashed the money orders: "I did mail the books. I was glad to mail them their books. I wish to get the greatest publicity to my work!" He isn't hiding anything.

The tone then shifts to cloudy menace. There is no fictitious business, and no duplicitous business dealing but has there been fraud? Legman says he's not really clear what he has been charged with, and what possible outcomes there might be. Examiner Haynes takes the hearing off record at this point and explains to Legman that so far nothing prosecutable has been detected. "We have no jurisdiction, we have no interest... in this case... in presenting those facts to the United States Attorney".

But, on the other hand, Haynes continues, the hearing on obscenity will proceed. Several people in the room deem *Love & Death* obscene. Although Haynes won't say so, what is being explored here is the question of how far the Post Office can intimidate Gershon Legman into dismantling his own business.

We slip through the looking glass. If Legman's book is found obscene, he might lose his second-class mailing privileges, might after all be referred to the United States Attorney for prosecution. If he should be convicted of obscenity, he might even be jailed. Even if he is not prosecuted, the Post Office can and probably will continue to harass him. The Post Office can continue to keep him from sending out his book, or block his incoming mail, all on its own authority.

Legman objects that "these [fraud] orders are in the nature… of an harassment of a publisher". When it's his turn to cross-examine Chester Battles, Legman goes on the offensive. "I would like to know who complained about me", he demands. Battles refuses to answer. "Does the Examiner know", Legman asks, "that I myself mailed copies of *Love & Death* to several postal officials?" In fact, "I mailed them to whatever person I knew to be in any sort of charge in the Post Office Department".

Can it be that the author himself is the source of the complaint?

Battles, with Melaugh objecting, argues first that he had never received a copy, and then, doubling back, that he has no idea who has been sending copies of *Love & Death* to him. "They simply arrive".

Legman demands to know whether Battles has read his book. Battles, irritated, asserts he's never opened the covers of *Love & Death,* and implies he never wants to. Legman insists that he's been careful to send (yet another) free copy to one of Battles's agents. And hadn't they discussed the book when Legman visited him at his office about the complaint earlier that February? And isn't a copy with passages underlined lying right there on Haynes's desk?

Legman pushes harder: "And isn't it true that Inspector Battles has himself been collecting reviews and newspaper notices of the book?" Hasn't he seen the positive reviews in *The New Republic* and *Harpers?* Melaugh objects that Legman is "running riot". Battles says nothing.

Legman lunges again. Does Battles have any idea what the book is about? Melaugh objects that "it isn't Inspector Battles's job to know the content of the books". Legman retorts that "if the hearing's purpose is to determine whether I am sending obscene material through the mail, certainly somebody has or ought to have looked at the contents of the book". Hasn't the inspector underlined parts of it? Chester Battles allows that he's "brought certain parts of the book to the attention" of his superiors.

Legman charges on boisterously: "The reason I asked is because the complaint, as I received a copy of it, states that 'this book is obscene and of an indecent character' and 'contains vulgar, obscene, indecent and morally offensive words and phrases'. Now there's no recommendation there for [which] those words and phrases are. It is difficult for me to prepare to defend words, phrases and so on if I don't know what they are.... If I am to oppose, and I believe I have the right to oppose this fictitious order, [and] I am told there's something, but I don't know what it is, in a manufactured book containing maybe a quarter million words". So, how can I defend my book?

Examiner Haynes dismisses the problem of words and phrases as irrelevant: recent legal decisions mean that words and phrases by themselves can no longer be used to brand a book obscene. (No one seems to note that this raises the question whether the case should have been brought at all.) At any rate, says Haynes, "I am capable of reading the book myself, and I will". He's arguing it's just a matter of judgement—his Post Office judgment. He also tells Legman that he's not interested in his blustery assertion that Morris Ernst and the ACLU are "taking an interest" in this case. (In fact, they are.) But Haynes and Melaugh are taken aback by Legman's unorthodox behavior. Clearly, he knows he's being spied on, and instead of hiding like a suspected criminal, he's been sending complimentary copies of his work to men he knows are trying to catch him in a crime.

By sending his book to Battles and his superiors, Legman may have been trying to get an opinion, an idea of whether his work was going to draw down postal wrath. Many publishers held meetings with postmasters in cases they thought were "iffy", and this led to what was essentially prepublication self-censorship. It was like asking, "If I do this, will you punish me? What if I do that?" Legman execrated censorship and self-censorship, so another explanation seems more likely. His book was an argument about sexual censorship. He was trying to bring a test case against the Post Office, to show how irrational it was. Jay Landesman later wrote that Legman had added the words "prick and balls" to one chapter just to catch the Post Office's attention. But perhaps Legman misjudged his antagonist and its resources, because now they're going after him ferociously.

The hearing goes deeper and focuses on the question of obscenity. No one reads from the book, and when Legman tries to explain his thesis, he's cut off. The hearing gets personal. Perhaps Legman has a tendency to publish obscene works? Melaugh inquires into his previous writing and publishing activities, but evidently he has not done very much research about these, since the questioning stays close to only one article, the book and *Neurotica*. Legman keeps mum about his confiscated on oral sex, and many of his other writings.

Examiner Haynes questions Battles: "Do you know whether he ever published any article entitled 'Sex Variants'?

"I guess he said he had", Battles replies.

Legman interrupts to point out that *Sex Variants* is actually the title of a book by Dr. George W. Henry, published in 1941, and that it contains an article by him, but that is not the article's title. It is a glossary—the first—of American homosexuality and homosexual slang, and "that was the part which I contributed and designed. I have contributed many other lists of books [bibliographies] and some poetry ... as an expert on certain subjects related to sex and censorship".

Now it's Legman's turn to cross-examine himself, which he admits is a little silly. All he can do is explain his work and he begins by offering his credentials as a scholar, one who finished high school in Scranton and educated himself in the New York Public Library. He has worked for Alfred C. Kinsey, of Indiana University. He has researched for Dr. Robert L. Dickinson, head of the American College of Gynecology and the Committee on Maternal Health. He asserts the intellectual seriousness and social importance of his writings.

About *Love & Death*: "The writing of this book is the result of nearly 10 years or more of thought and discussion and pre-publication on the subject [mostly in *Neurotica*]. Almost everything I've done in the past is in some way related to it, and this comes as a final flowering of my purpose". All of his work takes up the same theme: sexual censorship. He is preparing "a history of sex censorship in the English language, not political and not religious censorship which have been covered by very great scholars", but sex censorship, a "subject which has been difficult until the present time for people to discuss without excessive emotion". "As it happens, the *Dictes* [The Sayings] by Caxton, the first dated book printed in England [1477], is also the first expurgated book printed in England". Censorship is there from the beginning.

It's Melaugh's turn to jump in.

Perhaps Legman's work is obscene because of his own character. Isn't it true, Melaugh asks, that Legman was arrested in New York in 1944 for draft evasion? Legman denies this. Here's what really happened: he was picked up in some sort of a sweep, and arrested and held for not carrying his draft card.

Isn't it true, Melaugh grinds on, that he consorts with known homosexuals? This is in fact true: Legman has been researching the gay culture of New York since the middle 1930s. He has gay consultants and gay friends, but in 1950 it is too dangerous to answer frankly. With the introduction into evidence of his interest in homosexuality, the investigators now have a weapon to threaten Legman with—his own morality and political loyalty.

This is a dicey time for such questions. In February 1950, Senator Joseph McCarthy began an investigation of subversion in the State Department, and one witness testified that it was a nest of homosexuals, thus potentially disloyal. At almost the moment Legman is testifying, the Senate is holding a formal inquiry into the employment of "homosexuals and other moral perverts" in government. People are losing their jobs.

Legman explains that homosexuals seek him out for information, sympathy and psychological advice, comforts in short supply for gay men in 1950. Does Legman present himself as a psychologist or psychiatrist, Melaugh demands? Legman answers that he knows psychiatrists, and, indeed, during this period his interest in psychoanalytic thought has been growing. Thinking that perhaps he could offer some useful expertise on homosexuality during this recent scare, he has pulled together his notes and written an article "On the Cause of Homosexuality". It appears to be more Dad's fault than Mom's... Melaugh and Haynes are uninterested.

What about his arrest for waving a loaded pistol in a restaurant? Melaugh asks. Legman replies that he wasn't waving a pistol, the pistol wasn't loaded and he wasn't threatening anyone but trying to prevent an anguished suicide attempt. Does Legman know, as the postal inspector certainly knows, that he has a NYC police department "B" or registration number? Yes. Does Legman know that he has an FBI number? An FBI number is a centralized way of keeping track of people who've been arrested around the country, the way state and federal authorities can access a "rap sheet". Legman shrugs this off—but it's a threat.

What Legman doesn't know but may suspect is that the FBI has started a dossier on him. In fact, the file was initiated at the request of a postal inspector, probably Chester A. Battles, though his name has been blacked out in the redacted Freedom of Information Act version of the file. The FBI told Battles they had no independent information to share on Legman, but they opened the file anyway, just to be on the safe side.

After a long morning and afternoon Haynes closes the hearing, saying in effect, "We'll be in touch". Legman can file a brief, a written defense of *Love & Death* in two weeks time if he wishes. He can have a transcript of the hearing if he needs it. These are new rights for the complainant (or is he the defendant?) forced on the postal examiner's office by the courts after objections about arbitrariness.

Throughout the hearing, Legman seems alternately defiant and frightened. Certainly, it is a terrifying affair. He has not been charged with a crime, and he can't confront his accuser, but the burden of proving innocence is on his shoulders. Although Legman maintains a belligerent stance, he's plainly concerned that federal charges may follow. From what I've been able to find in Justice Department records, no charges were sent up. Maybe Legman was small potatoes compared with Samuel Roth, who would be tried, convicted and jailed a few years later. Maybe the point was just harassment. Maybe they had him where they wanted him anyway.

A few months after the hearing the fraud and unmailability decision was upheld and the Post Office stopped delivering mail to 858 Hornaday Place. Legman could not receive answers to advertisements for *Love & Death,* and he could not mail the book out, although he could sell it if he could get it into stores. He urged the ACLU to keep following the case.

Years later Legman wrote to Landesman, that from that day in June, 1950 "our bags were packed". Legman couldn't know how much worse things would get, but the McCarthy Red Scares were well under way and he correctly surmised that his life and work would get harder. The 1940 Brussel raid, the ups and downs of publishing and bookselling friends, the civil service purges of "sex deviants" and radicals, all added up to a very nasty intimation of the future.

Legman was born in 1917, so anti-radicalism had been raging for his whole life. Each new anti-subversive crusade added to the smog that hung thick over the New York publishing world. Just as Legman did not know about his own slim FBI file, he was similarly ignorant of the extent of the dossiers the agency was gathering on other writers, editors, artists, folklorists, anthropologists and cultural workers, as well as political activists. Though he had no direct left connections, as part of the intellectual world of New York he could feel anti-subversion filtering into the general culture, feel how it was affecting the lives and work of people who never thought of themselves as radicals in a political sense. And among the politically active, teachers were losing their jobs, librarians being fired, professors asked to take loyalty oaths, unions purged. A dead weight, anti-subversion was like censorship; it limited peoples' personal and cultural options, closing off possibilities by narrowing the range of what could be thought, said and done. Legman was an expert on the limits of what could be said and done, and he knew the limits were pressing in on him.

In 1950, anti-smut and anti-communism infused each other. As anti-communism began to run out of steam, its cheerleaders turned their searchlights on moral and sexual perversion, focusing on mass culture and its corrupting effect on the American family. Legman was aware of this too: he had watched congressional investigations of juvenile delinquency unfold since the Clark conference in 1946; in 1950 the Kefauver committee was probing the extent of juvenile crime in America. Ironically, the prevailing view that came out of expert testimonies since the mid-1940s was a nearly complete inversion of the point Legman was trying to make in *Love & Death*.

Legman argued that the suppression of images of sexuality resulted in a sadistic and violent mass culture that could harm children, even lead to fascism as it asked them to identify with vigilantism, "the institutionalized lynch". The smut vigilantes, fascists to Legman, argued that any depiction of sex, and especially "perverted" (nonmarital, nonprocreative) sex, led to violent crime committed by children and a loss of social order.

But, Legman argued, why were bitch heroines, Superman and grisly murder comics acceptable substitutes for love? What if Americans dropped censorship altogether?

Fear of smut reigned. Several states enacted new and stricter anti-porn laws and demanded that police and postmasters enforce them, despite the Supreme Court's moves toward a more restrained and precise definition of obscenity. By 1953, Estes Kefauver was investigating the relationship between smut and crime, with a special emphasis on youth and pornography. The subcommittee's work would last well into the 1960s. We are supposed to remember the 1960s as the years when the clouds lifted, but in this very decade Arthur Summerfield's Post Office would achieve the apotheosis of Comstockery, as it fought the courts to extend its control over words and images.

So, their bags were packed. Gershon Legman probably thought of the decision to move to France both positively and negatively. The United States was becoming an impossible place for him to work. He didn't necessarily link this to political repression, so closely was he focused on sex, its bibliography and its folklore. But if *Love & Death* was "him", his very self, and if the government allowed no chance for people to read his most heartfelt writings, that was political repression.

He must also have thought of this positively. There was honor in being an expatriate. There were, after all, hundreds of other interesting Americans living abroad; there were French, Dutch and Swiss intellectuals with freer attitudes. There were the great libraries, some newly on the market because of the war. Somehow, all their books, files, manuscripts and tens of thousands of Gershon's note cards were either stored or shipped, and he and Beverley sailed in 1953. For a while they kicked around Paris, then different coastal towns in the south of

France. They fell in love with the climate, the flowering trees and blooming vines.

Then, as so often with Legman, the impossible happened. A distant relative—improbably, a Hungarian count—had actually made some money on racehorses and, even more unlikely, had willed it to Gershon. Or so one someone told me. It's only one of many wild stories about Legman. In fact on a small legacy from Beverley's wealthy Canadian family she and Gershon were able, just barely, to buy a bit of land with an old, old building on it in the village of Valbonne in Alpes Maritimes, not far from Cannes. In truth, the building had been a fort of the Knights Templar. And weren't the Knights Templar known for their odd initiations, sexual rituals? And weren't they brutally suppressed by the Catholic Church? Wouldn't that be a wonderful history to investigate? Wouldn't an olive grove be a lovely place to read and write all those volumes on dirty jokes and bowdlerized ballads? Do you suppose they ever thought of Chester Battles, stuck in the Bronx?

STEVE J.B.

Prison Bitch:
Nothing Funny About It

"PRISON BITCH" IS A SONG ABOUT PRISON RAPE, heard on the *Bob & Tom Show* on radio station WFJX, FM 105.7.

They say our love is taboo, that what we're doin' is wrong,
But I don't care what they say, 'cause my love is so strong.
They tell us we should be ashamed, we're not husband and wife,
But I cherish each moment with you; I'm so glad you're in my life.

You're my prison bitch, my prison bitch, you're not like other men.
I'm glad we share a prison cell when lights go out at ten.
I can't escape the way I feel, now that would be a crime.
As long as I am doin' you I don't mind doin' time.

Cause you're my prison bitch, my prison bitch, and I have no regrets.
I got you for a candy bar and a pack of cigarettes.
At first you were resistant, but now you are my friend.
I knew that I would get you in the end....

I first heard this song several years ago when I was incarcerated in Ohio. An officer had downloaded it to his workstation computer, and he played it nearly every day, often several times in a row. Inmates and guards laughed and laughed. It made me feel sick. I still hear it in my head many times a day.

I asked the officer not to play the song but he couldn't resist. Maybe he didn't realize that I'd find it offensive. Maybe he didn't know about me—but how could that possibly be, with the super efficient prison grapevine, everyone knew my history.

I first went to prison in 1979, because I shoplifted a goose down sleeping bag. It cost $150, which made it grand theft, a felony. Had it cost $149, I'd probably have got 30 days in jail instead of four years in prison, of which I served three. The judge said he didn't like people hitchhiking in from up north and going on crime sprees in Florida. He was going to make an example of me.

Sexual assaults began the day I arrived at the Alachua County Jail. By the time I made it to prison I was known as Stephanie.

I made a very rapid transition to being an alternative woman, probably because I was simply unable to defend myself. I had never really been in a fight and was not the slightest bit tough.

The only way that a person can be reasonably safe from assault is to acquire a reputation. Often this is done by stabbing someone. If one is successful, it can mean additional time in prison. It can also get one killed. Some people are willing to pay this price. For me, it just didn't seem like an option.

What happens when you're sexually victimized in prison? In my case, besides using a feminine version of my name, I began shaving my legs and other body hair, and wearing female attire and make-up. As the abuse went on unabated for several years my original identity seemed to disintegrate.

Necessity is the mother of invention. An inmate can make a fake gun out of a bar of soap and some black shoe polish. It might not shoot, but it looks real enough and has, on at least one occasion, gained an inmate his freedom.

I guess the next best thing to breaking out of prison is settling down with a wife. An inmate can't make a convincing one out of soap, but there are countless true stories of inmates making a wife using everyday items such as Kool-Aid, a razor, a sewing needle, Vaseline, a toothbrush and a cellmate. Typically the cellmate is someone small and frightened, who doesn't know how to defend himself.

The Kool-Aid is for making pigment to be used in place of
eye shadow and lipstick. The razor is for removing body hair so
that the skin is smooth. The sewing needle is for making halter
tops, sexy underwear, and short skirts, out of old T-shirts or
whatever. Usually this is done by the wife once the vows have
been spoken, often at knife point. A knife can be made by
attaching a razor blade to a toothbrush handle. It might not be
great for stabbing, but it will slice open an uncooperative
person's neck.

Everyone knows what the Vaseline is for.

When women are raped in the free world they are trauma-
tized. But at least they can try coping strategies. They may be
able to change their phone number or their residence, or to
travel. They may turn to friends or family for support. They may
take self-defense courses designed for rape survivors.

When men are raped in prison or forced into regular sexual
service there is little they can do. Often all they can do is try not
to think about the next attack. In my case I quickly learned that
the best way to deal with the situation was to become skilled at
pleasuring my attacker so that he would "finish" as soon as possible. I would try to become involved in choosing the time,
method, etc., so that I would feel that I had some control. I made
the best of what I had to put up with.

While many studies have been done of the impact of rape on
women in the free world, none, to my knowledge, has been done
on prison rape. What are some of the possible long-term psychological effects? How severe and long-lasting might they be
when a person was assaulted every day for several years? What
might be the effects on a person who was periodically "gang-
banged" by multiple attackers? Might the effects be exacerbated
by the knowledge that people are laughing about it, and believe
the attacks are deserved? What kind of life can a prison bitch
expect to lead once he is released?

I can only use myself as an example. And I cannot be absolutely sure which if any of my symptoms stem from my experiences in prison. But I strongly believe that many of my symptoms are the direct result of repeated sexual assault by persons with whom I was forced to live in a small cell for a long period of time.

I've been diagnosed as having Post-Traumatic Stress Disorder. The symptoms are too numerous to list, but here are some of the most important ones:

- Recurrent and intrusive recollections of the event, including distressing images, thoughts, perceptions and dreams
- Reliving the experience and having "flashbacks"
- Intense psychological distress at exposure to cues that symbolize an aspect of the event
- Efforts to avoid activities, places or people that arouse recollections of the trauma
- Diminished interest in participation in significant activities
- Feelings of detachment or estrangement from others
- Sense of foreshortened future (e.g., no expectations of a career, marriage, children, or a normal life span)
- Difficulty falling and staying asleep
- Difficulty concentrating, hyper vigilance and an exaggerated startle response.

I experience a lot of anxiety and, often, panic attacks. I am very uneasy around men. This may be because when I was in prison I learned that almost any man would take advantage of me sexually given the right set of circumstances. Since nearly all men are bigger and stronger than me I view them as potential attackers. I may reason that men in the free world are different, but I do not feel it inside. I do not feel safe around any of them. I am also very uncomfortable around gay men. Simply being around men can make me feel like running away.

I have cognitive problems. I seem not to be able to focus on what I am doing at any given moment. I misplace things, look for things in the wrong places and have trouble identifying objects that I'm looking for. (I may scan a shelf several times looking for an object without seeing it, even though it's in plain view.) I have great difficulty doing tasks that used to be fairly easy, such as typing. I had to correct mistake after mistake while typing this.

I could go on but by now the picture is probably coming into view. I have issues that may take a long time to resolve. Some may not be resolvable. Is my condition a result of the fact that I was recreation for sex-starved inmates? I think that a lot of it is. Are other people being affected in a similar way? I feel that they must be. And what about the lessons being taught to inmates who are allowed to take advantage of their cellmates when lights go out at 10? Will years of indulgence in forced sex have a reha-bilitative effect on them?

The prison industrial complex is supported by tax dollars. It operates the way that it does because people don't object. I was in prison for shoplifting. Should I have been locked in a cell with a guy twice my size and weight who was doing life for a violent crime?

I don't object to having been incarcerated for committing a crime, but I don't think it was right that I was made a gift to another inmate.

I don't think "Prison Bitch" is a very funny song.

ALEXANDER COCKBURN

Pee Wee, Townshend and Ritter

T HE WORSE THE STATE TREATS KIDS, THE MORE THE state's prosecutors chase after inoffensive "perverts" in the private sector who have committed the so-called crime of getting sexual kicks out of images downloaded into their computers or bought as part of an archive of archaic soft-core porn.

Before we get to Paul Reubens, aka Pee Wee Herman, pause to consider the Bush administration's proposed cuts in social services affecting youth, as passed by the Senate in January:

- $60.9 million cut from childcare, meaning access cut for 38,000 kids;
- $29 million cut from after-school programs;
- $13 million cut from programs that help abused and neglected children;
- $3 million cut from children's mental health funding;
- $42 million cut from substance-abuse treatment programs.

All this and more from a president who had the effrontery in his State of the Union address to proclaim the ringing lie, "We will not pass along our problems" to future generations, even as the future generations are scheduled to pick up the tab for his proposed disbursements to the very rich.

Meanwhile, out in California a prosecutor is trying once more to destroy Pee Wee, who took a hit back in 1991 for the awful crime of jacking off in a Sarasota film theater during a showing of *Nancy Nurse*. Reubens pleaded no contest and slowly hauled himself out of the ditch, but last year the shadows gathered round him once more.

His travails were recently described by Richard Goldstein in a brilliant piece in the *Village Voice*. A teenager complained to the LAPD about Reubens and a friend, the actor Jeffrey Jones. Though the complaint was dismissed, cops took occasion to search the homes of both men. Jones is charged with taking pornographic pictures of a juvenile, a felony. Reubens faces a lesser charge: possession. Both have pleaded not guilty.

But what exactly does Reubens "possess"? He collects vintage erotica, mostly gay, with copies of those old physique mags that slaked covert gay fantasies the same way Women of Borneo in *National Geographic* helped out straight kids in the same era. The cops took away 30,000 items for leisurely perusal, leaving behind a further 70,000. The DA concluded there was no case, and it looked as though Pee Wee was in the clear.

Enter a zealous Protector of Youth in the form of the city attorney, Rocky Delgadillo. One day before the one-year statute of limitations expired, Delgadillo issued a warrant for Reubens's arrest. If Reubens gets convicted he could go to prison for a year, and whatever public career he was reconstituting after the Sarasota mishap will no doubt be history. Goldstein writes that the cops told him Reubens had 6,500 hours of videotape, including transfers of vintage 8-millimeter gay films, with some minutes of teenage boys masturbating or having oral sex. Remember, in 1982 the Supreme Court declared child pornography unprotected by the First Amendment, with "porn" encompassing even clothed images of children if they are construed as arousing. "Child" means anyone under 18.

Collectors buy archives in bulk. An archive comes up and you grab it quick. Goldstein cites a California dealer of vintage magazines, who has sold to Reubens, as saying "there's no way" he could have known the content of each page in the publications he bought. In other words, Reubens may get cooked for images he didn't even know he had.

But what if he actually did know what he had? So what?

The state these days nails people for what they have in their computers. Poor Pete Townshend draws a well-publicized escort of no less than 12 police officers to drag him off when he's arrested and absurdly accused of "incitement to distribute" (also a crime here) because the silly ass used a credit card to download images from pedophile sites, which are monitored by the FBI in a vast operation involving multilayered schemes of entrapment. Small wonder the G-men and G-women were too busy to spare any time for urgent memos about Middle Easterners learning how to fly 747s.

In England it's now a criminal act to look at, receive or send any pictures or electronic images of children that the police or other authorities construe as sex related. These photos can be computer-generated, with no relation to any physical being. Scan a hot little Cupid from Bouguereau, tweak it around in Photoshop, and if the cops find it on your laptop you're dead meat.

We're in the twilit world of the "thought crime". Have a photo of a kid in a bath on your hard drive, and the prosecutor says you were looking at it with lust in your heart, and that is tantamount to molesting an actual kid in an actual bath. The possibilities for entrapment are rich indeed. The FBI could send pedophilic images to a target, then rush around, seize his laptop and announce that porn has been found on the hard drive.

Once you're defined as a dirty beast in a raincoat, it's hard to fight back. Look at what's happening to Scott Ritter, entrapped in another Internet sting operation, with the feds now shopping for a suitable jurisdiction in which to nail him again, even though his case was settled and sealed at the state level, before some kind soul in favor of bombing kids in Baghdad leaked the file to the press.

In an admirable article in the London *Daily Telegraph* apropos the Townshend case, Barbara Amiel recently wrote thus:

"Behind our own attitudes lurks a recurring insistence that violent images create violent social behaviour. Since we can't outlaw urges, including urges of paedophilia, we throw our resources into preventing any way in which urges can be gratified. But, if gratification involves nothing else than the viewing of pictures or textual descriptions of the act, making that a criminal offence strikes one as completely insane.

"Shouldn't we start by decriminalising every human act that does not go beyond reading, viewing or listening to representations of acts that if engaged in might be unlawful? Then we could punish with various degrees of severity any deviant acts that cause actual harm".

Sure, there are predators out there, seeking to do young people harm. But don't confuse dreams with deeds, no more than with George Bush's pledge to future generations that "we will not pass along our problems" while his budgets and his war plans inflict on so many young lives.

STEVE PERRY

Unsafe at Any Speed: Youth, Sex and the Heresies of Judith Levine

O N THE SHELF IN MY FOURTH GRADE CLASSROOM— north wall, near the front—there sat the obligatory set of junior encyclopedias. Now and again during lulls in afternoon study time, either Brenda S. or I would go and retrieve the R volume. Then, sitting across the aisle from each other near the back of the room, we proceeded to inspect together the diagrams of the human reproductive system.

The details of interior plumbing were of no particular interest to us, but we always lingered over the sketched male and female forms that surrounded them like sausage casings—the ample, pendulous breasts on one side, the dejected-looking penis on the other—while exchanging the occasional meaningful look.

I remember it as well as Proust recalled his madeleines; it was one of the more worthwhile experiences of my elementary school years. Nowadays, alas, it would be grounds for throwing one or both of us in the kiddie calaboose and tattooing "Sex Offender" on our foreheads.

Do I exaggerate? Not by much.

Judith Levine's endlessly reviled *Harmful to Minors: the Perils of Protecting Children from Sex* contains numerous stories of youngsters branded sexual predators and forced into humiliating regimens of "counseling" for behavior no less benign. Surely by now you have heard of Levine's book, published a couple of months ago by the University of Minnesota Press after being declined by a string of commercial publishers; before the ink was dry, pols and shrinks were rising as one to condemn it.

The charge? Soft on child sex abuse, which in the present climate is as good as being soft on communism (and lord, how we miss communism) or brown-skinned terrorists.

Levine's book is actually a fine and brave effort at putting into perspective various matters regarding children, adolescents, sex, sex abuse and sex education.

It's true that Levine seeks to debunk much of the child sex-abuse hysteria that has been causing convulsions all round the US since the spate of day care sex abuse scandals in Jordan, Minnesota, and across the country in the 1980s.

Although those cases proved to be fictions promulgated by zealous interrogators and small children anxious to please them, the stranger with candy—the adult predator seeking children to sodomize, or worse—has become one of our more durable icons and useful political props.

Levine commits two principal heresies against right-thinking. First, she asserts that the stranger with candy is not really the problem we make him out to be. (On the special matter of priests with candy-who can scarcely be called strangers-more in a second.) She notes that a great many reports of extrafamilial "sex abuse" involve consensual liaisons between adolescents a little below the age of consent and boyfriends or girlfriends a little above it.

As regards the great bogeyman in all this, the pedophile moving with stealth through Internet chat rooms, she makes two interesting points: first, that the manufacture and distribution of kiddie porn through the Internet is controlled almost exclusively by police agencies running sting operations (an LAPD detective is quoted boasting as much); and second, that the National Center for Missing and Exploited Children places the total number of reported adult/adolescent assignations arranged through the Internet from 1994-96 at a whopping 23. The Internet was young then; if you assume the number has tripled or quadrupled with the growth of online households since then, you come to 50 or so cases a year across the entire country.

Hardly the epidemic we're led to believe, particularly when you bear in mind that a high proportion of these involve nerdy guys not much over the age of consent and lonely girls not much under. (And no, I am not saying I'd like to see my own child in one of those relationships—but then again it's hardly the portrait of the Internet Stalker we are routinely presented, is it?)

The grand and terrible irony is that child sexual abuse remains as real a problem as ever. But it's not the stranger with candy putting kids at risk; the vast majority of such abuse occurs in or near the home at the hands of male adults in positions of authority and trust-the father, the uncle and, to a far greater extent than even the most cynical supposed, the parish priest.

Levine's second heresy is her belief that post-pubescent teens are bound to explore sex, entitled to do so and perfectly capable of having constructive sexual experiences. In these abstinence-only days, parents do not like the idea that their kids are sexual beings for many reasons, some practical and worthy and some selfish and narrow. The abstinence movement, notes Levine, is partly about "reversing, or at least holding back, the coming of age, which for parents is a story of loss, as their children establish passionate connections with people and values outside the family".

This being America, we should also ask how many parents do not feel a pin-prick of resentment over their kids' newfound power to explore pleasures unsanctioned by the parent. So it's hardly surprising they'd rather tell their kids not to think of it.

But in the age of AIDS and of dwindling abortion rights, "child protection" of this sort comes at a terrific cost.

JoAnn Wypijewski

It's a Sex Thing

TOWARD THE BACK OF THE GAY PRIDE PARADE IN NEW York on June 29, 2003, a group of rickshaws tooled around bearing happy couples, some with wedding garb or at least flower bouquets, followed by a white stretch limo draped in pink net and paper bells. They called themselves The Wedding Party and passed out stickers saying "It's a Love Thing", and, as if with a clear of the throat, "and a legal thing".

A few days earlier I was in Sheridan Square amid the throng celebrating the Supreme Court's 6-3 decision in the case of *Lawrence v. Texas*, striking down the nation's remaining sodomy laws and overruling the odious 1986 decision in *Bowers v. Hardwick*. There was a lot of talk of love and legality that evening too, references to wedding rings as the next battle cry, bows to Vermont and Canada—though City Councilwoman Margarita Lopez raised a cheer too with her drawn-out and vaguely dirty-sounding pronunciation of "for-ni-ca-tion!" Love and sex, liberty and law, yoked in the eternal push-pull. The other day *Newsweek* had a cover story bemoaning sexless marriage, apparently become the norm among straight professionals too exhausted by the job, the house and the endless round of children's activities; now the people who brought us sexual freedom, gender-bending and a new definition of family are plumping for the marriage contract.

Of course, expecting gay people to be society's sex mavericks is a little like expecting black people to be its social conscience. It's not homosexuals' life mission to provide heterosexuals with models for the myriad possibilities of human sexuality. (Though who but the most pinched fundamentalist couldn't take delight in contemplating the cultural etymology of the film *Bend Over*,

Boyfriend, which a couple of years ago became the top-selling straight porn video, as marrieds in the Heartland discovered the joys of the strap-on?) And, of course, gay people want to get married for the same reason straight ones do: the health insurance, the tax benefits, the children, the property rights. Like any dewy-eyed romantic, the woman who publicly proposed to her girlfriend at the end of the Pride parade probably wasn't thinking about legal separation, divorce, lawyers' fees, the piece on the side or any of the other less-alluring accoutrements of state-sanctioned union. No one likes to dwell on it, but the marriage system could survive just fine without white tulle and roses; it would collapse without divorce and adultery.

It's unlikely gay marriage would change that, though things are clearly desperate in the straight world when no less a conservative than *New York Times* columnist William Safire hopes it will. The family's a wreck, spouses are splitting and people don't even have Thanksgiving at home anymore. In this dire situation, "maybe competition from responsible gays would revive opposite-sex marriage", Safire writes, imagining a new kind of keeping up with the Joneses. He must have missed the recent report in his own paper about the tribulations of out-of-state couples who journeyed to Vermont for their civil union a few years ago and now, their bliss gone bad, are hard-pressed to get out of it because dissolution requires state residency. "There's a thin line between love and hate", as the man sang, and no law or convention has yet been devised to make it otherwise. On the heels of The Wedding Party in the Pride parade came the Anti-Violence Project with its banner on domestic abuse. Vickie, a counselor with the project, reported what I've heard from people who do the same work among heterosexuals: especially since 9-11, battering cases have spiked up. What with economic calamity and fear of life-out -of-control, love is too thin a reed to hold all it's expected to, with or without devotion by legal contract.

It's all too bad that the *Lawrence* decision has devolved to a discussion of marriage, because what it articulated was far more profound. It no more suggested a right to marry than it asserted a right to engage in sodomy, but it did affirm something that has been at the core of gay liberation, and that has been unappreciated by many straight leftists and liberals who always thought the sex talk was secondary to the really big issues. Justice Kennedy, who wrote the majority opinion, is too starched to say "Everything begins with sex", but how else to interpret his assertion that "when homosexual conduct is made criminal by the law of the state, that declaration in and of itself is an invitation to subject homosexual persons to discrimination both in the public and in the private spheres"? In other words, if the state can criminalize and demonize, control, threaten and persecute persons in the most intimate sphere of life, it can do anything: deny them jobs, housing, equality, respect, safety, liberty, happiness. Indeed, it does all those things. What the Court did was pull out one of the major struts supporting compulsory heterosexuality; by embracing Justice John Paul Stevens' dissent in *Bowers,* which asserted that the Due Process Clause of the 14th Amendment "extends to intimate choices by unmarried as well as married persons", it also rang a chime for sexual freedom against the claims of conventionalists, straight and gay, who would have us all in little boxes run round with the picket fence.

After the Sheridan Square rally, I bumped into a friend of *CounterPunch,* an adamant sex radical with a highly developed sense of the sour. He was fulminating that people were celebrating even though "if I pulled my dick out in Washington Square right now I could still be arrested!" What he meant, upon clarification, was that were he discovered having sex in the park Men's Room, the police could cart him and the other fellow off to jail and the Court's decision would not affect that in the least. Moreover, the gay cheerleaders for marriage would let them rot. He's quite right, but then who would expect the Supreme Court, establishment poo-bah of probity, to sanction sex in public toilets? Who would want it to? Most people who have sex in such private public spaces, whether Washington Square or the Oval Office, don't do so because they have no bedroom. It's all about the danger, the allure of anonymity, the prospect of getting caught but not quite. Domesticate that and the thrill really is gone. It is an exquisitely delicate game, to be sure. Dangerous desires are not usually the same as wanting actual danger. Police in New York once understood this and looked the other way; not so since Giuliani time, with "quality of life" policing, sex district demolition and vice busts. But it will take something more thoroughgoing than a Supreme Court decision to put that kind of fun back in Fun City.

As it is, Justice Antonin Scalia, writing for the dissent, recognized the potential reach of the decision more than even many of those who praised it. The State of Texas had claimed that it had the right to control anyone's sexuality outside of marriage; homosexuals just happened to be the target here. And Scalia, for all his ranting about the "homosexual agenda", was angered fundamentally by the majority's rejection of that control. Sanction sodomy, he said, and you might as well eliminate laws against adultery, masturbation, bestiality, prostitution. Privilege privacy, he didn't quite say, and you might as well uphold abortion rights. Champion liberty, and you undermine the repressive power of the state. "There is no right to 'liberty' under the Due Process Clause", he flatly stated.

And then, proving that there really is a syntax of bigotry which sustains itself across the eras and that the next logical battle is over full civil rights, he wrote, "Many Americans do not want persons who openly engage in homosexual conduct as partners in their business, as scoutmasters for their children, as teachers in their children's schools, or as boarders in their home." As it happened, the same day he made that declaration from the bench, Strom Thurmond died in South Carolina. And the same day's paper that reprinted Scalia's dissent remembered the old racist's stump speech for president in 1948: "On the question of social intermingling of the races, our people draw the line.... All the laws of Washington and all the bayonets of the Army cannot force the Negro into our homes, into our schools, our churches and our places of recreation and amusement." When Strom said that, an awful lot of white folks of means had Negroes in their homes, cooking their food, tending their aged, rearing their children. They just didn't have Negroes in their beds, which was always a prime fear. Then as now, it was a sex thing.

As the parade ended and people poured into the Greenwich Village streets, I saw a skinny white boy and a skinny black boy, maybe 16, both shirtless, arm in arm, looking around in wonder. Anywhere else in the city, or any other time, they couldn't be so street-innocent, never mind so sweetly affectionate. What was remarkable for me, not having been to a Pride parade in a few years, was that they, we, were walking in a sea of youth and color: all these little hip-hoppers with baggy basketball jerseys and cubix zirconia ear studs; Asian boys with slim hips and spikey hair; butch black and Latina girls and their fem-boy or girl friends all in a gang; big nut-colored women, fleshy and some without shirts, only bright pink stickers on their nipples saying "My Bedroom, My Business"; beautiful young black men exercised to a heroic ideal, raggedy deaf kids of indeterminate race; dred-locked Caribbeans, an Asian drag queen done up in peacock feathers; a white bearded guy done up like an aging Guinevere; a Venezuelan crew, outfitted in tight faux tiger skins, their chests a-glitter, their skulls crowned by pre-Columbian-style feather headdresses, their hands gripping staffs topped with arcing black marabou and a tiger 's face. Note to Al Sharpton: the young brothers and sisters are out and many (and had only Dean and Kerry signs to look at). Note to the peace crowd: "Feygelehs Against the Occupation" cut neatly through the "complexities" of the Middle East; "Israel Out of Palestine", "More Fucking, Less Killing", "Sodomy, Not Imperialism" were their frisky cries. Note to the marriage crowd: the young things I spoke with weren't convinced their heart's desire lay in replicating straight coupledom.

As I headed home, I saw an overweight leather man leading his masked "slave", mostly naked but for a few well-placed strips of black leather, by his neck chain through a crowd of lusty lesbians and into a bar. It was bracing to see some things haven't changed.

Dr. Susan Block

Covering Justice:
Ashcroft's Breast Fetish

S EEMS OL' CRABBY, CRAFTY AYATOLLAH ASHCROFT IS
testing our ability to withstand his craftiness, and
proving himself to be every bit the Ass 'n' Ayatollah we
were afraid he'd be. Over the past few months, especially since
9/11, he has been doing this in some serious life- and liberty-
threatening ways.

But Ashcroft's latest destruction of liberty and justice
involves suppression of liberty for the Spirit of Justice. That is,
he has ordered to be covered up a rather large, lovely statue
named the "Spirit of Justice" that has towered behind American
attorneys general for some 70 years. With a set of $8,000 drapes
(prudery isn't cheap), he has turned the Spirit of Justice into the
Spirit of Censorship.

See, the "Spirit of Justice" is naked. Well, topless. Actually,
half-topless. One breast (looking to be a rather nice, round, C
cup complete with perky nipple) is revealed, the other concealed
by a Grecian-style tunic, giving our gal just a bit more coverage
than her male counterpart, the "Majesty of Justice", who has
nothing but a loincloth sheathing his majestic manhood. These
huge aluminum statues were constructed during the 1930s
under FDR, and were strongly influenced by the Art Deco movement of the times, as well as, perhaps, the taste of certain
Democrats. According to Beverly Lumpkin of ABC News, the
lady statue has been fondly referred to for years as "Minnie
Lou".

Minnie Lou is not exactly a sexpot. I imagine that the Art
Deco sculptor who created her had more than pure prurience on
his or her mind. More of an Athena (Warrior Goddess of

Wisdom) than an Aphrodite (Sexy Goddess of Sex), she exudes power and dignity. Minnie's partial nudity is part of her power, her purity, her naturalness, her truth and, thus, her spirit of justice.

Now, thanks to the American Ayatollah, Minnie and her counterpart (Mickey?) have both been covered up, shrouded like ghosts, depriving the common people of our right even to glimpse these glorious feminine and masculine symbols of American Justice rising up out of the deep Depression in all their shiny aluminum splendor.

What kind of prudish, priggish, self-conscious ass would do such a thing?

Even former Attorney General Edwin Meese didn't cover up the perennially half-topless Minnie Lou. Of course, her gloriously bare boob did seem to mock the presentation of Meese's report on his commission on pornography. Minnie Lou has been in the Great Hall for over 70 years to remind us that the Spirit of Justice is naked, at least partially.

Ashcroft has already shown himself to be awfully Ayatollah-like in his draconian Patriot Act, which strips civil liberties from American citizens, and in his Torture-Lite approach to the "detainees" at Guantanamo Bay. Now he appears to be adopting the mullahs' mode of dealing with the complexities posed by the human female body: Cover it up, get it out of sight, and get on with the manly business of oppression, power-grabbing and punishment.

I can just imagine him thundering to his staff (pun intended): "If the Taliban can cover up their women, then by God Almighty, we can cover up our half-topless female statues!!"

After all, Ayatollah Ashcroft is just one man, and he can't run around this great gigantic country of ours covering up the millions of bare bosoms of nudists, topless dancers and sculptures throughout the US (though that's coming...). But, by Jesus, he can cover up the flagrantly bare bosom of the lady statue that

towers over him during his all-important speeches to pesky journalists and left-leaning photographers who like nothing better
than to snap a nice shot of Minnie Titty rising above the dour
Ashcroft visage.

But $8,000 for drapes? Whew, that's an expensive burka.

I guess we should be grateful he didn't blow Minnie up like
the Taliban did the Bamian Buddhas.

But it makes you wonder. Does Ashcroft's cover-up of the
Spirit of Justice signify his tendency to "cover up" other things?
Though the Spirit of Justice is more Athena than Aphrodite, she
is a beautiful, powerful woman. Covering her and her consort
up in this already Dark Age projects gloom and oppression. Is
that the message Ashcroft wants to send? Or is it that he just
can't help himself?

Obviously, he's got a problem with nudity. Now, I would
never force a person to stand in front of a naked statue if it really
made him or her uncomfortable. But Ashcroft knew all about
the Spirit of Justice when he accepted the job of Attorney
General. He shouldn't have taken the job if he didn't like the
trappings. But of course, one of the reasons Ashcroft probably
wanted the job (other than the fact that he'd just lost the
Missouri Senator's race to a dead man) was because of his
driving lust to cover up Minnie and generally restrain all liberties, except the freedom to pray.

Extreme prudery in any religion is fertile soil for fanaticsm,
just a hair's breath from terrorism. The most successful and
despicable alleged terrorist of our time, Mohammed Atta, is a
case-in-point for prudery gone amok. Here was a man who
wouldn't even shake a woman's hand (though there are rumors
of him hiring hookers), wouldn't even look at a woman. A room-
mate's girlfriend taunted Atta by hanging a reproduction of a
Degas nude above the toilet in their shared apartment. Atta tried
to ignore it for a couple of months, then tersely asked his room-
mate, not the girlfriend, to remove it. Many mysteries of 9/11

remain to be solved, and surely there are a multitude of personal, political and economic reasons why this atrocity occurred.
But one small yet powerful cause seems to have been the deep
anti-sex, anti-female feelings of this man, his abhorrence for
women, for nudity, for Eros, for life. It is ironic that the attack
would put another sexual repressive of a different religion into
the spotlight, enabling him to grasp greater powers than ever.

But, since irony is dead (long live irony), it just seems sadly
predictable. Thanatos leads to Thanatos. Atta leads to Ashcroft.
Until a preponderance of us are fed up enough to respond to
Thanatos with Eros. Things seem pretty bleak these days, but I
believe we can do it, even now, in the depths of our terror. Just
as there's a little bit of yin in every yang, there's always a little bit
of Eros in Thanatos times.

I call upon some brave and crazy soul, some truly patriotic
citizen to run into our Hall of Justice, tear down those $8,000
drapes (gently, please, don't damage them) and set the Spirit of
Justice and her beloved Majesty free!

And if that's considered a terrorist act, so be it.

Angelina Jolie and the French Revolution

INCE THE FINELY HONED INTELLECT, NOT TO MENTION exuberant body, of Angelina Jolie have become an object of vulgar interest to many of our associates, we turned eagerly to Britain's *News of the World* for an update on the star of *Tomb Raider*. Sunday's edition of the Murdoch-owned tabloid is full of ripe detail about Angelina's self-confessed sexual tastes, plus admiring commentary from her husband, Billy Bob Thornton, and former co-star Elizabeth Mitchell, who appeared with her in a movie about lesbian supermodel Gia Carangi, and who sighed to the *News of the World*: "Angelina's got such beautiful lips and they're all her own. She's all real. She's a work of nature".

It depends how you define nature. Perhaps they were still part of the original bodywork when Angelina and Elizabeth embraced each other, but since then Angelina's breasts have clearly been into the bodyshop for an upgrade. Part of our painful duty as investigative journalists has been to spend wearisome hours comparing various photographs of Angelina's breasts, as available for inspection on the internet. Clearly, one set has the tedious soup-plate symmetry of artificial enhancement, in contrast to the somewhat less ample, but erotically more pleasing tits of an earlier era.

It seems that Billy Bob hires a nurse to extract his blood so he can send droplets to Angelina when she is away filming. She wears it in an ampule around her neck. Chic, and reminiscent of the red threads the fast set of young aristocrats used to wear round their necks in late eighteenth-century France, in the

Directoire period. The threads were an ironic homage to the guillotine on which many of their relatives had perished.

The *News of the World* tells us that this daughter of Jon Voigt and French actress Marcheline Bertrand, born in Los Angeles, "spent much of her childhood living out of suitcases. At 14 she began to rebel and had a live-in boyfriend at her mother's house. She also began mutilating herself with knives". Tattooing is another enthusiasm. An inventory: 1) Dragon on left arm; 2) Cross on thigh; 3) H on left wrist; 4) Dragon with tribal design on lower back; 5) Japanese symbol for death on shoulder; 6) Cross on lower front hip; 7) "Quod me nutrit me destruit" on stomach [Latin for What nourishes me also destroys me]; 8) Courage ... was removed 8) Blue box on lower back, center; 9) "A prayer for the wild at heart, kept in cages",Tennessee Williams quote on left inside forearm; 10) Billy Bob above dragon on left shoulder.

In harmony with her teenage habit, Angelina and Billy Bob keep a knife under their pillow to slash at each other during sex sessions. They spent last Christmas happily cutting their fingers and daubing messages in blood on the walls above their bed. "I was looking at her asleep", Mr Thornton confides to the *News of the World* reporters, "and I had to restrain myself from literally squeezing her to death. Sex for us is almost too much. It's so intense that sometimes we can look at each other and think, 'We can't get into this right now or something's going to happen.'"

Over the breakfast table, the *News of the World* reports, he confessed to her that he had come close to doing her in the night before. "Angelina added: 'You know when you love someone so much you can almost kill them? I nearly was killed one night, and it was the nicest thing anyone has ever said to me!'"

Oh well, knives for some, ear plugs and eye blinders for others. Angelina and Billy Bob's stated preferences somehow made us think of Balzac's novella, *La Duchesse de Langeais* in which a beastly sensualist called Montriveau plots to turn the duchess into his love slave. Irked by her caprices Montriveau has her abducted from a ball to his apartment where he informs her that as a punishment she is to be branded on the forhead with a red-hot iron (shaped as a cross of Lorraine), which three masked pals of his are even now heating up in the next room.

Greatly to Montriveau's mortification the duchess is thrilled with the plan. "Ah! My Armand, mark, mark quickly your creature as a poor little possession.... When you have thus marked a woman as your own, when you have an enslaved creature wearing your red cipher, oh, then you can never give her up, you will be forever mine.... But the woman who loves always marks herself. Come gentlemen, come and mark, mark the Duchesse de Langeais. Come quickly, all of you, my forehead burns hotter than your red brand".

Under this eager torrent of verbiage Montriveau's ardor wilts and he loses "faith" in his whole plan. We think there could be the germ of a script here for Angelina and Billy Bob, though maybe they're more interested in Geoffrey Wolf's book *Black Sun: The Brief Transit and Violent Eclipse of Harry Crosby*, about the love-unto-death affair of Harry Crosby and Josephine Bigelow, in the months after the stock market went through the cellar in the fall of 1929.

In December, Crosby and Mrs. Bigelow took a five-day trip to Detroit. Wolff writes: "...they checked into the Book-Cadillac [Hotel] on December 3, registering as Mr. and Mrs. Harry Crane in a twelve-dollar-a-day room on the twentieth floor. Most of their meals they took in bed, where they also smoked opium, made love and battled".

On December 7 the lovers returned to New York where they agreed that Mrs. Bigelow should return to Boston to her husband. But Josephine did not return to Boston and on December 9 she had delivered a 36-line poem to Crosby who was staying with his wife Caresse at the Savoy-Plaza Hotel. The last line of the poem is: "Death is our marriage".

On December 9, Harry Crosby made the following entries into his notebooks: "One is not in love unless one desires to die with one's beloved. There is only one happiness it is to love and to be loved". These were Crosby's very last entries into his journal, because on December 10, after shooting Josephine, Harry Crosby shot himself a few hours later. Wolff sums it up thus: "He had meant to do it; it was no mistake; it was not a joke. If anything of Harry Crosby commands respects, perhaps even awe, it was the unswerving character of his intention".

Crosby always struck us as a horrible little twerp, but Angelina and Billy Bob could surely make something of all this.

Returning to that red thread and the guillotine, the common view is that many thousands of French aristos perished under the blade. Not true. Greer's statistical study *The Incidence of the Terror,* published in 1935, shows that 666 nobles got the chop in Paris and another 1,543 in the rest of France. Compare that with the carnage after the destruction of the Paris commune of 1871 when some 20,000 Communards were executed.

The best defense of the French Revolution and its excesses is surely that of Mark Twain in *A Connecticut Yankee:* "There were two 'Reigns of Terror' if we would remember it and consider it; the one wrought murder in hot passion, the other in heartless cold blood; the one lasted mere months, the other had lasted a thousand years; the one inflicted death upon ten thousand persons, the other upon a hundred millions; but our shudders are all for the 'horrors' of the minor Terror, the momentary Terror, so to speak; whereas, what is the horror of swift death by the axe, compared with lifelong death from hunger, cold, insult, cruelty and heart-break? What is swift death by lightning compared with death by slow fire at the stake? A city cemetery could contain the coffins filled by that brief Terror which we have all been so diligently taught to shiver at and mourn over; but all France could hardly contain the coffins filled by that older and real Terror—that unspeakably bitter and awful Terror which none of us have been taught to see in its vastness or pity as it deserves".

And to think that Lewis Lapham dared put Tom Wolfe on the cover of *Harper's* next to the man who wrote those tremendous lines! Come to think about it, Angelina and Billy Bob could do a movie about Charlotte Corday's stabbing of Marat in his bath. Corday was a counterrevolutionary of course. Despite this the crowd around the guillotine was shocked when the executioner had fun with her severed head and pulled her features about. Supposedly, Corday's face blushed, prompting two centuries worth of debate on whether the guillotine was, in fact, a quick death or a kind of vivisection.

The Jacobins were terrified of female radicals. Olympe de Gouges, author of *Les Droits de la femme et de la citoyenne* (1891), perished on the guillotine not long thereafter, as did Madam Roland. St Just invoked the "male energy" of the Republic.

In his interesting 1993 book *Bodywork*, Peter Brooks wrote, "In the cult of Marat Charlotte Corday is present only in that gash in Marat's breast, a kind of displaced representation of her woman's sex as a wound on the martyred man. David's painting, *Marat Assassiné*, says it all: the ecstatic face of the martyr, the drops of blood on the immaculate sheet, the quill pen still grasped next to the kitchen knife fallen on the floor, the bathwater become a pool of blood... all these elements suggest the intrusion of ungoverned female sexuality on a life dedicated to the higher cause". And now, with Angelina, ungoverned female sexuality and the higher cause are one!

Epilogue: BillyBob was untrue and Angelina threw him out. He's gone into eclipse. She's doing fine.

SUSAN DAVIS

A Visit to the Kinsey Institute

I AM OFF TO BLOOMINGTON IN SOUTH-CENTRAL INDIANA, further on the trail of Gershon Legman, social critic, sex researcher, writer and folklorist. In the 1940s, before his exile in France, Legman worked in New York as a book buyer, a bibliophilic-go-between and researcher for Alfred C. Kinsey, the Indiana University biologist whose *Sexual Behavior in the Human Male* blew open American ideas about what people do behind closed doors. There's an especially rich trove of Legman's brilliant, polemical letters and folk pornography at the Kinsey Institute here.

Indiana 41 is a dangerous road, and I'm a danger to myself when I stop to photograph the frequent roadside crosses, so I push on, cutting through the faded limestone glory of Greencastle, over the bench land to the White Valley. The smoky bottomlands, where they're burning slash, are lulling, and I'm listening to Ralph Stanley, hallowed banjo player and high-lonesome singer, trying to decide which is the best on his new album of old songs. They're all good, but "False Hearted Lover's Blues" is a classic, a "come all ye" warning about the faithlessness of women in general:

> *They'll bite the hand that feeds you,*
> *Spend the money that you save.*
> *With your heart strings and silk garters,*
> *They'll build a doghouse on your grave.*

From Ellertsville it's all strip services into Bloomington. I find my way to the Memorial Union, next to Ernie Pyle Hall, his typewriter on display in the window. There's still time to change clothes and catch a few hours at the Archive.

But getting into the Kinsey Institute is harder than it looks. The collections and research work there are so provocative that gentle barriers have been set up to make sure no one wanders in casually. I've been here before, and I've called ahead, but it's still surprisingly tricky. You go in the front door of Morrison Hall, the biology building, and the Archive is on the fourth floor. But there are no stairs after the second floor, and the Kinsey Institute is walled off from the rest of the building, as if its contents could not be allowed to seep into other scholarly operations. You have to take an elevator to the third-floor so a receptionist can look you over; but since the elevator doesn't go to the fourth floor during working hours, you have to work your way up a tiny set of winding stairs, through more doors and then into the reading room.

Unexpected developments interfere with my work. The Archive is having its annual unannounced book sale (no dealers invited), clearing out its duplicate copies of everything from Krafft-Ebbing to eighth-rate porn. It takes time to figure out what I might want to buy. "We've got to get this stuff out of here!" Shawn Wilson, user services coordinator, tells me. "We have such a space problem". They do, because Kinsey collected everything remotely relevant to human sexuality, from personal diaries to pre-Columbian sculpture. For decades many other collectors of material considered obscene, illegal or degenerate have sent their treasures here, knowing they would not be burned or thrown out with the trash. The ice sheet of the 1950s pushed a lot of eccentrics Kinsey's way.

The archive isn't just a remarkable collection of books about sex, and it doesn't just contain Kinsey's voluminous papers. It's jammed with scrapbooks and manuscripts of all kinds. Then there's his data reservoir of tens of thousands of face-to-face interviews with people about their sexual histories. Kinsey's interview technique, carefully designed to preserve total anonymity, tried to break down reserve and banish embarrassment. He fired the questions at his subjects, relentlessly corralling unanswered questions ("let's try this again: when was the first time you had sex with an animal?") but his sympathetic acceptance produced unusual honesty on touchy subjects.

Over the years, Kinsey and his staff compiled an enormous and liberating database of information about what people actually did, rather than what they were supposed to do. It was Kinsey's research that demonstrated that about 10 percent of the US population was homosexual; bisexual himself, he revealed the frequency of bisexuality. He helped people accept masturbation as a normal adult practice, not a disease of childhood. He drove the final nail in the coffin of the myth of the vaginal orgasm. He found that a lot of people rarely have sex. Some of his interviewees were willing to keep sex diaries for him. And there are endless letters, because Kinsey encouraged people to stay in touch with him. Especially after the publication of *The Human Male*, people often wrote asking if their behavior, or their children's behavior, was normal.

This can seem like a collecting mania, but in many ways it made sense. Kinsey started his career as a field biologist, a positivist par excellence, spending years chasing down every subspecies of gall wasp. When he changed his focus to sex he followed the same strategy, operating on the vacuum cleaner principle, scooping up information and artifacts almost indiscriminately, on the theory that no one could know what might prove useful in the future. Towards the end he seems to have been unable to stop collecting. He most likely worked himself to death. Still, vacuum cleaner mode is not a bad scientific method when the problem is range and variation. Five decades after his death provocative books on previously unthought-of topics are still coming out of the Kinsey.

Because the book sale takes up so much of the reading room, they've assigned me to work in the John Money seminar room, two floors down (elevator and stairs again), back through con fusing corridors. Every day I must lock up everything except the tape recorder I use to take notes, collect a pile of old letters from Shawn, and zigzag through this labyrinth to the Money room, making the same journey in reverse at the mandatory lunch hour, back again after 1 PM, and repeat the same route at closing time.

But it's more than inconvenient, it's disorienting because along those two back hallways are displayed samples of Alfred Kinsey's remarkable collection of erotic art. Images of every sort of sexual activity, solitary, coupled or group, fantastic or realistic, have been pulled from the vaults and put up on the walls. I almost can't make it to the Money room, the display is so distracting. There are cheap French postcards, portraits of strippers, and posters for 1950s B movies like *I Want More!* There are Picasso lithographs, and paintings by Matisse and Chagall, and silver gelatin photographs of the imaginable and the unimaginable. There's a Michel Fingesten bookplate showing a woman watering a phallus tree; it sprouts little penises. I'm especially struck by an urgent ink brush close-up of a man, fully clothed, masturbating in a street. And an etching of a reclining nude, an odalisque. She spirals, pointing her face, an elbow and one breast upward, her back and heart-shaped rump to the artist. It's obvious he loved her.

The Money room is distracting, too. Money was an early expert on transexualism. Not only is it full of his books, but it contains his own erotic art collection, and here I am trying to concentrate on publication dates. I rush through that first afternoon feeling overwhelmed. Tonight as every night when I leave, exhausted from staring at dead people's handwriting, a weird carillon begins to play. It must be an experimental music project, but it sounds like a child whacking an out-of-tune xylophone as it echoes through the campus woods. But Bloomington has reasonable restaurants and bars, and I can recuperate with a glass of wine over Thai or Yugoslav food, or just a steak. Then to bed, sleeping uneasily and longing to head out to Bean Blossom, an hour away, where Ralph Stanley and the Clinch Mountain Boys are playing this weekend.

Over three days I make the corridor trip at least 24 times, and its effect on me begins to shift. At first I'm stopped in my tracks by the frankness, the beauty of pictures of people making love or simply displaying their bodies in so many different ways. Later I'm distracted by them, wanting to read the carefully composed labels about the artists and subjects. The next thing I know I'm taking notes. And I'm not supposed to be taking notes on erotica this trip, but concentrating on some finer points of folklore publishing history.

At the outset, working at the Kinsey comes as a relief. Everyone is so matter of fact about sex. You could ask to see a manuscript on anything—bestiality among the industrial elite of Indianapolis, for example—and the staff wouldn't bat an eye. They would simply drop it on your desk and say, "Anything else we can get you?" There's a kind of comfort in this, given our Puritan inheritance. Catherine Johnson, curator of the art collection, is kind enough to give me a personal tour of the locked museum, which includes an amazing collection of colored, specialty condoms preserved in glass vials of nitrogen gas and an extensive selection of fetish footwear. Kinsey's art collection, she tells me, holds 7,000 works and artifacts, 48,000 photographs and documents. And that's not counting films and "special collections". I retreat to my room for a nap. Don't let anybody tell you it's easy working immersed in erotica.

Then, a day later, I begin to get giddy, as if I've had too much champagne. I make a crude joke to Shawn about the Money room's decor: "What is this, the Penetration from the Rear Room"? Shawn's not getting my joke. "No", he answers, puzzled. "I told you, it's the Money room". Does this mean that after a while it all becomes just wallpaper to the Kinsey staff? Not really, director Liana Zhou says. "It becomes normal to us because it's part of life. We just think it's really beautiful". Lucky Liana. Her office is adorned with Japanese color wood block prints, pages from giant pillow books.

Finally, on day three, it all starts to grate. On my final exit, as I glance at the headless masturbator and my charming odalisque, a voice inside me snarls, "Oh, why don't you just COVER UP!" Where did that voice come from?

The problem is displacement. Everything stashed at the Kinsey was once stashed somewhere else. In a shoe box in the back of a closet, in a vault, under the bed. Whether fine art or junk, it was originally somebody's "special stuff", used who knows how—as a turn on, entertainment or consolation. Now the catalogs and exhibits throw neutral museum light on what was once trash, or delectably furtive, but here promoted to Art. "All of the fingerprints have been cleaned off; there are no tattered corners, no signs of use and love. I guess the Kinsey's walls say "It's all really okay". It's okay to have this stuff, and it's OK to do this stuff. Certainly that was what Alfred Kinsey's published research said, and what he wanted to say, as he sought to breach every sexual boundary of his own. And yet, there are still all those barriers and locked doors and special permissions needed...

I scoop up my tapes and hike over to First and Jordan to take a look at the house Kinsey built. Just an ordinary brick ranch house but here, in a special room, Kinsey began to add film of people having sex to his databank: an assistant shot untold reels of film of people, sometimes Kinsey's graduate students, sometimes Kinsey himself with a volunteer, getting it on. Sometimes he simply watched and took notes.

Few of Kinsey's methods would pass muster with the prudish and litigation-phobic University Human Subjects Committees today, including his apparent stipulation that men who worked with him prove they were "unbiased" about homosexuality by having sex with him and each other. It's unknown whether the few female members of his research team had to pass similar tests. If wives and girlfriends objected to the bisexual group marriage of the research team, as they occasionally did, their feelings were largely ignored.

A young man comes out of the house to ask if I need help. "Can I take a photo?" Sure. "Do a lot of people stop to ask if this is Dr. Kinsey's house?" All the time, says the blasé college student.

Then I head home, this time straight on I-74, listening to Ralph Stanley again and contemplating traditional music's view of sex. It's graphic, but it's not about how many rules can be broken. Dr. Stanley has been recently saved in the Primitive Baptist Church, and some fans say it's opened up his vocal style. For Ralph Stanley there are only the 10 old rules and the old songs are terse stories about people who break most of them. When Lord Arnold's wife seduces Mathie Grove right there in church one Sunday "the like had never been done", that's all. There are the brusque consequences. When Lady Arnold defies her husband,

> He took her by the hair of her head
> And led her through the hall
> With his sword, cut off her head
> And kicked it against the wall.

The old story songs have a matter-of-fact brutality, even though they're worn smooth from years of singing.

At 75 Ralph Stanley is more than a generation younger than Alfred Kinsey. Stanley grew up in Virginia. Kinsey was originally from the East Coast, practically a New Yorker, but he did his real work from then-provincial Bloomington. As I cruise down towards the Wabash, I ponder the two men: Kinsey the modernist, building a sexual science, Stanley, the traditionalist, reinterpreting an old sound and present at the birth of a new one, bluegrass. Each did his own most creative work in the cold, cold years of the middle twentieth century. How was it that the heartland made a home for them both?

JoAnn Wypijewski
Let Them Perfect Love-Making...

SOMEWHERE IN ROME, CUTTING A PATH, IF MEMORY serves, from the area of Largo Argentina to the Pantheon, is a mere sliver of a street whose shops cater to the trade of the Catholic religious. One finds there a representation of the psychosexual orders of the church as exquisite as the real-life manifestation is corrupt. In one half of a typical shop-front window might be a grey lambswool cardigan, mannish overcoat, sensible black shoes, maybe a bit of pale blue amid the white cotton blouses; in the other half, yards of draped brocade, a fringed stole, silken colors as glistening as the arrangement of silver and gold rings and the beautifully turned chalices. "Male and female he created them", here with a twist.

Perhaps it was on this street that the cardinals who staged fashion shows at the Vatican for one another in the time of Paul VI (aka "the Red Queen of Milan") purchased their finery; likewise the bitter campophobes clustered around Cardinal Ratzinger under John Paul II. Gay or straight, they and the whole priestly cohort at least dress the part that the two Popes have articulated for them: that of "eunuchs for the sake of the kingdom of heaven", guardians at the gate of the Vatican's own special seraglio, where sex is banned unless one can get away with it, and women are confined without pleasure, powe or even, since the scuttling of habits for these true adherents to the vow of poverty, a consoling ostentation.

Now some Catholics are calling to shut down the seraglio—to free men of the cloth for manhood, women for ordination and both for marriage. Others, notably the Ratzinger wing of the hierarchy and its most rabid supporters, urge a redoubling of efforts toward repression. They also propose a purge of homosexual priests, a move that would complete John Paul's triumph over the Red Queen's old twirlers but also decimate America's dwindling priesthood (estimated to be 35 to 50 percent gay) and probably much of Europe's.

As in the past when the subjects of celibacy and ordination of women have threatened to be raised within the church, the Pope's reflex, like that of his predecessors, has been to stifle discussion before it begins. So it was at the recent conclave of cardinals in Rome to address the gathering scandal. Since then there has been more dissension among the American faithful, more lay meetings to discuss reform, more ad hoc groups of high donors urging a withholding of tithes. There have also been more lawsuits, more "recovered memories", more outrage that the victims and their lawyers might not extract all the money they had anticipated to make up for their suffering. From every direction the response seems naive or repellant.

In a sense, the priest scandal is the churchly equivalent of the Clinton impeachment. Here is a hierarchy that is totalitarian in perspective and actual practice, brooking no opposition, no equality and no voice of the people, to whom it has lied and whose liberty it has been intent on squelching for centuries. Piously proclaiming its fealty to Jesus, it long ago abandoned his commands to poverty, simplicity and love in the fullest sense. "My kingdom is not of this earth", Jesus said, but the Vatican ranks among the richest and most stratified kingdoms in the world. "Judge not", but from the earliest days of their consolidation of power the Church Fathers took obsessive interest in the sexual practices of the people and assumed an authoritarian prerogative to control their bodies and their minds. "Love one another", but they made sin, not love, the cornerstone of their teachings; and pride, not sympathy, their guiding star. "Be of good cheer; I have overcome the world", but they took those words and perverted them for worldly power, and with it pressed upon the people a faith in conformity and an acceptance of a lordly priesthood.

How pinched, then, to regard the sexual crimes or pervy behavior of a priestly minority as the ultimate abuse. "Anything to bring him down", left opponents of Clinton used to say, and one hears the same about the church now. But the sex panic around Clinton was dangerous because it did nothing to upset the structures of power and deceit imbedded in the presidency while it emboldened society's most straitened elements, the enemies of human weakness and freedom. The sex panic around the church is not too different. When American bishops meet in June to resume discussion on the priesthood scandal, the most that can be hoped is that someone will broach the subject of heterosexual marriage.

Out of the frying pan and into the fire...

Let's put aside for the moment the obsessions and hypocrisies of the church, and return to that street in Rome with its projections of male-female performance. Like stage costumes, those vestments suggest life at an angle to the universe of the everyday. They are alluring in the same way that communities of religious men and women are alluring—not because they provide the best model but because for so long they provided practically the only model of adult life distinct from Married With Children. Growing up Catholic in the sixties, I'm not sure I understood this, but my gay contemporaries did. Even after gay and women's liberation, these communities have retained, at least in theory, a kind of radical essence, standing as they do outside the systems of advertised desirability, coupledom, love under contract, property exchange and primo- or any geniture.

Because, in practice, priests throughout the world have wives, children, concubines and gay lovers, it's sensible enough to suggest, as Jon Meacham did in a recent issue of *Newsweek*, that the church should recognize these relationships, extend the opportunity to all priests and join the twenty-first century where women and homosexuals are concerned. But the church isn't sensible, and wouldn't be even if it shed every taint of corruption and made itself a union of equal spirits. So long as it exists, the question What should it do about priests and sex? is therefore best answered in the form of a mind game rather than with a list of helpful hints. People seek religion for transcendence, not for an approximation of the ordinary. For the old ascetics, ecstatic experience more than substituted for sex, and then became part of church iconography. But now, imagine the neutered parish priest, the Pope's "eunuch", performing Mass within eyeshot of Bernini's statue of "St. Theresa in Ecstasy". For him, where is the transcendent sensual experience? Not in the drear of enforced celibacy or secret gropings and certainly not in marriage.

I turn this question over in my mind and imagine one path: a priesthood of men and women, gay and straight, freed for sex but barred from marriage. And not just any sex (remember, this is a mind game); rather sex as a pure act of love, of giving, giving and expecting nothing in return. No vows, no bargains, no possibility for betrayal or divorce, for tearful children standing in the doorway as mummy or daddy explains it's not their fault; no "relationship" except with all of humanity, wherever there is the need for tenderness, for affection, for spiritual and physical intimacy. Let them perfect lovemaking as they strive to perfect love, living in such a way as to belong to no one and to everyone, missionaries without aim of converts; their satisfaction, their happiness derived from the comfort and pleasure, indeed ecstasy, of another.

"She's mad", I hear the readers clucking. Very well, for this is a religion whose adherents are enjoined to "Love your enemies, do good to those who hate you. Bless those who curse you, pray for those who calumniate you. And to him who strikes thee on the one cheek, offer the other also; and from him who takes away thy cloak, do not withhold thy tunic either. Give to everyone who asks of thee, and from him who takes away thy goods, ask no return. And even as you wish men to do to you, so also do you to them. And if you love those who love you, what merit have you? For even sinners love those who love them. And if you do good to those who do good to you, what merit have you? For even sinners do that. And if you lend to those from whom you hope to receive in return, what merit have you? For even sinners lend to sinners that they may get back as much in return.

"But love your enemies, and do good, and lend, not hoping for any return, and your reward shall be great, and you shall be children of the Most High, for he is kind towards the ungrateful and evil. Be merciful, therefore, even as your Father is merciful. Judge not, and you shall not be judged; condemn not , and you shall not be condemned. Forgive, and you shall be forgiven; give, and it shall be given to you; good measure, pressed down, shaken together, running over, shall they pour into your lap. For with what measure you measure, it shall be measured to you".

Who may wonder that the Church Fathers run from the complexities of sex and take cover behind their rules? For what domesticated sexuality, what sensual abnegation or soul-smothering celibacy can possibly meet the radical demands of such love?

ALEXANDER COCKBURN

The Hoofprints of Lucifer

THE HOOFPRINTS OF LUCIFER ARE EVERYWHERE. AND since this is America, eternally at war with the darker forces, the foremost Enemy Within is sex, no quarter given (or asked for, when you think about it). Here are some bulletins from the battlefront, drawn from a smart essay on "Sex & Empire" in the March issue of *The Guide* (www.guidemag.com), a Boston-based monthly travel magazine that has "about the best gay sex politics around", according to Bill Dobbs of Queerwatch, whom I take as my adviser in these matters.

In February 2000, Matthew Limon, an 18-year-old, had oral sex with a 14-year-old schoolmate. A Kansas court sentenced him to 17 years in prison, a sentence duly upheld by a federal court in February. Last July, an Ohio court sentenced 22-year-old Brian Dalton to seven years in prison because of sex fantasies he wrote in his diary. A woman teacher in Arizona faces 100 years in prison for having an affair with a 17-year-old boy. Frankly, I'd have risked two centuries in prison to have sex with Miss Hollister when I was in school.

Apropos the triumph of identity politics across the past 30 years, Bill Andriette, the author of "Sex & Empire", remarks that "the same PR machinery that produces all these feel-good identities naturally segues into manufacturing demonic ones— indeed, creates a demand for them. The ascription of demonic sexual identities onto people helps drive repression, from attacks on Internet freedom to sex-predator laws. Identity politics works gear-in-gear with a fetishization of children, because the young represent one class of persons free of identity, the last stand of unbranded humanity, precious and rare as virgin prairie".

This brings us into an Olympian quadruple axel of evil: sexually violent predators (familiarly known as SVPs), preying on minors of the same sex. There's no quarreling between prosecutor and judge, jury and governor, Supreme Court and shrinks. Lock 'em up and throw away the key.

The other day I listened to Marita Mayer, an attorney in the public defender's office in California's Contra Costa County, describe the desolate business of trying to save her clients, SVPs, from indeterminate confinement in Atascadero, the state's prime mental bin. Among Mayer's clients are men who pleaded guilty to sex crimes in the mid-1980s, mostly rape of an adult woman, getting a fixed term of anywhere from 10 to 15 years. In the old days, if you worked and behaved yourself, you'd be up for parole after serving half the sentence.

That is all changed. In California, as in many other states, SVP laws kicked in in the mid-1990s, crest of the repressive wave provoked by hysteria over child sex abuse and crime generally: mandatory minimum sentences, erosion of the right to confront witnesses, community notification of released sex offenders, surgical and chemical castration, prohibition of mere possession of certain printed materials, this last an indignity previously only accorded atomic energy secrets.

So California passes its SVP law in January of 1996, decreeing that those falling into the category of SVP have a sickness that requires treatment and cannot be freed until a jury agrees unanimously that they are no longer a danger to the community. (The adjudicators vary from state to state. Sometimes it's a jury, or merely a majority of jurors, sometimes a judge, sometimes a panel, sometimes a "multidisciplinary team".)

Instead of being paroled, Mayer's clients, serving out their years in Pelican Bay or Vacaville or San Quentin, counting down the months, suddenly find themselves back in jail in Contra Costa County, told they've got a mental disorder and can't be released till a jury decides they're no danger to the community.

Off they go to Atascadero for a two-year term, at the end of which they get a hearing, and almost always another two-year term.

"Many of them refuse treatment", Mayer says. "They refuse to sign a piece of paper saying they have a mental disease". Of course they do. Why sign a document saying that for all practical purposes you may well be beyond reform or redemption, that you are Evil by nature, not just a guy who did something bad and paid the penalty?

It's the AA model of boozing as sin, having to say you are an alcoholic and will always be in that condition, one lurch away from perdition. Soon everything begins to hinge on someone's assessment of your state of mind, your future intentions. As with the damnable liberal obsession with hate-crimes laws, it's a nosedive into the category of "thought crimes".

There the SVPs are in Atascadero, surrounded by psych techs eager to test all kinds of statistical and behavioral models, along with phallometric devices designed to assist in the persuasion of judge and jury that, yes, the prisoner has a more than 50 percent likelihood of exercising his criminal sexual impulses should he be released.

Thus, by the circuitous route of "civil commitment" (confining people deemed to be a danger to themselves or others), we have ended up with a situation that from the constitutional point of view, is indeed absolutely Evil: people held in preventive detention, locked up twice for the same crime.

"It's using psychiatry, like religion, to put people away", Mayer concludes. "Why not hire an astrologer or a goat-entrail reader to predict what the person might do? Why not the same for robbers as for rapists? What's happening is double jeopardy. People don't care about child rapists, but the Constitution is about protections. How do I feel about these guys? When I talk to my clients I don't presume to think what they'll do in the future. I believe in redemption. I don't look at them as sexually violent predators, I see them as sad sacks. They have to register; they could be hounded from county to county; even for a tiny crime they'll be put away. Their lives are in ruin. I pity them".

But not goat entrails, surely. The animal rights crowd would never stand for it.

A final bulletin on the hoofprints of Lucifer, leading to a memory of my dear departed sister Sarah, and her mother, Jean, the supposed origin of "bad girl" Sally Bowles, of *Cabaret* notoriety.

The *New York Times* has been at the forefront of a drive to rid midtown of sex stores, thus enhancing the value of its own real estate. And here's an editorial outburst from the *Daily News's* at the start of this year: "The city is still plagued by 142 pornographic video stores, topless bars and other X-rated businesses— 73 in Manhattan, 42 in Queens, 14 in Brooklyn, nine in the Bronx and four on Staten Island. In the past two years, the Giuliani administration has padlocked dozens of porn shops and dragged their owners into court. But once there, tenacious smutlords and their lawyers have been able to find enough wiggle room in the city's zoning rules to stay in business and continue blighting neighborhoods".

The *News'* beef was that the number of "smut shops" had been reduced by only two since the Mayor embarked on his anti-porn rampage. On January 3 the *News's* editorialist cheered Giuliani's renewed efforts to shut down the crafty operators of porn video stores who've been trying "to pass themselves off as straight businesses by putting a few spaghetti westerns and kung-fu movies on the shelf". How about that for respect for freedom of expression?

A few weeks ago I found myself at a small theater in SoHo, attending what had been billed to me as a re-creation of Weimar and the world of Sally Bowles. This same Sally Bowles, as first created in a short story by Christopher Isherwood, then in *I Am A Camera*, a stage version that transmuted into *Cabaret*, was based on Jean Ross, my father's second wife, a very charming woman. So I've always taken an interest in the fictional versions of her time in Berlin.

The production in SoHo turned out to have nothing to do with Berlin and everything to do with Giuliani, since the strippers ousted from gainful employment in their usual premises were regrouping under the banner of Art. In fact it was a big relief not to listen to pastiche songs in the manner of Kurt Weill. It was the night of the much-heralded snow storm that menaced New York the day of George Bush's inauguration, so the audience of six was heavily outnumbered by the strippers. The acts were okay, though not particularly rousing. The star of the evening didn't take off so much as a petticoat, being a magician who, since we're on the subject of Weill, looked slightly like Lotte Lenya in her cameo appearance as the KGB officer in *From Russia With Love*. She ogled the sparse audience gloriously as she bumbled her way through her tricks.

Jean Ross was a gentle, cultivated and very beautiful woman, not a bit like the vulgar vamp portrayed by Lisa Minelli. Jean died early, at the age of 62. Her daughter Sarah, my half sister, wrote wonderful detective stories under the name Sarah Caudwell: among them *The Shortest Way to Hades, The Sirens Sang of Murder, Thus Was Adonis Murdered* and, posthumously published, *The Sibyl in Her Grave*. Before she turned to crime Sarah was a barrister, and a very good one. She used to negotiate my contracts with Verso, and I'd pay her by taking her to lunch at the Ritz in London. As in any other venue she'd light up her pipe, then when waiters rushed up to protest, fling the thing into her handbag, from which smoke would soon begin to wreathe our table.

Sarah felt strongly about Isherwood's use of her mother, and wrote a piece about it in the British weekly, *The New Statesman*, in the mid-Eighties. Her mother Jean, she wrote, never liked *Goodbye to Berlin*, or felt a sense of identity with the character of

Sally Bowles, which in many respects she thought more closely modeled on one of Isherwood's male friends. (His homosexuality could not at that time be openly admitted.)"

Sarah's point was that Isherwood, supposedly so avant garde, was actually very conventional: "The convention does not permit an attractive young woman to have much in the way of intellectual accomplishments, and Isherwood follows it loyally. There is nothing in his portrait of Sally to suggest that she might have had any genuine ability as an actress, still less as a writer. My mother, on the other hand, was at least talented enough as an actress to be cast as Anitra in Max Reinhardt's production of *Peer Gynt* and competent enough as a writer to earn her living, not long afterwards, as a scenario-writer and journalist.

"Above all, the convention requires that a woman must be either virtuous (in the sexual sense) or a tart. So Sally, who is plainly not virtuous, must be a tart. To depend for a living on providing sexual pleasure, whether or not in the context of marriage, seemed to [Jean] the ultimate denial of freedom and emancipation. The idea so deeply repelled her that she simply could not, I think, have been attracted to a man who was rich, or allied herself permanently to anyone less incorrigibly impecunious than my father. She did not see the question as one of personal morality, but as a political one".

The pipe smoking did in Sarah in the end, presumably causing the cancer in her esophagus that killed her at the age of 60, last year. I knew her best at Oxford in the early sixties ,where she intrigued successfully to have women admitted to the Oxford Union. She was always exclaiming about so-and-so's "wonderful profile", pursuing dons with this particular asset. One don was known for watching television and Sarah, amid the ashes of her love, sent him this verse:

> *I cast aside my modesty, I laid aside my shame*
> *And on my knees I offered love or something much the same.*

You brushed my powder from your sleeve, with elegant precision
And murmured: 'Conversation is killing television'.

Death

BEN SONNENBERG
Ted's Spell

OUR FRIENDSHIP BEGAN IN LONDON AT BILL AND DIDO Merwin's house in 1959. Ted Hughes was twenty-eight years old and I was 22. I had never met anyone I admired so much who was at the same time so approachable. Ted's voice was a level baritone with overtones of his birthplace in the northwest of England. I listened to him so intently, literally on the edge of my seat, that I fell off my chair. When he helped me up from the floor, he didn't stop talking and I felt the vibration of his voice running down his arm. To borrow words from his poem "Pike", his voice seemed to come from a "Stilled legendary depth:/ It was as deep as England".

We took long walks together, Ted with his daughter, Frieda, in a baby carriage, gossiping some (quite a lot, actually) but talking of poetry mostly. Ted would declaim long passages of Chesterton and Kipling. He would quote at length from Lawrence and the poets of the First World War. His quotations from Shakespeare, by contrast, were short. "As the Clown says in *Measure for Measure*...". I remember that last quotation. I remember Ted's voice as he spoke it. "Groping for trouts in a peculiar river." I wish I could remember of what it was apropos.

TED AND I WERE GOOD FRIENDS IN THOSE DAYS. NOT CLOSE friends exactly, not intimate friends; but good friends nonetheless. I remember encountering him in Marylebone Road one fine fall day. I was in a jaunty mood. "Where are you off to?" I asked him. He told me he was heading for the bookseller Bertram Rota, then in Vigo Street, to sell him some manuscript pages. I said, "How much does he give you for them?" Five pounds, Ted said. I said, "I'll give you ten." I enjoyed transactions like that. I also gave Ted money to help start up *Modern Poetry in Translation*. I was quite the debonair young patron of the arts at that time.

There were two main obstacles to a deeper friendship between us. One was geography. Ted moved to North Tawton in Devon in 1961; for most of the 1960s, I was living in London and in the south of Spain. The other was Sylvia. I didn't take to Sylvia. We were cordial to one another at first, but after she discovered that I knew people in New York who had once known her, she became distinctly cold to me. And yet, in his letters to me from Devon, Ted sends me her love and tells me of her interest in my work.

I never doubted Ted's feelings for me. Like an ideal older brother, he showed real interest in my work, always overpraising it and encouraging me to write more. Not only did Ted pay attention to my writing, he also asked my opinions about his own. In his foreword to *Difficulties of a Bridegroom*, he tells of showing me his story "The Suitor" and of me saying "You should have called it 'Death and the Maiden'". That would have been during the winter of 1962, after his son, Nicholas, was born. "Your signsake", he wrote of Nicholas, born under Capricorn. At times Ted's belief in astrology seemed almost mediæval to me. At other times it seemed of a piece with his scholarly interest in spirits, witches, magic, alchemy: elements of understanding the Elizabethan world picture. It was different with Sylvia. Or so I gathered from Ted. "She *witched* herself into that building", he said one day as we passed 27 Fitzroy Road, the house where Sylvia died (and where, as has often been noted, William Butler Yeats once lived).

Ted could be teased about his beliefs. (I doubt you could tease Yeats.) When he offered to cast the horoscope of my daughter Susanna, who was born in London in September 1965, I said, "You really believe in that stuff, don't you, Ted?"

"Sometimes it's a useful way of focussing one's attention on a person."

"So is a kiss, Ted."

"Well, you've got me there, haven't you, Ben?" he said.

I MOVED BACK TO NEW YORK CITY IN JANUARY 1966, AND TED and I kept up our friendship exclusively by letters. Ted's are fitful, apologetic, often beginning with phrases like "Long time since I wrote you" or "Sorry for the long delay." He writes me explications of *Wodwo*, *Crow* and *Orghast* and as always expresses interest in my work in the theater. Most of his letters are hand-written on both sides of the paper, sometimes extending up the left-hand margin and ending upside down on the top. Rereading them, I hear his voice: energetic, hypnotic, unstoppable.

Ted came to New York in September of 1986. Except for a brief visit in 1984, this was the first time I'd seen him in almost 20 years. He was here representing the Plath estate in an action concerning the 1979 movie of *The Bell Jar*. The action was brought by Dr. Jane V. Alexander, a psychiatrist in Brookline, Massachusetts, who figured in both the movie and the book as a character called Joan Gilling. A scene in the movie shows Gilling making homosexual advances toward Esther Greenwood, as the Plath character was named. Dr. Alexander claimed that her reputation had been damaged by the movie and she was asking $6 million in compensation, not only from the Plath estate but also from 14 other defendants, including Harper, the publisher of *The Bell Jar*, Avco Embassy Pictures and various other corporations. The trial was expected to last six weeks.

Ted arrived with his sister, Olwyn, at about 4 in the after-noon. We had tea in my living room, a long bright room on the Upper West Side with an oblique view of the Hudson. Ted and Olwyn were in New York in order to find a lawyer. Before them was the prospect of a long, expensive trial. Both of them were under strain, Ted the more visibly so. His complexion was pale and his long hair unkempt. In the States, he explained, more even than in England, he had to contend with the "maenads", his term for those devotées of the cult of Sylvia Plath who blamed him for her suicide. I said I was sorry to see him so beleaguered. He said,"And I'm sad to see you in a wheelchair, Ben". At our last meeting, three years before, the symptoms of my multiple sclerosis had not been so advanced.

Ted was back in New York in January of 1987. The whole affair was over almost before it began. There was to be a settlement of $150,000. "All that the doctor wanted, Ben, was to have her day in court", Ted said. None of the judgement was chargeable to the Plath estate. Nevertheless, he told me, the costs to the estate had been considerable. "One year's earnings", he said. The amount was large. I forget how much exactly. It astonished me, though.

Olwyn wasn't present that afternoon. A disappointment to me. I feel a bond with Olwyn. Ted came with the aptly named John Springer, a New York publicist. Christopher Hitchens was also there. Ted spoke of the lawyer, Victor Kovner, who'd represented the Plath estate. "Very good lawyer, wonderful man."

I asked him how much trouble the "maenads" had been. "No more than usual, Ben", he said. "I've got John to thank for that." Then he told me of Ted Cornish, a healer in Okehampton, Devon. "He has helped people over long distances, "Ben", he said. "I'll give you his telephone number." Nobody spoke for a moment. My wife, Dorothy, gave me a skeptical glance. I fancied I saw Christopher making a scornful mental note. Not for the first time in my friendship with Ted, I thought of that passage in *Henry IV, Part I* when Glendower says, "I can call spirits from the vasty deep" and Hotspur replies:

> *Why, so can I, or so can any man;*
> *But will they come when you do call for them?*

I promised I'd call Ted Cornish.

IN 1990 I GAVE UP THE MAGAZINE GRAND STREET, WHICH I'D started in 1981. Failing health, rising costs. Ted wrote that he was sorry to hear that the magazine was folding. He went on to write: "In retrospect, I see I have submitted very little. Partly out of the wish to spare you having to turn down work from a friend." But Ted's contribution of three poems to the first issue of *Grand Street* was exceedingly important. It helped establish the magazine, and his second contribution, "Sylvia Plath and Her Journals", in the third issue of *Grand Street*, made me feel that the magazine was indeed established. Ted had blessed the magazine, which was exactly the kind of privilege I had from Ted from the time of our first meeting, through our correspondance, up to the time he died: a beneficence, a blessing on everything I did.

AFTER TED DIED, HIS WIDOW, CAROL, SENT ME MANY photographs: Ted with the Poet Laureate's stipulated cask of sherry; Ted fishing in Cuba, in Scotland; Ted with an aged Leonard Baskin; Ted with Carol over the years...My favorite is of Ted holding the case containing the Order of Merit as the Queen looks on with a genial smile. Ted smiles too, like a small boy who's gotten the Christmas present he wants. Physically, he looks strong. In 12 days he was dead. Olwyn to me: "It's almost as though he was suddenly shot."

On October 11, 1999, about a year after his death, I went with my wife to a tribute to Ted at the 92nd Street Y. Here is where I first saw him, in the Winter of 1956. He read then from *The Hawk in the Rain*, which had been given a prize that year for the best first book of poems. Now several famous poets were reading from his numerous books, and a famous actress was reading from his dramatic works. When they were done, the lights came down, and, over the sound system of the auditorium, we heard

Ted's spellbinding voice. He read "The Thought Fox", from *The Hawk in the Rain*, with its last line, "The page is printed."

ALEXANDER COCKBURN
Edward Said, Dead At 67

A mighty and a passionate heart has ceased to beat.
Edward Said died in hospital in New York City
Wednesday, September 24, 2003: at 6.30 PM, felled at
last by complications arising from the leukemia he fought so
gamely ever since the early 1990s.

We march through life buoyed by those comrades-in-arms
we know to be marching with us, under the same banners, flying
the same colors, sustained by the same hopes and convictions.
They can be a thousand miles away; we may not have spoken to
them in months; but their companionship is burned into our
souls and we are braced by the knowledge that they are with us
in the world.

Few more than Edward Said, for me and so many others
beside. How many times, after a week, a month or more, I have
reached him on the phone and within a second been lofted in
my spirits, as we press through our updates: his trips, his tri-
umphs, the insults sustained; the enemies rebuked and put to
flight. Even in his pettiness he was magnificent, and as I would
laugh at his fury at some squalid gibe hurled at him by an
eighth-rate scrivener, he would clamber from the pedestal of
martyrdom and laugh at himself.

He never lost his fire, even as the leukemia pressed, was
routed, pressed again. He lived at a rate that would have felled a
man half his age and ten times as healthy: a plane to London, an
honorary degree, on to Lebanon, on to the West Bank, on to
Cairo, to Madrid, back to New York. And all the while he was
pouring out the Said prose that I most enjoyed, the fiery dia-
tribes he distributed to *CounterPunch* and to a vast world audi-

ence. At the top of his form his prose has the pitiless, relentless clarity of Swift.

The Palestinians have lost their greatest polemical champion. A few weeks ago I was, with his genial permission, putting together from three of his essays the concluding piece in our *CounterPunch* collection, *The Politics of Anti-Semitism.* I was seized, as so often before, by the power of the prose: how could anyone read those searing sentences and not boil with rage, while simultaneously admiring Edward's generosity of soul: that with the imperative of justice and nationhood for his people came the humanity that called for reconciliation between Palestinians and Israeli Jews.

His literary energy was prodigious. Memoir, criticism, homily, fiction poured from his pen, a fountain pen that reminded one that Edward was very much an intellectual in the nineteenth-century tradition of a Zola or of a Victor Hugo, who once remarked that genius is a promontory in the infinite. I read that line as a schoolboy, wrote it in my notebook and though I laugh now a little at the pretension of the line, I do think of Edward as a promontory, a physical bulk on the intellectual and political landscape that forced people, however disinclined they may have been, to confront the Palestinian experience.

Years ago his wife, Mariam, asked me if I would make available my apartment in New York, where I lived at that time, as the site for a surprise fortieth birthday for Edward. I dislike surprise parties but of course agreed. The evening arrived; guests assembled in my sitting room on the eleventh floor of 333 Central Park West. The dining room table groaned under Middle Eastern delicacies. Then came the word from the front door. Edward and Mariam had arrived! They were ascending in the elevator. Then we could all hear Edward's furious bellow: "But I don't want to go to dinner with ******* Alexander!" They entered at last and the shout went up from 70 throats, Happy Birthday! He reeled back in surprise, recovered himself, then saw about the room all those friends happy to have traveled thousands of miles to shake his hand. I could see him slowly expand with joy, at each new unexpected face and salutation.

He never became blasé in the face of friendship and admiration, or indeed honorary degrees, just as he never grew a thick skin. Each insult was as fresh and as wounding as the first he ever received. A quarter of a century ago he would call, with mock heroic English intonation,"Alex-and-er, have you seen the latest *New Republic*? Have you read this filthy, this utterly disgusting diatribe? You haven't? Oh, I know, you don't care about the feelings of a mere black man such as myself." I'd start laughing, and say I had better things to do than read Martin Peretz, or Edward Alexander, or whoever the assailant was, but for half an hour he would brood, rehearse fiery rebuttals and listen moodily as I told him to pay no attention.

He never lost the capacity to be wounded by the treachery and opportunism of supposed friends. A few weeks ago he called to ask whether I had read a stupid attack on him by his very old friend Christopher Hitchens in the *Atlantic Monthly*. He described with pained sarcasm a phone call in which Hitchens had presumably tried to square his own conscience by advertising to Edward the impending assault. I asked Edward why he was surprised, and indeed why he cared. But he was surprised and he did care. His skin was so, so thin, I think because he knew that as long as he lived, as long as he marched onward as a proud, unapologetic and vociferous Palestinian, there would be some enemy on the next housetop, down the street eager to dump sewage on his head.

Edward, dear friend, I wave adieu to you across the abyss. I don't even have to close my eyes to savor your presence, your caustic or merry laughter as we gossiped, your elegance, your spirit as vivid as that of d'Artagnan, the fiery Gascon. You will burn like the brightest of flames in my memory, as you will in the memories of all who knew and admired and loved you.

Contributors

Steven J. B. lives in Ohio.

Dr. Susan Block is a sex therapist and talk show host in Los Angeles. She is the author of *The 10 Commandments of Pleasure.*

Lenni Brenner is the author of *Zionism in The Age of The Dictators* and *51 Documents.* He lives in New York City.

Marsha Cusic writes about music and culture. She lives in Detroit.

Susan Davis teaches at the University of Illinois. She is the author of *Spectacular Nature: the Seaworld Experience.*

Michael Dickinson lives in Istanbul, and his dark asrts can be studied at http://carnival_of_chaos.tripod.com

Bruce Jackson is Samuel J. Carpen Professor of American Studies at the University of Buffalo and author of numerous books, including *Wake Up Dead Man: Hard Labor and Southern Blues.*

Ron Jacobs is the author of *The Way The Wind Blew: a History of the Weather Underground.* He lives in Vermont.

Vanessa Jones lives in Canberra, Australia.

Peter Linebaugh is author of *The London Hanged* and, with Marcus Rediker, of *The Many-Headed Hydra.*

Dave Marsh is publisher of *Rock and Rap Confidential* and author of *The Heart of Rock and Soul: the 1001 Greatest Singles Ever Made.*

Susan Martinez writes about culture and music for *CounterPunch* and *Rock and Rap Confidential.* She lives in Berkeley.

Vicente Navarro is the author of *The Political Economy of Social Inequalities: Consequences for Health and Quality of Life* and *Dangerous to Your Health.* He teaches at Johns Hopkins University.

Steve Perry is the editor of *City Pages,* the alternative weekly published in Minneapolis.

Sigrid Miller Pollin has an architectural practice based in Amherst, MA. She teaches design in the Fine Arts Center at UMass Amherst with an emphasis on cross media transformations.

Max Page teaches urban, architectural and public history at UMass Amherst. He is the author of *The Creative Destruction of Manhattan 1900 to 1940*.

Ben Sonnenberg is the former editor of *Grand Street* and the author of *Lost Properties: Confessions of a Bad Boy*. He lives in Manhattan. Before being published on the *CounterPunch* site, his essay first appeared in *Raritan*.

Ben Tripp is a screenwriter, satirist and cartoonist. He lives in LA.

David Vest is a writer and blues pianist. His latest CD is *David Vest and the Willing Victims* from Trillium Records. He lives in Portland, Oregon.

Daniel Wolff is the author of *You Send Me: the Life and Times of Sam Cooke* and *The Memphis Blues Again: the Photographs of Ernest Withers*. He lives in Memphis. Before appearing in *CounterPunch*, his essay, nominated for a Grammy, was published as the liner notes to *Sam Cooke With The Soul Stirrers, The Complete Specialty Recordings*.

JoAnn Wypijewski is a former editor of *The Nation*. She is the creator of *Painting By Numbers: Komar and Melamid's Scientific Guide to Art* and editor of *The Thirty Years Wars, the collected work of Andrew Kopkind*. She lives in Manhattan.

Alexander Cockburn and Jeffrey St. Clair coedit *CounterPunch*, both the newsletter and the well-known site, www.counterpunch.org. They live, respectively, in Petrolia, Northern California and in Oregon City, Oregon.

MICHAEL DICKINSON
A Note on The Cover

CLUED THAT THIS BOOK COVERED TOPICS AS VARIED AS the lifelong fascism of Salvador Dali, Dylan going electric at the Newport Folk Festival, Angelina Jolie's breasts and a "minor" blood-based fetishism she had with her ex, Ashcroft covering up the breasts of a statue outside the Department of Justice, the Court decision on gay marriage, a piece on how the CIA might have killed Paul Robeson, black blues and soul singers—but also aware that the basic take of the book is liberation and repression as reflected in imperial and popular culture, I set to work and came up with this picture for the cover.

The owner of the lovely face which adorns the reclining statue whose breasts have been bra-covered by American Justice Prudery is Ms.Angelina Jolie. She's listening intently to Dylan's early sixties album "The Times They Are A-Changin'". Ain't they just? Some minor cuts around her navel imply the blood-based fetishism. Her lover slumps naked at the foot of the couch—rejected? ashamed? looking for his socks?

A nightmare pale horse from Dali's "Temptation of Saint Anthony" leaps hooves high, flashing its fascist white underbelly, desperately fleeing the fire in the looking glass. The image brings Baldwin's passionate "The Fire Next Time" to mind, the title taken from an African-American slave song, mother of soul and blues, warning: "God gave Noah the rainbow sign, no more water, the fire next time!"

The eye looks on.

And on the gentleman's dressing-table/coffin? nearby sit a pair of familiar figures, popular and imperial, the Prince and the Showgirl, Britney Spears wears well the body of the Willendorf Venus, that paleolithic fertility-sex goddess, very big in her own time. Beside sulks the Prince in suspenders. Flick flick. Charles here represents Repression... And it's quite a funny picture. (And he believes in the Divine Right of Kings, for God's sake! Do me a favor! No monarchy!)

And what's on telly down there under the console? Why it's "Ole Man River", Paul Robeson, the first American to be banned from TV when he was barred from speaking on NBC's "Today with Mrs Roosevelt" in March 1950, under the New Internal Security Act. Sound familiar? Robeson said, "The artist must elect to fight for freedom or for slavery. I have made my choice. I have no alternative."

Moving on, we pass the headless, limbless and dickless torso of a Greek statue, an albino python rearing from its loins, signifying...?, on to a gold-framed wedding photograph—two brides in white! But no, it's a picture of Bush and Blair committing unlawful gay wedlock, aided and abetted by the Pope, who holds aloft a pink condom like the holy sacrament itself!

That blue and white glazed object parked up at Ms. Angelina's comfortable couch is a seventeenth-century joke drinking-vessel uncovered recently during sewage excavations under a pub in London's East End. Dirty!

Index

AK Press

ORDERING INFORMATION

AK Press
674-A 23rd Street
Oakland, CA 94612-1163
USA
(510) 208-1700
www.akpress.org
akpress@akpress.org

AK Press
PO Box 12766
Edinburgh, EH8 9YE
Scotland
(0131) 555-5165
www.akuk.com
ak@akedin.demon.uk

The addresses above would be delighted to provide you with the latest complete AK catalog, featuring several thousand books, pamphlets, zines, audio products, video products, and stylish apparel published & distributed by AK Press. Alternatively, check out our websites for the complete catalog, latest news and updates, events, and secure ordering.

Also Available from AK Press

The first audio collection from Alexander Cockburn on compact disc.

Beating the Devil

Alexander Cockburn, ISBN: 1 902593 49 9 ● CD ● $14.98

In this collection of recent talks, maverick commentator Alexander Cockburn defiles subjects ranging from Colombia to the American presidency to the Missile Defense System. Whether he's skewering the fallacies of the war on drugs or illuminating the dark crevices of secret government, his erudite and extemporaneous style warms the hearts of even the stodgiest cynics of the left.

Next from CounterPunch/AK Press

COMING SUMMER, 2004

A Dime's Worth of Difference:
Beyond the Lesser of Two Evils
Edited by Alexander Cockburn and Jeffrey St. Clair

The hot how-to-think collection on the presidential stakes and the two-party pantomime. Cockburn and St Clair steer past the hand-wringing and the what-ifs into the clear, bright uplands of reason about what's really at stake.

COMING FALL/WINTER, 2004

The CounterPunch Book of Monsters:
The Empire's Willing Executioners
Edited by Alexander Cockburn and Jeffrey St. Clair

The gang's all here! The Dulles Brothers, Edward Teller, The CIA's Top Poisoner, Albert Wohlstetter, the Neo-Cons Favorite Philosopher, Kissinger and his Mentor, Jeane Kirkpatrick and scores more! Who dreamed up the Tuskegee Experiment? Who Devised the Bravo H-Test? Order the CounterPunch Book of Monsters and explore the heart of darkness.

Also Available from CounterPunch and AK Press,
(call 1-800-840-3683 or order online at www.akpress.org)

Whiteout: the CIA, Drugs and the Press
by Alexander Cockburn and Jeffrey St. Clair, VERSO.

The involvement of the CIA with drug traffickers is a story that has slouched into the limelight every decade or so since the creation of the Agency. In Whiteout, here at last is the full saga.

Been Brown So Long It Looked Like Green to Me: the Politics of Nature
by Jeffrey St. Clair, COMMON COURAGE PRESS.

Covering everything from toxics to electric power plays, St. Clair draws a savage profile of how money and power determine the state of our environment, gives a vivid account of where the environment stands today and what to do about it.

The Golden Age Is In Us
by Alexander Cockburn, VERSO.

Cockburn's classic diary of the late 80s and early 90s.
"A Patchwork Paradise Lost", Times Literary Supplement.
"A literary gem", Village Voice.

Why We Publish CounterPunch
By Alexander Cockburn and Jeffrey St. Clair

Ten years ago we felt unhappy about the state of radical journalism. It didn't have much edge. It didn't have many facts. It was politically timid. It was dull. CounterPunch was founded. We wanted it to be the best muckraking newsletter in the country. We wanted it to take aim at the consensus of received wisdom about what can and cannot be reported. We wanted to give our readers a political roadmap they could trust.

A decade later we stand firm on these same beliefs and hopes. We think we've restored honor to muckraking journalism in the tradition of our favorite radical pamphleteers: Edward Abbey, Peter Maurin and Ammon Hennacy, Appeal to Reason, Jacques René Hébert, Tom Paine and John Lilburne.

Every two weeks CounterPunch gives you jaw-dropping exposés on: Congress and lobbyists; the environment; labor; the National Security State.

"CounterPunch kicks through the floorboards of lies and gets to the foundation of what is really going on in this country", says Michael Ratner, attorney at the Center for Constitutional Rights. "At our house, we fight over who gets to read CounterPunch first. Each issue is like spring after a cold, dark winter."

YOU CANNOT MISS ANOTHER ISSUE

Name _____

Address _____

City _____ State _____ Zip _____

Email _____ Phone _____

Credit Card # _____

Exp. Date _____ Signature _____

Visit our website for more information: **www.counterpunch.org**

☐ 1 yr. **$40**   ☐ 1 yr. email **$35**   ☐ 1 yr. both **$45**

☐ 2 yr. **$70**   ☐ 2 yr. email **$60**   ☐ 2 yr. both **$80**

☐ 1 yr. low income **$30**   ☐ 2 yr. low income **$65**

☐ Supporter **$100**   ☐ Donation Only

Send Check/Money Order to: **CounterPunch, P.O. Box 228, Petrolia, CA 95558**
Canada add $12.50 per year postage. Others outside US add $17.50 per year.

The Politics of Anti-Semitism

Edited by Alexander Cockburn and Jeffrey St. Clair

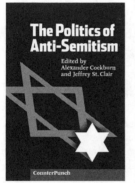

What constitutes genuine anti-Semitism—Jew-hatred—as opposed to disingenuous, specious charges of "anti-Semitism" hurled at realistic, rational appraisals of the state of Israel's political, military and social conduct?

There's no more explosive topic in American public life today than the issue of Israel, its treatment of Palestinians and its influence on American politics.

Yet the topic is one that is so hedged with anxiety, fury and fear, that honest discussion is often impossible.

The Politics of Anti-Semitism lifts this embargo.

Powerful Essays By

Michael Neumann	Scott Handleman
Alexander Cockburn	Lenni Brenner
Uri Avnery	Linda Belanger
Bruce Jackson	Robert Fisk
Kurt Nimmo	Will Youmans
M. Shahid Alam	Norman Finkelstein
Jeffrey St. Clair	Jeffrey Blankfort
George Sunderland	Kathleen and Bill Christison
Yigal Bronner	Edward Said

Reviews

"Michael Neumann's essay, "What Is Anti-Semitism," by and of itself is worth forking over the $12.95 to get a copy of The Politics of Anti-Semitism. ...There is much more in The Politics of Anti-Semitism that deserves attention. ... But, of particular note are the essay of Yigal Bronner, a member of Ta'ayush, the Arab-Jewish Partnership, and professor at Tel Aviv University, and one of the last essays of Edward Said, before he lost his life to cancer. Both of them offer a sane and humane vision in which Israelis and Palestinians are able to live together, side by side, with all their diversity and commonality, in peace. They conclude the collection fittingly, with hope for the future."

Gilles d'Aymery: www.swans.com

"This is a superlative discussion, with important lessons for all. Many of the essays in this book have appeared on the CounterPunch website—an important online magazine which is edited by the editors of this book. Cockburn, St. Clair and the other authors must be commended for addressing this important topic with this collection of excellent essays. Unfortunately, criticism of Israel is still a taboo topic, and the first ones to raise questions will probably attract a significant amount of abuse. One must remember this when appreciating the courage of those who have produced this important book."

Paul de Rooij: Washington Report on Middle East Affairs

Available from CounterPunch and AK Press
(call 1-800-840-3683 or order online at www.akpress.org)

Other Titles from AK Press

Books

CDs

DVDs